Six from Leipzig

To Caio and Rafaela,
With best wishes,
Sig Arther

Six from Leipzig

GERTRUDE DUBROVSKY

VALLENTINE MITCHELL
LONDON • PORTLAND, OR.

First published in 2004 in Great Britain by
VALLENTINE MITCHELL
Crown House, 47 Chase Side, Southgate
London N14 5BP

and in the United States of America by
VALLENTINE MITCHELL
c/o ISBS, 920 NE 58th Avenue, Suite 300
Portland, Oregon, 97213-3786

Website: www.vmbooks.com

British Library Cataloguing in Publication Data

Dubrosky, Gertrude W.
  Six from Leipzig
  1. Refugees, Jewish – England – East Anglia 2. Refugee
  children – England – East Anglia 3 Kindertransports
  (Rescue operations) 4. World War, 1939–1945 – Children.
  5. World War, 1939–1945 – Jews – Germany – Leipzig
  I. Title
  940.5′3′089924′0432122

ISBN 0-85303-470-2 (paper)

Library of Congress Cataloging-in-Publication Data

A catalog record for this book is available
from the Library of Congress

Typeset in 10.5/12pt Ehrhardt by Vallentine Mitchell
Printed in Great Britain by MPG Books Ltd, Bodmin, Cornwall

In Memory of the six million, among whom are

Rose Asman Schmulevitz
Leo and Eva Schmulevitz
Yetta Ribetski
Trude and Abraham Grünbaum
Clara and Adolph Koppold

and

In celebration of the survivors, among whom are

Vera Ribetski Nussenbaum
Paula Grünbaum Balkin
Edith Grünbaum Maniker
Tsvi Koppold Shdaimah
Sigmar Koppold Silber
Zilla Koppold Weininger

The publication of this book has been helped by the generosity of
Sir Bernard Schrier and his family

Contents

Acknowledgements

———•◆•———

There are two wonderful things about writing a book. One is its completion. (There is a caveat: history is always a work-in-progress – without beginning and without end.) The other is being able to thank those who made the book possible.

Always, I am reminded that we are not alone in the world, lonely though it sometimes is. My work would not have started if I had not met Greta Burkill. And it might not have continued were it not for the constant support and encouragement of several people whom it is now my privilege to thank. Harry and Jean Burkill gave me initial and crucial support by granting me access to the Burkill papers in their possession and those in the Cambridge University Library. They have become very dear friends and have been my hosts in their lovely home in Sheffield. They have spent countless hours with me, recounting their memories, feeding me, and taking me on excursions. If this work has any merit, much is due to both Harry and Jean. A thank-you is entirely inadequate and entirely sincere.

I also have been encouraged and nurtured in this work by the six from Leipzig: Paula Balkin, Vera Nussenbaum, Edith Maniker, Tsvi Shdaimah, Sigmar Silber, Zilla Weininger. They have shared their painful memories with me, have been generous with their time and their own memorabilia, and also have become special friends. I have tried to be as accurate and honest as I can in interpreting the papers and the interviews from which I have extracted this history. Whilst the history is theirs, any mistakes made are mine.

I started the research for this book with the help of a fellowship from the Oxford Centre for Hebrew and Jewish Studies. The continuing encouragement of David Patterson, the founder of the centre and its president, has been most gratifying and I thank him for it. An invitation from Clare Hall, Cambridge University, to spend a fellowship year helped me continue the research and begin the serious writing. The genuine interest of Professor Gillian Beer, President of Clare Hall, and the help of Elizabeth Ramsden, College Secretary and friend of all the Clare Hall visiting fellows, are remembered with pleasure. Both made my stay memorable.

The Littauer Foundation, New York, provided the necessary funding for me to have the German-language letters from Leipzig translated into English. I thank the Foundation for its support.

Throughout my work I have had the support and encouragement of my three sons and their families. They are the blessings of my life.

Gertrude Dubrovsky
2003

List of Illustrations

―――――•◆•――――

became his parents. He is now Reader in Mathematics at Sheffield University.

18. Harry with his wife, Jean, Oxford, 1994.
19. Ann Sofier, foster mother to Harold Koppold (now Zvi Shaimah). 'Fostering Harold was one of the most wonderful experiences of my life,' she said. He changed his name when he moved to Israel and called his foster mother every Friday night.
20. Zvi Shaimah on his kibbutz, Nir Oz, Israel. A self-taught artist and sculptor, his work beautifies the kibbutz – much of it reflects his *kinder-transport*/Holocaust experiences.
21. Siegmar Koppold Silber in his New Jersey law office. 'The simple home I had with Elsie Mansfield was the best home I ever had.' He was adopted at the age of 12 by the Silbers of Patterson, New Jersey, USA.

List of Abbreviations and Terms

AAC	Academic Assistance Council
AJDC	American Joint Distribution Committee
CBF	Central British Fund
Central Committee	Government agency established 1940
CGJ	Council for German Jewry
CRC	Cambridge Refugee Committee
CRCC	Cambridge Refugee Children's Committee
CRREC	Chief Rabbi's Religious Emergency Council
CUJS	Cambridge University Jewish Society
Hilfsverein der deutschen Juden	eastern European Jewish aid organization
IAC	Inter-Aid Committee
ICA	Jewish Colonization Association
Israelitische Religionsgemeinde	Jewish communal organization
JRC	Jewish Refugee Committee
Judenrat	German social services organization for Jews
Kindertransport	children's transport
Kristallnacht	(lit. Night of the Broken Glass) 10 November 1938
MCC	Movement for the Care of Children
RCM	Refugee Children's Movement
Reichsvereinigung der Juden in Deutschland	
Reichsvertretung der Juden in Deutschland	
UPA	United Palestine Appeal
Yeshiva	orthodox Jewish rabbinical seminary or day school

Preface

Six from Leipzig is a story of young children, cousins 'untimely ripped' from their European nests and sent alone to unknown relatives in a foreign country perched on the edge of war. Their story reflects, in some measure, the experiences of some 10,000 children who had a similar history. The book also tells of the hundreds of people working tirelessly on behalf of refugee children to help them grow into mature and stable citizens.

For those in the refugee children's committees, the real work started after the children arrived in England. The young refugees were no longer numbers or statistics or names; they were bewildered children of various ages, sizes, abilities and apprehensions. They had in common a need for reassurance, nurturing and education. Behind their survival in England lies the dedication, selfless labour and enduring concern of a valiant and able army of women and men.

Cambridge had two working committees responsible for the well-being and safety of refugees who arrived in the city. The Cambridge Refugee Children's Committee, composed primarily of women, was concerned with the welfare of unaccompanied refugee children; the Cambridge Refugee Committee, primarily men, raised the funds, controlled the money and were responsible for the needs of refugee families. Both committees met regularly, cooperated, and were pulled in all sorts of directions at one and the same time.

In Cambridge there was an outpouring of community support for the refugees – for families, single adults and unaccompanied children. But also there were those who feared that refugees would inevitably take away jobs from English men and wondered publicly why there was so much concern for them.

The Cambridge Refugee Children's Committee worked tirelessly for the good and welfare of the children in their care. The fact that so many grew to be healthy and contributing members of the societies where they found themselves speaks volumes for the effectiveness of the care they initially received at the hands of strangers to whom their parents entrusted them.

INTRODUCTION

———•■◆■•———

Getting Started

I thought I knew everything I had to know about the Holocaust: the concentration camps, the death marches, the brutalization of decent law-abiding citizens by governments gone mad, and the victims – 11 million of them. In addition, there are those who fled the madness and escaped with their lives. Though they did not go up in smoke, they lost their homes, their families, and their places in society. Among them were children who had been sent from Germany, Austria, Czechoslovakia and Poland to Britain, Sweden, Holland, France, Switzerland, Israel (then Palestine) and elsewhere just before Germany marched into Poland and Great Britain entered the war.

For a long time I knew nothing about the children. Nor did I know of ordinary citizens groups who organized rescue operations in England and elsewhere to save young refugees. From December 1938 to September 1939 about 20,000 children, ranging in age from a few months to 17 years, were placed on trains and boats in the middle of the night or in the early hours of the morning by parents who were not granted permission to enter the countries to which their children were being sent. Fully half, or 10,000, came to Great Britain; of these, about 2,000 came to Cambridge or other parts of East Anglia and were under the supervision of volunteers.

Most of the parents who registered their children for the *Kindertransports* were confident their sons and daughters would live. They also knew that separation meant a better chance for the children. In reality, the children who came to Britain did survive; but most of them never saw their parents again. The refugee children transported to Britain are the focus of this book. I use the experiences of six cousins from Leipzig, who were supervised by the Cambridge Refugee Children's Committee (CRCC) to illustrate the issues facing both the children and the voluntary committees.

I am often asked how I happened to become interested in *Kindertransport*, a seeming departure from my previous work on Yiddish literature about America and the social history of American Jewish farmers.

They have in common the immigrant experience, the pain of loss, disloca-tion, and the need to make difficult adjustments to gain a new life. But, while I chose to do my previous work, the subject of *Kindertransport* was thrust upon me by a woman I met only once in my life.

The children caught up in the Nazi excesses were grouped together in my mind as a category of 'victims', but I had heard little about them. I knew about dreadful decisions parents often had to make. I heard more than I wanted to know from survivors of the Holocaust who had settled in substantial numbers on farms in the community where I also lived. Because I could speak and understand the Yiddish language of these newcomers, I was aware of some of their stories. But I never solicited them. The new settlers were from a world completely foreign to my own, although it was once the world of my parents. They came with regularity to our home and I overheard their conversations with each other or with my parents.

The refugee neighbours who settled on farms in America in the late 1940s brought extraordinary experiences with them. Building new lives on the ruins of their old lives, they carried their pasts with them – in their eyes, in their voices, and in their trembling shoulders during the Kaddish recita-tion at the synagogue. In my mind's eye, I still see them on Yom Kippur, their backs draped in the stained and tattered prayer shawls they somehow managed to preserve and carry to America.

One particularly horrendous story I heard was from a survivor of a small rural village in an area of the Ukraine not far from the Russian border. She was a young mother during that fateful time in 1941, with two young children who must have been about the ages of my own two boys when I heard the tale. When the Germans arrived in her town, cheered on by some local Ukrainian hooligans, she knew she had to leave quickly. With her children and nothing else she headed for the thick woods which were every-where and not too far away. She ran and fell, got up and ran, keeping pace with the older of her two sons, dragging the younger one by the arm, and then picking him up and running some more. Safety was deep in the forest. She was desperate to save her child and herself. But it soon became clear to her that the younger child simply could not keep up and she could not carry him and run. They were all in jeopardy. Making a decision that marked the rest of her life, she left her baby sitting under a tree while she and the older child took off. In America, years later, she was haunted by the child's screams: 'Mamma, Mamma, wait! Wait for me!' Every night she woke, hearing the last words of her child as if for the first time.

As a young mother myself, I identified with the terrible dilemma of that unfortunate woman who survived, but at what a price. Her life was perma-nently damaged. I asked myself what I would have done, and concluded that I probably would not have had the courage. I am sure I would have decided that we all live or we all die together. To think about the child was too painful for me. I carry my own childhood memory of being abandoned by a mother who left to go to a hospital from which she never returned. After more than three-score years, I still cry remembering how my beautiful young mother parted from her four children, the oldest of whom was 9. She said goodbye to each of us in turn, and, sobbing, made a painful journey across the room and out of the house to a waiting car, leaving us forever bereft. So, on a personal one-to-one level, I identified with a mother and with a child. But beyond the singular, I did not think about children of the Holocaust.

Growing up Jewish in a non-Jewish environment at a time when fascism became an attractive ideology was bad enough. I must have been 10 or 11 when I became vaguely conscious of ominous events happening somewhere in Europe. Disasters. Murders. Pogroms. I thanked God that I was born in America, under luckier stars. But we were not free of the poison. I still remember how frightened I and everyone in the community was when swastikas and a crude depiction of a figure hanging from a gallows appeared on the exterior wall of our synagogue/Community Centre. I was a child, but the incident made a deep impression. I didn't want strangers to know I was Jewish.

The unfortunate mother's story stayed with me. It gained fresh poignancy years later, when I interviewed Holocaust survivors to understand their motivations for settling on farms. Without my intending it to happen, I was drawn even deeper into the dark world of Holocaust memories. I heard of trips in boxcars, of children crawling out from under dead bodies in mass graves, and of terrified innocent people running in forests, pursued by bounty hunters. Of the survivors, I knew who had survived in bunkers in the woods, who had served in the *Judenrat* and who had been in the concentration camps. In fact, I knew more than I wanted to know.

The survivors did not easily talk to strangers about their experiences. Nor did the established Jewish farmers of the community, once émigrés themselves, necessarily understand what their new neighbours had endured. The two groups often eyed each other with suspicion and were careful in their dealings one with the other.

It was language that connected me to them. My children were grown up when I needed to interview the last group of people to settle on the farms in the community I was studying. I approached them speaking Yiddish. They protested, and said it would be easier for me if they spoke English. I invited them to speak in whatever language they were comfortable with, and invariably the interview started in their new English. But within minutes, without their even realizing it, they slipped into Yiddish, and seconds later they left the farm experience I was trying to capture and were back in the dark world they always remember, to the woods where they lived like animals, and to the camps, from where their previous 'animal-like' life in the woods seemed like paradise.

'I became an animal,' said one man, 'and I no longer cared about anything, I did not think about anything, I was no longer human.'

Once, when a man began describing the scene inside a boxcar on his trip to Auschwitz, I could not bear to hear any more, and I begged permission to return the following day to complete the interview. The survivors I spoke to represented the whole of the Holocaust experience to me. I did not need to look for more witnesses; these sufficed. They struggled to forget and remembered everything, every night and every hour.

But I never heard from them about children placed on trains by their parents and sent to foreign countries. Very likely, information about *Kindertransports* never reached the small Polish, Russian and Ukrainian villages where the majority of Europe's Jews lived. It took another project, and a different group of interviewees, for me to learn about an entirely different Holocaust experience.

But I am getting ahead of my story. Years after I left the farm, after my book on Jewish farmers was written though not yet published, I went to Cambridge on a holiday. It was May 1984. I had been invited by Renford and Moira Bambrough, whom I had met at the Carnegie Foundation for the Advancement of Teaching in Princeton, where I was working and where Renford was a visiting scholar for a short period.

More considerate hosts I could not have had. They wanted my week with them to be as full as possible and they were eager to show me all of Cambridge and its environs. Every day I was taken on a new excursion. As my visit drew to a close, Moira asked if there was something special I wanted to see and I suddenly confessed: 'Moira, when I go somewhere new, I also like to see something Jewish.'

Moira, a bit astonished, thought about it and said, 'There is nothing Jewish in Cambridge.' She then remembered a Mrs Greta Burkill, who had something to do with Jewish refugee children.

'Well, if that's all you have,' I said, 'let's go visit Mrs Burkill.'

Moira, bless her, called Mrs Burkill and the next day, one day before I was due to leave Cambridge, we knocked on the door at 4 Archway Court. A small, cheerful, grey-haired woman let us in. Margreta Burkill spoke with an accent I recognized as eastern European; Russian icons shared the mantelpiece with family photos and specimen pieces of china. Much later I learned that Greta had spent her childhood years in her mother's native Russia after her parents divorced. She was totally fluent in Russian, and indeed, in spite of years in England, retained an accent.

We got through the pleasantries of introduction very quickly. Greta, as she asked to be called, immediately started talking about 10,000 children who came to England and needed to be taken care of. She talked about local community groups, composed primarily of women, who worked around the clock finding places for these young refugees and supervising, as best they could, their educational process. The Cambridge group set up a school in nearby Ely so that children from religiously observant homes would get kosher food, Hebrew language skills and Bible instruction. Nevertheless, religious groups, concerned about the many Jewish children in Christian homes, tried to entice the young people away from their resident placements. Rabbis petitioned Parliament for guardianship of the children and went so far as to publish a pamphlet accusing Christians of proselytizing Jewish children.

What Burkill was telling me was mind-boggling: 10,000 children, some infants, placed on trains by their parents and shipped to England; responsible people assuming on-going commitments to the well-being and education of foreign children; Rabbis enticing children away from the homes in which they were placed.

Having done much oral history, I only half-believe what I am told. People tend to say what they think the interviewer wants to hear. Further, memory is not reliable; it shifts and is different at different times; remembered facts often are not facts at all but instead are related to a layer of personal and/or psychological narration more akin to poetry than to history. Nor can remembered events always be verified. I need corroborating evidence before I take at face value what I am told. And so, as politely as I could, I asked Greta Burkill if there were any documents to support what she was telling me.

'Not very many,' she said. 'We worked outside of official circles by making private contacts with Members of Parliament and other influential individuals. People in England, generally, were against having refugees come into the country, even children. What few papers we had, we put in the Imperial War Museum and in the Manuscript Room of Cambridge University Library. Except for these.' At that, she handed me a pack of papers covered with hand-drawn charts on which were noted the names of children, where they came from, their ages, their parents' names, their religion – Catholic, Protestant or Jewish. (If Jewish, whether orthodox, liberal or reform.) There was a column to indicate where the children were placed in England, and remarks.

I have done enough historical research to recognize genuine and valuable documents when I see them. And I also know what happens to papers when relatives must clear out an estate. Mrs Burkill was 86 years old and told me she had had some heart problems. I was emphatic when I said, 'Mrs Burkill, you must put these papers into an archive or a library.'

'I cannot,' she protested. 'Each of these children came through my hands. It's as if each one were mine. This is all I have of that time.'

As earnestly and emphatically as I could, I repeated, 'Mrs Burkill. You must! These documents must be preserved.' And just as emphatically, she responded, 'I cannot.'

My effort to protect and preserve historical documents appeared futile. Our visit was over; we left. The next morning Moira took me to the airport bus and I went on to Frankfurt to visit my sister and brother-in-law on a sabbatical in Heidelberg.

It was my first visit to Germany, where I went with great trepidation, knowing I would hate the whole experience. The encounter I had the day before with Greta Burkill was still fresh in my mind. In Germany, I told my sister that we had to visit places of Jewish significance. We owed our relatives and the Jewish people who had perished there, and all the children who had suffered, that much respect. And so we went searching for hidden and/or abandoned Jewish cemeteries ... Jewish schools ... synagogues ... Dachau.

Dachau made me numb. On the day we appeared there, the place was full of schoolchildren on a field trip, sharing their candy and bubble-gum and laughing their innocent laughter. I saw the infamous square described to me by Yakov, one of my farm interviewees. According to this man's testimony, the inmates were regularly called out to be counted at night, in freezing winter. They were forced to stand for four hours or more at attention, wearing thin prison uniforms if they were lucky, or, if unlucky, naked. At one roll call, Yakov felt himself freezing and began reciting the Shma, the prayer of faith. Those standing next to him began rubbing him with snow; miraculously he survived. I stood in that square and remembered Yakov's words; and yet, I had no reactions. I could not connect with feelings of any kind. And then I saw large photographs of children being herded into the camp. Two children looked out towards me. I had a sinking feeling that they were my own innocent grandchildren, who I had assumed were safe in America. They were begging me with their eyes to save them. All the children I had thought about and heard about came together in that one photograph. Finally, as if a wall of ice had dissolved within me, I broke into uncontrollable weeping.

Germany was a difficult place for me. Everywhere, disturbing evidence of both the ghastly Holocaust history and the more recent signs of prosperity. I was more than ready to return to Princeton, to my work at the Carnegie Foundation and my other work on Jewish farmers.

One week after I returned home, I received a letter from Moira Bambrough telling me that Mrs Burkill had called her to say she had all the papers copied for my benefit. I gulped, not really able to comprehend why

Mrs Burkill had done that. Exactly one day later, and before I could respond to Moira's letter, I received another communication from her, an envelope with an enclosure – a clipping of a newspaper obituary. Mrs Burkill had died. When Moira went to pick the papers up, she found a package addressed to me on a chair.

I was probably the last person to whom Greta Burkill spoke about her most meaningful work. And one of the last things she did before her death was to bequeath a project to me. I am not a religious person. That is, I know little about the nature of the supernatural, nor do I think about it much. Yet, I saw in this remarkable set of circumstances the hand of God. Somehow, Mrs Burkill picked me out to do a job. But I already had a job; I could not turn my attention to the CRCC. I was not even sure how I felt about the whole thing. Was it a reward or a punishment? I still do not know. I kept the papers in my file, and moved the whole incident to the back of my consciousness.

But, in the fullness of time, my foundation work ended, my book was published and the documentary film I had been working on at the same time was almost complete. I began to feel the inevitable low that accompanies endings when my son Benjamin happened to call. Sensing my mood, he asked me what the problem was. I told him my work was done.

'How can you say that?' he asked. 'You still have the Cambridge project to do.'

I finished talking to Ben, and as I put the phone down, my hand landed on an announcement of a fellowship offering in England. It had been on my desk for a while; I just had not paid attention to it. The Oxford Centre for Jewish and Hebrew Studies was inviting applications for fellowships in modern British history. Serendipity. I cannot really explain it as accidental; I no longer believe in accidents. Certainly the Cambridge project, if it was to be done, had to take me to England. The fellowship offered five months in England with housing and a stipend, enough to start the research. I called immediately to find out about the deadline, and I was told it was in three days. 'That's ridiculous,' I was actually indignant. 'I can't get anything to you in three days.'

'Sorry, the Board of Governors meets then. You can fax an application if you'd like.'

So, I faxed my application and a few weeks later was notified that I had been awarded the fellowship. It was then that I really became scared. I am not trained in history. Did I really want to do this job? What nerve, for a woman I met for three hours once in my life to give me a piece of work! And why didn't I think it through before I applied? The next day I sent my acceptance letter to the Oxford Centre. I committed myself. I had a job to do.

CHAPTER ONE

Cambridge Daily News:
Mirror of the Community

According to one inhabitant's evaluation, the number of Jewish families living in Cambridge in 1938 could be counted on the fingers of one hand. She was talking about the townspeople, not the university community. Whilst she may have understated the case, the Jewish community was small by any standard and it kept a low profile. Indeed, a fair number of ordinary townspeople may have only been acquainted with Jews of the Bible, having never seen or met any contemporaries. The Jews of Cambridge lived quietly and, for the most part, modestly. Like much of the community at large, they were preoccupied with their economic survival and increasingly concerned about the fate of family in Germany and Austria.

Kristallnacht – 10 November 1938, the Night of the Broken Glass – burst upon the scene like a bolt out of the blue, sending shock waves through the entire population. The Cambridge Refugee Children's Committee (CRCC), in the planning stage since 1936 and engaged in preparing to accommodate refugee children in Cambridge, could no longer afford the luxury of rationally deliberating. Greta Burkill and other members of the CRCC immediately stepped up the tempo of their work. In a memo Burkill describes their reaction:

> On we worked, finding homes and jobs until November 1938 [when] *kristallnacht* made the goal of the Nazis unmistakably clear ... The Nazis ran amok, killing, destroying and rounding people up for Concentration Camps ... The urgency piled up, the whole of Great Britain was aghast – the horror of it all went like an electric current through every town and village. The feeling was 'we must save the children'.[1]

The *Cambridge Daily News* reflects this time in Cambridge as only a local newspaper can. Like most such papers everywhere, the *CDN* typically focused on local events: news of the cricket club; the proceeds of the handicraft sale; sports; marriages and deaths; drownings; unfortunate accidents;

accidental fires – the ordinary and extraordinary joys and traumas of life lived in a community. Events elsewhere in England or on the Continent did not necessarily get front-page treatment. But on 10 November 1938 and for a week following, the front page of the *Cambridge Daily News* was preoccupied with *kristallnacht* and its after-effects. In one-inch letters, a banner headline across the top of the first page seemed to blare out the news: 'German's Terrible Revenge of Jews'. Subhead: 'Bomb used in Orgy of Destruction. Thousands arrested.' The story follows.

> So terrible is the revenge that Germany is taking for the shooting of Herr Von Rath, one of her Paris Embassy officials, that it seems impossible that in a few more hours there will be one piece of Jewish property unwrecked or unpillaged. All over the country today, synagogues have been fired. In some cases, bombs have been used for the destruction, Jews being forced to remove the wreckage. Of eleven synagogues in Berlin, nine are either burned down or are in flames. Shops and homes are being wrecked, people, including children, are being turned from their beds into the streets. In Vienna, 5,000 Jews have been arrested including many waiting outside British consulates for Visas to enable them to leave the country. Suicide among Jews is rife – 22 have occurred in Vienna alone ... The wave of terror bears every mark of being organized. Jews not [allowed to] defend themselves. Jews caught with arms will get 20 years in a concentration camp. Jewish houses and shops have been wrecked and pillaged in Nuremberg and all synagogues set on fire in Frankfurt.

In the days following the uninhibited rioting and abandonment of human decency in the brutal treatment of Jews and Jewish property, the news of *kristallnacht* and its after-effects continued to get prominent front-page coverage in the *CDN*. On 11 November 1938 the headline informed its readers that Germany had arrested hundreds of Jews. As if reticent to cast any blame on neutral powers who were reluctant to intercede at an earlier date, the paper begins its story with a Reuters release published in the *New York Times*: 'Recently this [German] government has extended its domain with the <u>consent of Western Powers</u> [emphasis added] who acquiesced in its bloodless victories as a prelude to scenes yesterday which no man can look upon without shame for the degradation of his species.' On 12 November 1938, the *CDN* ran another front-page banner headline that identified German restrictions on Jews:

> [Jews are] excluded from Cinemas and May not Visit Theatres – Milliard [a thousand million] Marks Penalty. [Jews had to pay for the damages the Nazis had inflicted on Jewish-owned shops and buildings.]

Jews forbidden to visit theatres, concerts, cinemas, music halls, dancing performances or exhibitions of any kind by order of Dr Goebbels, the Propaganda Minister. Jews attending them will be punished severely – All Jewish men between ages of 18 and 60 who are German in Frankfurt are taken by police in Frankfurt to concentration camps.

On the same day the *CDN* published a letter that had first appeared in the *London Times* by the Archbishop of Canterbury, deploring 'the cruelty and destruction visited on the Jews'. The archbishop is quoted as saying that the most sinister aspect of all was the fact that the police 'either acquiesced and/or participated in the devastation or were powerless to stop it. Just when there seemed to be a general desire to be on friendly terms with the German nation.' The Independent Labour Party expressed its outrage at 'a crime against the whole human family'.

On 14 November 1938 the *CDN* reported: 'Jews must pay immediately for the damage caused to Jewish shops in the November 10th rioting; the Berlin Bourse is closed to Jews; and the "race" is banned from universities. All Deans in [German] universities were to ban Jews from attending lectures.' On 17 November 1938 the *CDN* reported that 'Cambridge students protest by formal letter to the German Ambassador in London [against] the treatment of the Jews.' Finally, on 18 November a 'Letter to the Editor' appeared in the *CDN* in which the writer, T.M. Pilkington of Bentley Road, explores the question: 'Why do we not like the Jews?' Calling attention to the pressing need for 'friendly hospitality' if children and old people 'are to be saved from a terrible fate', the writer asks, rhetorically, 'Why do we not offer our help?' He answers, '[Because] we ourselves do not like the Jews very much more than Hitler does. Can we not … remember that the German Jews are just ordinary peace-loving people like ourselves?'

Three days later, the Bishop of Ely, Dr B.O.F. Heywood, made the front page of the *CDN* with his plan/request to the church assembly and its board of finance to raise £50,000 for the relief of non-Aryan Christians (baptized Jews), who are also being persecuted in Germany. On the same page there is a parallel article reporting that since 1933, 11,000 men, women and children have been given permits to enter England. There is also a report stating that Prime Minister Chamberlain had asked voluntary organizations to do a survey of land in British Guiana for Jewish refugees. Whilst Palestine consistently offered to take in any and all refugees, the prime minister claimed that Palestine was 'too small to immediately provide a solution to the refugee problem'.[2]

Between 23 and 25 November 1938 a Franco-German pact was signed, cultural relations between Germany and Italy were strengthened, and a German-Japanese pact was confirmed. For the Germans, things seemed normal once again, according to the *CDN*. But in England the momentum was growing for the English to do something more than passively sympathize with the victims of German aggression. On the day the German-Japanese pact was signed, Lord Baldwin made an impassioned radio appeal to his compatriots on behalf of the refugees and the Baldwin Fund was born. It ultimately raised millions of pounds for refugees to come to England.

On 1 December 1938 the first transport of 500 refugee children from Germany left the Hook of Holland for Harwich. Up until then not a word had been reported by the *Cambridge Daily News* about the imminent arrival of foreign children. It is not clear whether the newspaper knew it was about to happen and chose to remain quiet for the safety of the children or that the Cambridge Refugee Children's Committee purposely kept the news to themselves. Given the ambivalent feelings in England about refugees arriving on their land, the CRCC reasonably may have decided the less known the better and thus did not issue press releases. However, on 2 December 1938 the front page proclaimed the arrival of these young 'victims of Nazi anti-Semitism'. Large, bold headlines on the front page told of the 'First of 5,000 Jewish and non-Aryan children who will find a home in England. Next batch of 300 Jewish children from Germany is expected to arrive in England next Friday.' Eventually 9,354 unaccompanied and 'unguaranteed' refugee children came to England.[3] The entire *Cambridge News* story of the first transport's arrival follows.

Two hundred boys and girls, sad-eyed and pursued by the shadows of unseen grief, sighed as they trod on English soil. Looming through the darkness of a bleak winter morning. Pakeston Quay at Harwich was as unlovely as any British or Continental post could be, but for them today – refugees from a storm more fierce than the North Sea gale through which they had sped during the night – it was home, the spot of earth supremely blest. They were the first of the 5,000 Jewish and non-Aryan children who are to find refuge immediately in England from the Germany that they can no longer call their home. Out of the North Sea mist they came in the LNER liner, *Prague*, before daybreak this morning – as tragic a freight as ever set forth across the sea to a strange new land. Many of the children are fatherless and motherless, and come with vivid memories still lurking of the orphanage where they were sheltered in Berlin, fired above their heads, and of their dash for life from the only home they could remember as it crashed in flames. The others, about half of the total, came from the Hamburg district.

The children were enabled to enter England and a brave new world today by a form of permit which has never been used before – a printed form bearing simply each child's photograph, together with his or her name and those of the parents. 'The Home Office have been simply marvellous. We cannot thank them too much,' said Major G.H. Langdon, who was in charge of the landing arrangements …

The refugees are to be provided for at a holiday camp at Dovercourt Bay, near Harwich, until accommodation can be arranged for them in private houses. A reporter who toured the camp, found the children eating a breakfast of porridge, bread and butter and jam, and tea or cocoa – the first hot meal they had for more than 24 hours. One room was stacked from floor to ceiling with brand new garments sent by Jews. The next batch of 300 Jewish children from Germany is expected to arrive in England next Friday.[4]

After the arrival of the children, the Chief Rabbi, Rabbi Joseph Hertz, wrote to Lord Samuel. Instead of expressing appreciation for the efforts made on behalf of the children, the Chief Rabbi voiced displeasure because he had learned that the next transport was due to leave on Saturday, 10 December.[5] For religiously observant Jews, travel on the Sabbath is not permissible. As a result, the next transport was delayed and arrived on Monday, 12 December. Perhaps in reaction to Hertz's letter, the import of which may have been privately communicated to the editor of the *Cambridge News*, only a very short article headed 'The Parting' reported the second arrival of children. Although it appeared on the front page, the reader could easily miss the small article taking less than two inches of column space and squeezed between 'Moral Rearmament in Holland' and a lottery story, 'A Quick Million'. The report tells of the separation of very young siblings, a painful consequence of the *Kindertransports* and the chaotic pressure of the times. Some siblings, thus separated, never saw each other again. The *CDN* story reads:

> Slightly bewildered by a new country, a young refugee from Nazi perse-cution of the Jews in Austria stood on the quay at Pakeston, Harwich, today. He had just said an affectionate goodbye to his sister. 'I'll see you again, soon,' she comforted him, as she left with compatriots to the camp at Lowestoft. Brother and sister were two of 527 refugees who reached Pakeston today from Vienna. Many can speak English. The boys were sent to the Dovercourt refugees' camp.

On the same day that the second transport of children arrived,[6] Eva Hartree, chairperson of the children's sub-committee of the Cambridge Refugee Committee (CRC), announced in a letter to the editor of the *Cambridge Daily News* the formation of another sub-committee to find homes in and around Cambridge:

... for the unfortunate children who are obliged to leave their homes and parents in order to escape from misery and hardship inflicted upon them in their own homes. We would greatly welcome offers to take one or more children for what, we hope, will be a limited time, until arrangements can be made for their parents to rejoin them, either in Great Britain or elsewhere. Most of the children are of the Jewish race, but there are also many 'non-Aryan' Christians among them and these, as the Archbishop of Canterbury has said, are a special responsibility of the Christian community. There are also orphans (... a large proportion of the party which arrived recently at Dovercourt are from an orphanage in Berlin which was burnt over their heads, leaving them homeless) and it may be that some will wish to take a child more permanently. We should be especially pleased to receive such offers. We have received many kind offers of help, e.g. medical and dental supervision ... and educational facilities either free or at reduced fees; also special classroom accommodation, where they can assemble together to learn English during the first weeks of their arrival before entering school among English companions. The children will be able to go to the elementary schools where this is desired, so the cost of education need not be taken into consideration by those who feel that they would like to do their share in this work of mercy. We have every hope of being able to allow a small sum per week to those who have accommodation but feel that they cannot afford the extra expense of having a child to feed and clothe. The amount of such allowances and the number of them which we can give will depend on the response to the appeal of Lord Baldwin and our local appeal for financial aid from those who are not able to help by providing accommodation. All offers of homes should be sent to Mrs Hutton, 1 Chaucer Road, who will send a form to be filled in by the applicant in order that all particulars may be registered. Donations and subscriptions and promises of financial help should be sent to Mr R.G.D. Laffan, Queen's College.

Yours, etc. Eva Hartree[7]

At this time the CRCC was a sub-committee of the CRC and did not, as yet, have its own office. Offers of homes were to be sent to the residence of Mrs Hutton, and promises of financial help were to be sent to the office of Mr Laffan. Given the difficulty of coordination, it is remarkable that the CRCC accomplished what it did.

As a seeming follow-up to Mrs Hartree's letter in the *CDN*, there appears an announcement from the executive committee of the Cambridge Borough Liberal Association.[8] The association, at its weekly meeting, expressed, by resolution, its conviction that 'the people of Britain would support His Majesty's government in offering asylum to a large number of refugees from Nazi tyranny'.

On the day the second transport was to have arrived (10 December) a meeting scheduled by the United Council of Christian Witness was held in Cambridge at the Emmanuel Congregational Church schoolroom, where a plan to help refugees was to be presented. It was preceded by Mary Campbell's eye-witness account of the plight of Jewish refugees in Vienna. Campbell is identified as 'a Cambridge girl', recently returned from a tour of duty at a Quaker office in Vienna. During his introduction, the Master of Selwyn College spoke of a 'centralized committee concerned with refugees', referring, no doubt, to the local CRC or the CRCC or both.[9]

The CRC/CRCC had received from a Mrs Lilley the offer of a home at Hunstanton to be used for the next four months by 20 young adult refugees (up to the age of 30), who would get training in 'English ways' of cooking and some training in the English language. Domestics and farmers were permitted entry visas to England and a number of refugees from Germany and Austria willing to be trained for those positions were given entry visas and thus were spared the Holocaust. The chairman of the meeting hoped the congregations in Cambridge would 'adopt' the refugees and see them through financially. 'We want this to be part of Cambridge's contribution to the refugee problem', the Master declared. Presumably, when the training was completed, the refugees would be qualified to serve as maids or butlers in Cambridge homes. A resolution in favour of the scheme was unanimously passed.

Miss Campbell then gave an eye-witness account of the Jews' plight in Vienna, where continuous streams of refugees from various countries were searching for some means of leaving but finding all doors closed to them. Campbell directly blamed pernicious and pervasive anti-Semitism for keeping England from doing what was demanded:

> Up to the present there had always been some place to which [refugees] could go, if not in Europe to some undeveloped country elsewhere, to start life afresh … It was not that there was no longer room; there was plenty of room in our own British Empire. But the doors [are] closed, and it [is] the duty of those interested in the problem to see that the doors [are] opened. It depends on us to show that public opinion demands these refugees should be given shelter, at least for some time, in our own country … Within the larger problem of the refugee [is] contained the whole problem of anti-Semitism and the Jewish problem. At the moment, the refugees suffering most [are] perhaps the Jewish ones. It [is] by no means only the Germans who [hate] the Jews: there [are] plenty in other countries. There [are] some in our own East End and in other parts of the country.[10]

By her own admission, Mary Campbell is not talking about the 'full Jews' in desperate straits, but those who had converted, the non-Aryan Christians, whom she considered to be in the most difficult position of all because they belonged neither to the Jewish community nor to the Christian community:

> The full Jews said, 'You don't belong to us, you have left the Jewish faith', and the German government replied, 'You are all Jews.' In Austria, where a great number [of non-Aryan Christians] were members of the Catholic Church, the church had not lifted a finger to save them because it dare not. Individual Catholics, however, had been extraordinarily brave.[11]

At the Friends' Centre in Vienna, where the speaker had been working, the staff considered Austrians as 'kindly, happy-go-lucky people and different from the Germans'. The Quakers were confident that if National Socialism were to come to Austria at all, it would be in a 'milder' form. Sadly, Ms Campbell declared, they were all wrong. 'The behaviour of the Austrians towards the Jews was worse than that of the Germans.' The Nazis in Austria had accomplished in days what had taken years in Germany. Campbell graphically described the unbridled plundering and the incomprehensible sight of Hitler Youth members forcing elderly Jews to scrub the pavements.

'When all "full" Jews lost their jobs, the non-Aryan Christians hoped they would be treated differently but they were not.' Campbell then continues talking about Jews without discriminating between non-Aryan and non-baptized. 'Hardest of all for the Jews was the economic pressure, their losing all means … or hope of livelihood.' Jews were told that they had to leave the country within a certain time or risk imprisonment. Searching for help, they appeared at the Friends' Centre, but unless they had influential contacts, the Quakers were helpless in the face of the desperate situation. 'Many people were turned out of their homes. If they asked where they could go, the official answer was, "The Danube is big enough for you all".'

Mary Campbell urged Cambridge citizens to help refugees obtain visas quickly by offering or guaranteeing them hospitality for an indefinite period or by providing jobs such as domestics. All a prospective employer would need to say, she claimed, was that he/she had tried, but had not succeeded, to find a suitable English servant. She advised immediate action, because 'tomorrow it might be too late'. The proposed plan would allow a small number of people into the country immediately for training as domestics. Short-term hospitality in England was also needed for people who had affidavits to go to America, but who had to wait for permission to leave. Accommodation in a more neutral place than Austria was needed for them while they were waiting. At the end of her talk, Ms Campbell referred to help being given to child refugees, but she did not elaborate. In fact, from mid-December until the end of 1938 the *CDN* published items almost daily about refugee foster and adopted children who were injured, abused or killed.

On 14 December 1938 a small item on page 1 of the *CDN* was entitled 'Jewish Children'. Ambassador Malcolm MacDonald stated in the House of Commons that the British government could not agree to authorize the immediate immigration to Palestine of 10,000 German Jewish children, but 'this did not necessarily mean that the request would be permanently refused. It would be considered during the London conference on Palestine, which it is hoped will begin next month'.

On 15 December 1938 the arrival of a third group of refugee children at Pakeston Quay was reported in a small article on page 3: 'Youngest Refugees Arrive/Twins from Hamburg'. Like so much of the reporting about the children at this time, the description is highly idealized:

> Three hundred and fifty boys and girls, whose ages range from 3 to 17, arrived from Germany via the Hook of Holland. The most popular members of the party were Samuel and Jacob, 3-year-old twins, who had come from Hamburg. Smartly dressed in navy suits, with long trousers and navy and red hats, they were profoundly happy, and were met by a London women who is adopting them. They talked with everyone in the waiting room, and appeared surprised that the great majority were unable to converse with them. They were the youngest refugees yet to arrive in England.

On 30 December 1938 forty-eight more Jewish child refugees from Berlin arrived via Hamburg at Southampton on the US liner *Washington*. Some of the young newcomers were sent to family friends or relatives, others were assigned to English homes. The older ones were to get training to prepare them for overseas settlement. The children, aged 3 to 17, were reported to be well dressed and looking well cared for. Repeated attention in the press to the appearance of the children points out the seeming incompatibility between the children's clothes, their healthy looks, and their 'refugee status'. Further, each one had a sponsor who signed guarantees for them. The implication a reader might reasonably draw is that the children came from affluent homes and were well connected. Neither the reporters nor the readers of the *CDN* had any idea of the sacrifices parents may have made in order to send their children to England properly outfitted. Nor did they know how hard the CRCC worked to get guarantors in an effort to save the maximum number of children. The guaranteed children were not counted against the imposed quota of 1,000 unguaranteed children per month.

The civil war being waged in Spain for the maintenance of democracy against the forces of fascism contributed to the turmoil of the times. In the same issue of the *CDN* (30 December 1938) that reported the happy arrival of refugee children, there was a letter to the editor from Joseph Needham, a world-renowned scientist and distinguished master of Gonville and Caius College in Cambridge. Needham asks readers to join him in 'a solemn protest [against] the granting of belligerent rights to General Franco's rebellion against the legitimate and democratic government of Spain'. On 6 February 1939 a memorial service was held at the Corn Exchange in memory of five Cambridge men, members of the International Brigade, who died in Spain in an effort to preserve democracy. A few weeks later, in ironic contrast, a front-page headline told *CDN* readers that Britain's House of Commons recognized General Franco's administration as the legitimate and sovereign government of Spain.

As 1938 drew to a close, the *Cambridge Daily News* cited as the story of the year the fact that the nations of Europe had come to the brink of war and at the eleventh hour had turned back. Across the Channel, the *Berliner Börsen Zeitung*, in its review of the year, accused Britain of 'attaching more importance to the friendship of Jewry than that of Germany'.

In the first two months of 1939 the news coverage of refugee children in Cambridge is muted, squeezed out perhaps by the ominous 'gathering storm' on the horizon. One would never know, from reading the newspaper, the kinds of issues both the CRC and the CRCC were confronting. Nor could the casual reader guess at the frenzied activities of volunteer workers in Cambridge and London in anticipation of more children arriving.

The *Cambridge Daily News* did reflect a world hovering at the edge of war and reported events related to it. Facing an uncertain future, local couples decide not to delay their wedding plans, but instead to marry before the prospective husband leaves for army or navy training. Week after week wedding photos of a smiling bride and groom surrounded by family are on the front page, together with stories of other young Cambridge men leaving to serve their country or asking for conscientious objector status.

In a letter to the Editor, Mrs Hartree of the CRCC criticized the British public for hanging on to the words of Hitler: 'It is bad for the people and bad for Hitler.' On the other hand, in January 1939 there is a complaint in the 'London Letter' (a regular column in the *CDN*) that there is too much broadcasting of appeals on behalf of refugees:

There is now a real danger of a general revulsion of feeling for these appeals for the refugees. [They] are doing real harm to home causes. For one thing, it is checking the flow of subscriptions to our hospitals and charities ... The chairman of the London Philanthropic Society says that while British generosity has responded warmly to appeals made on behalf of victims of war and political persecution abroad, some deserving charities at home are feeling the pinch. Further notwithstanding assurances by Whitehall that foreign refugees will not be stayers and will not take jobs in Great Britain, there are numerous complaints that it is already happening ... One country corporation has just decided to engage refugee nurses for the hospitals under its control. It will need a good deal of persuasion to convince Britain's own unemployed that the refugees are not diverting help they would otherwise receive and possibly taking jobs which they should have.[12]

As if to reinforce the same sentiment, another item reports the protest of 200 members of Cambridge University by petition against 'the continued neglect of the problem of unemployment during the last seven years', claiming that unemployment had increased by 300,000 in one year.[13]

On 7 March 1939, the *CDN* printed on page 1 an item concerning the continuation of Anglo-German trade. Two members of the Board of Trade, President Oliver Stanley and Mr R.S. Hudson, secretary of the Overseas Trade Department, were questioned in the House of Commons concerning a forthcoming visit the two were making to attend a dinner in Berlin tendered by the Reichsgruppe Industries. Since trading relations between England and Germany were to be settled by agreements between the different industries represented by the Federation of British Industries and the Reichsgruppe Industries, the House wanted to know what the motives of the two were in attending. Oliver Stanley's answer, as reported in the *CDN*, is far from clear. It implies that establishing contacts with those prominent in German economic life and surveying general problems connected with Anglo-German trade is useful. Business goes on as usual – preparing for the evacuation of children in the event of a German attack; continuing trade negotiations with German business associates.

If in 1939 the general public were preoccupied with the social stresses growing out of the economic depression and the looming war, then government officials were sorely tried by their responsibilities to meet all crises at one and the same time. Whitehall anticipated attacks from Germany and, trying to minimize the potential human toll, put in place a plan for the evacuation of women and children from London and other vulnerable areas on the eastern coast.

Well in advance of the evacuation (September 1939) specific government-appointed agencies were lining up homes where children and others would be boarded. By law, every household with one or more spare rooms were required to take in children or evacuated adults in the event of an emergency. The Cambridge area became an evacuation destination and a survey was commissioned to determine how many evacuated British women and children could be accommodated there. It was concluded, for example, that the Cambridgeshire town of Huntington, with a population of about 5,000, would be able to accommodate 2,212 additional persons in the event of war – nearly equal to half the town's population.[14] The majority (1,129) would be children; the remainder comprised helpers, teachers and accompanying adults – some with infants. Accommodation for 157 had already been reserved by relatives of townspeople before the census was taken. According to a scale of one person per room, Huntington had room for 2,424 persons, but older citizens of the town would be excused from catering for children. In all, 16,000 schoolchildren were allocated for evacuation to the Cambridge region.[15]

On the day Hitler gave orders for the invasion of Poland, 1 September 1939, the British government ordered the evacuation of children, their attendants, and teachers from the vulnerable areas of the eastern coast to safer places inland. Within three days, 1.5 million persons were conveyed into the interior of the country.[16] On 3 September Britain declared war against Germany.

Evacuated with the children were government workers and essential government papers and files, causing great inconvenience, particularly to newly arrived refugees and to those trying to help family in Europe. On the whole, the stories of the evacuation in the *CDN* put a smiling face on a sad event: the children are happy; the Cambridge hosts are kind. In Germany, the political editor of the *Frankfurter Zeitung* was quoted as claiming: 'the longer the war lasts, the more likely it is to create the danger of Bolshevism'. And in London, the British Federation of University Conservatives and Unionists passed a resolution stating that the war must continue until the 'objectives for which we entered upon it are secured'.[17]

In another part of the world, within sight of the port of Haifa, over 400 desperate Jewish refugees from Germany were reported to be stranded in two small boats in the territorial waters of Palestine. They were prevented by British soldiers from entering the port or from landing.[18] The story on the front page of the *Cambridge Daily News* shared space with dramatic accounts of the war elsewhere: gun battles on ships and 'dog-fights' with enemy planes in the air.

Alongside the drama of the times captured on the front pages of the *CDN*, life in Cambridge went on and was recorded: weddings of the young; anniversaries of the old; parties to honour worthy citizens – defense workers, Air Raid Patrol volunteers and foster parents of evacuated children.

By early January 1940 no bombs had fallen on British soil, and parents in London and other places from which their children had been evacuated took them home against the advice of the government. Chief Rabbi Hertz also had been evacuated to Cambridge and was in residence at the Bull Hotel. From there, he expended much effort to secure Jewish education for evacuated Jewish children in Cambridge and grew extremely critical of London's Jewish parents, who took their children home. He accused the parents of sheer selfishness in their disregard of government advice. But, to the parents who came for their children, it did not matter that the Chief Rabbi was displeased, nor that they had to cope with the inconvenience and deprivations of food rationing. The bombs were not falling and they wanted their children home. Those who remained in Cambridge were the refugee children who had no parents to ask for their return and no homes to go to. In the evacuation area, they became the centre of an intense battle between the Chief Rabbi, his Religious Emergency Council and the leaders of the Refugee Children's Movement.

While the *Cambridge Daily News* was in no way responsible for the battle, it reported the event of 12 September 1943 that precipitated it. A Jewish evacuee/refugee boy living in St Ives was removed to a 'fresh billet' in a 'most irregular manner ... without any authority being given or asked of the St Ives billeting officer', who had responsibility for the children within his district. According to the story, the boy had been 'happily billeted' in St Ives for some time past and had been attending 'weekly Jewish classes in Cambridge by arrangement', returning to his billet at night.[19] But, on the day in question, the boy had been sent by 'Jewish authorities' direct from Cambridge to a hostel at Tyler's Green in London. He had left his clothes in St Ives, and did not inform either his hosts or the billeting officer in charge. The billeting officer asked the Minister of Health to have the boy returned. The harried man (the billeting officer) found the job of keeping track of the young people difficult enough; it would be impossible if evacuees were removed irregularly from the district without his knowledge. Furthermore, he claimed, the boy was 'very happy in his billet and had frequently expressed the hope to remain there until war's end'. To the officer, and to the council to whom he brought the complaint, it did not seem right for the boy to be sent away 'in this way ... without giving any kind of notice'.

The next day Eva Hartree wrote a letter to the CDN expressing the distress of the CRCC.[20]

> In view of the report of the evacuation officer of St Ives to his Council concerning the irregular removal of a Jewish boy from his care, I would like to make it clear that this action was taken without the knowledge of

the Regional Refugee Children's Committee, which, in the case of those refugees who are also evacuees, works in close collaboration with the billeting officers concerned. Yours, etc., Eva Hartree. Chairman, Regional Refugee Children's Committee, 13 September 1941.

At the same time, Greta Burkill sent a detailed report of the incident to Member of Parliament, Wm Seabourne Davies of Bournemouth. The resulting outrage led ultimately to the Chief Rabbi being denied his wish for guardianship of the refugee children. Parliament voted in 1944 for the guardianship to remain vested with Lord Gorell.[21]

NOTES

1. Greta Burkill, unpublished memoir, Add. MS 7485, Cambridge University Library.
2. *Cambridge Daily News*, 21 November 1938, p. 1.
3. A 'guaranteed' child was one for whom a sponsor provided a 'guarantee' bond of £50 to the committee to offset the costs of the child's remigration.
4. *Cambridge Daily News*, 2 December 1938, p. 1.
5. See Amy Zahl Gottlieb, *Men of Vision: Anglo-Jewry's Aid to Victims of the Nazi Regime, 1933–1945* (London, 1998), p. 113.
6. 12 December 1938.
7. *Cambridge Daily News*, 12 December 1938, p. 5.
8. The announcement is dated 9 December 1938.
9. Possibly the Master of Selwyn was referring to the newly organized Movement for the Care of Children from Germany and Austria (soon to be renamed the Refugee Children's Movement), which assumed administrative responsibility and coordination of the work of all the local committees. The movement's offices were in London.
10. *Cambridge Daily News*, 10 December 1938, p. 7.
11. Ibid.
12. Ibid., 21 January 1939, p. 4.
13. Ibid., p. 5.
14. Ibid., 8 March 1939, p. 3.
15. See Susan Isaacs *et al.*, *Cambridge Evacuation Survey: A Wartime Study in Social Welfare and Education* (London, 1941).
16. See Bob Holman, *The Evacuation* (Oxford, 1995), pp. 32ff.
17. *Cambridge Daily News*, 5 January 1940, p. 3.
18. Ibid., 8 January 1940, Reuters press release, p. 1.
19. Ibid., 12 September 1941, p. 3.
20. Hartree's letter was published in the *Cambridge Daily News* on 16 September 1941, p. 3. The same story subsequently appeared in the *Jewish Chronicle*, 19 September 1941, p. 27.
21. For a fuller discussion of the issues, see chapter 5 of this book.

CHAPTER TWO

Taking Responsibility:
An Organizational Effort

Great Britain has traditionally been regarded as an island unto itself, protected on all sides by water, its geography ensuring relative immunity from attack by foreigners. In the twentieth century the Sceptred Isle became a destination for colonials wanting a new life; for beleaguered people needing a safe haven; for those requiring an extended stopover on their way to elsewhere. In the 1930s it represented an eagerly desired refuge for Jews and others marked for extinction on the Continent. By the Second World War Britain's invincibility had gone. Aeroplanes, rockets and remotely powered vehicles made the formerly indomitable island refuge an easy target of missiles launched by Germany. London was blitzed, Coventry almost disappeared. Britain was not only vulnerable, it was in serious jeopardy of being blown away.

The British met the war with amazing courage and a firm determination to prevail. For Jews, as courageous and determined as any other people, it was more complicated. Lingering in Jewish memory was the uneasy history Jews had experienced in Britain, where they had been a presence since the time of the Norman Conquest. From their very early days in Britain, when their communities were miniscule, the Jews were subject to special taxes, their living space was circumscribed, and the conditions for their congregating to worship were controlled by government decree. Centuries later, they continued to be regarded as different and somewhat suspect. They were expelled from England in the thirteenth century, and invited back again in the seventeenth.

Their numbers remained small until the end of the nineteenth century, when Jews, fleeing persecution in their eastern European homes, migrated to Great Britain in appreciable numbers. In 1885 the Jews' Temporary Shelter (or simply Shelter) for poor eastern European Jews from Poland and Russia was established in London to provide refuge for the 'hapless wanderers'.[1] After a brief stay at the Shelter, the majority of the refugee Jews settled in the East End of London, where they created the institutions needed to live viable Jewish lives. Slowly, they began accommodating themselves to the life-style of the Jewish working class.

On 30 January 1933 Hitler was appointed Chancellor of Germany. The more astute German Jews realized that they needed to leave the country. In Britain Jewish leaders knew they had to take action. In March 1933, Otto Schiff, a stockbroker and president of the Shelter,[2] called a meeting of a diverse group of Anglo-Jewish leaders representing different religious and political orientations but united in their concern about the future of European Jewry.

The gathered leaders realized that the lives of their European co-religionists were at serious risk, and they had a special responsibility to help their kinsmen leave Germany. They also knew that those who came to England would need to be supported until they could find work and be self-sufficient. It was a daunting responsibility, especially at a time of worldwide economic crisis. Nevertheless, the precarious situation of German and Austrian Jews left their English relatives with no option but to offer assistance, even if they themselves feared for the safety of their own families.

At their first meeting, the Jewish leaders in England lost no time in organizing a Jewish Refugee Committee (JRC) and setting up a provisional office at the Shelter in London. The memorandum of association clearly states the purpose of the JRC: 'To relieve or assist Jewish refugees in any part of the world in such manner and on such terms and conditions (if any) as may be thought fit.' A parallel organization, the Central British Fund (CBF) was established at the same time. The CBF became the fund-raising arm of the JRC.[3]

The JRC was the 'hands-on' agency, taking care of the needs of refugees arriving in Britain with their families but dispossessed of their goods and homes. The CBF was the administrative and financial partner. Although the objectives and scope of the JRC and the CBF differed considerably, the two organizations were inter-dependent and worked in tandem, both on behalf of refugees in Britain and of those left behind in Germany. They had in common the following tasks:

(1) To facilitate the immigration into the UK of Jewish refugees, to help their absorption or re-emigration, and to provide them with financial and other assistance as needed.
(2) To assist the Jewish agencies in Germany and Austria in their pressing problems, particularly in their efforts to prepare young people for emigration.
(3) To use their connections with the British government to facilitate the admittance into Palestine of refugees, and provide financial and other assistance.
(4) To look after the refugees' interests *vis-à-vis* the Home Office, the Police and other concerned authorities.[4]

Even while the framework of these new committees was being drafted, Otto Schiff and others knew that to accomplish their goal of helping European Jewry they needed the cooperation of the British government. Thus, one week after their first meeting, a representative group – Neville Laski, Leonard Montifiore, Lionel L. Cohen and Otto Schiff – visited the Home Secretary. While pleading for a humane and generous response to the needs of the Jews in Germany, the group also assured the government that the Jewish community would bear the expenses for the refugees, who would not become a burden on the public treasury. This promise was based on an estimate that over the next few years 3,000 to 4,000 might seek admission to Britain. However, their estimate was hopelessly inadequate; before the end of 1933 alone, 2,274 German Jews were admitted.

Fortunately, the Shelter was in place as an absorption centre and a temporary home for the new arrivals. It was able to provide as many as five hundred people at a time with short-term housing and social services from an already functioning agency. However, it did not take long for the offices of the JRC and the CBF to outgrow the Shelter and a move was made to Woburn House, home of the Board of Deputies. Still later, when demand for its services increased significantly and more space was needed, the JRC relocated to Bloomsbury House, an old hotel in Bloomsbury, London, that had been converted into offices.

By the mid-1930s, coincident with the rise of Nazism in Germany, Jews were singled out and blamed for the world's economic collapse and later accused of responsibility for the war. Anti-Semitism was on the rise everywhere and the risk to European Jewry grew increasingly more serious. On the Continent Jewish academics were dismissed wholesale from their university positions, and Jewish professionals – doctors, dentists, lawyers, teachers, academics – were forbidden to practice. Whilst earlier German Jewish refugees came to Britain with enough funds to support themselves, the later ones arrived more destitute than those before them.

The Nuremberg Laws of September 1935 stripped German Jews of all their property and civil rights. Up until early 1936 the JRC was moderately successful in addressing both the needs and talents of new refugees and identifying sponsors and/or funds. Those émigrés for whom friends and relatives in the UK provided guarantees were helped by the JRC to secure entry permits; others were assisted in obtaining third-country visas and out-bound transportation. The Welfare Committee, a sub-committee of the JRC, found places for students in British institutions or apprenticeships, either in skilled trades or in agriculture. A resettlement committee provided a number of loans to businessmen among the émigrés, and helped their ventures get Home Office approval. The Professional Committee secured employment for men and women trained in a variety of professions. A domestic bureau helped several thousand refugees arrive as domestics, some bringing their children with them.

Hitler's annexation of Austria in March 1938, and the subsequent unprecedented reign of terror against the Jews, resulted in panic and more serious efforts by Jews to leave Germany and Austria. The British Jewish community actively sought government assistance to help the beleaguered Jews, and urged that no government limitations be placed on the number of refugees allowed to immigrate to the UK. On behalf of the JRC and the CBF, Schiff and a group of Jewish leaders again guaranteed the Home Office that no refugee admitted to Britain would become a public charge. After England was drawn into the war, substantial financial contributions from public appeals were difficult to secure and the CBF was forced to ask for government assistance on behalf of those struggling to gain a foothold.[5]

The Jewish community in Britain honoured its commitment to support the refugees until after *Kristallnacht*, 10–11 November 1938, when the need for European Jews to leave their homes became even more urgent. Demands on the resources of the JRC grew to breaking point, even as their decisions and actions were driven by the critical needs of their European relatives fleeing to safety in Britain.[6] The quandary of the Jewish community put British policy makers on the horns of a dilemma. Their humanitarian impulse to help the beleaguered was offset by their concern for the welfare of Britain, which was reeling under the impact of a major economic crisis and hardly prepared for the inevitable war.

In hindsight, it is easier to understand this dynamic. The time available for the making of crucial decisions did not allow for long deliberation. Government policies enacted at this time reflect the efforts to reconcile obdurate and/or contradictory facts and needs: refugee numbers in Britain were growing: visitors were applying for refugee status; getting rid of refugees was becoming more and more difficult; the number of stateless ex-Germans and ex-Austrians was growing. The last fact was especially difficult: once people are declared stateless, they become undeportable and it then would be difficult to enforce their expulsion or exclusion.[7]

To their credit, principled people in Britain fought on moral and humanitarian grounds for intervention and aid to the besieged and increasingly impoverished refugees in Germany and Austria. Colonel Josiah Wedgwood, Labour MP for Newcastle-under-Lyme, petitioned the Home Secretary, Sir John Gilmour, to relax the Aliens Act in order for people from Germany to have unhindered access to Great Britain. Gilmour, concerned with the economic condition of the country and afraid of the impact of a foreign labour force, declared that parochial interests had to take precedence over all other considerations. Yet, when a Conservative MP urged him to take all necessary steps to *prevent* German Jews from entering the country, Gilmour emphatically declared that there could be no discrimination against anyone on religious or racial grounds. Sir John Simon, the Foreign Secretary, requested that Germany be notified of the profound concern of English Jews for their co-religionists.[8]

In December 1938 Lord Baldwin, the former prime minister, made an impassioned radio appeal to the British public to support the refugees. He stressed that the Jewish community was caring for both Jewish and non-Aryan Christian refugees: 'Compared to their effort, the Christian contribution towards the aid of refugees ... had been insignificant.'[9] In response to the appeal, contributions were received from more than a million people, and government officials were both moved by the appeal and impressed by the results. The major portion of the funds raised was allocated to the newly formed Movement for the Care of Children (MCC).

In the years 1933–39 the CBF was the world's leading Jewish fund-raising agency assisting Jews in Germany and Austria and the one agency to which refugees and the communities caring for them turned. In the pre-war years the CBF understood that their organization could not serve Europe as a relief agency, but it could offer constructive alternatives in training or retraining in Great Britain and subsequent remigration for those forced to flee their homes.[10] The organization hoped, unrealistically, that monies could be raised locally in Europe to cover the cost of relief and organizational efforts.

In March 1939 Czechoslovakia was absorbed by the German Reich and the JRC was deluged by as many as one thousand desperate visitors a day who needed to help relatives and acquaintances on the Continent.[11] The steady stream of refugees coming to England and in particular to Bloomsbury House from 'almost all the countries of Europe' stopped only after the declaration of war.[12]

The JRC fulfilled its promise to the British government that refugees would be looked after. Its members met incoming trains carrying both Jewish and Christian refugees and their families from the Continent. They escorted the new arrivals, who had neither friends nor relatives in Britain, to the Shelter, provided them with food, short-term accommodation and help in planning for their future. The range of services provided to these new refugees grew with their needs. Whilst the majority of refugees were secular non-orthodox Jews, some were orthodox and had specific food and work restrictions; a number were non-Aryan Christians (baptized Jews and/or their children); some were Christians who opposed the National Socialist Party in Germany or Austria.

The initial rescue and relief plan had been for émigrés to stay a short period of time in Britain and then be moved to another destination. When it became clear that remigration was not an easy option, JRC members sought suitable housing for families, jobs for those old enough to work, and social opportunities. Their efforts were considerably hampered and compromised by a latent anti-Jewish prejudice the volunteers encountered and about which neither committees nor individuals could do anything. High unemployment created uncertainty and stress in the general public and exacerbated the feelings of 'otherness' in the refugees and in the Jewish community. The British Union of Fascists, under Oswald Mosely, exploited the anxiety and openly championed fascist ideology as a panacea. Popular British sentiment was against refugees coming into the country for fear that the newcomers would compete with the British for scarce jobs, and the Jewish community was understandably nervous about a possible outbreak of overt anti-Semitism.

Since 1934 plans had been advanced by various countries for the absorption of Jewish refugees and émigrés. Many of the plans came to nothing while good governments, like good people, stood by and did little. The *Jewish Chronicle* kept a close watch on events in Europe as they affected Jews and the wider world. From the early 1930s, this mirror of the Jewish world reflected the abysmal situation of desperate refugees. Without proper credentials, Jews were regarded as criminals, hounded everywhere, not permitted to enter into any country and not permitted to leave. When they could get passage on a boat, they were often not allowed to debark. The *St Louis* is one of several boats sharing this fate. The pages of the *Jewish Chronicle* read like a geography book: far-away places with unfamiliar names – Senegal, Uganda, Rhodesia – are considered as refuge for the desperate. But, invariably, governments offer reasons why they cannot tolerate more refugees.

The CBF administrative records make clear the constant preoccupation of members of the JRC with the onerous task of saving people.[13] Joan Stiebel, secretary first to Otto Schiff and then to the JRC, told how she and others worked often round the clock to prepare the files necessary to process the émigrés before they could be admitted to Great Britain. 'We worked in total pressure, often till 10, 11 or 12 o'clock at night. The only thing that mattered was getting people out. If we facilitated the paperwork, we could get a family out.'[14]

Whilst the CBF was greatly preoccupied with the raising and spending of funds, the leaders also were involved constantly with policy-making in response to the many and various kinds of problems needing attention. The CBF provided: (1) assistance to refugees either in transit or already in the UK; (2) grants to community agencies in Europe on behalf of émigrés; (3) ongoing allocations to Zionist organizations providing tools and equipment for agricultural trainees to go to Palestine; (4) assistance in the construction of housing in Palestine. In addition, money was made available to the non-sectarian Academic Assistance Council (AAC) (organized in May 1933) to absorb or place the 1,200 academics, jurists, physicians and other professionals summarily dismissed from their positions in German universities and institutes. CBF minute books[15] and AAC records[16] list a number of distinguished academics, both Jews and non-Jews, who were engaged in helping to place refugee colleagues in British institutions of higher learning.

After the outbreak of war the British government agreed to share the costs of maintaining refugees in England. Even so, by the end of 1939 the JRC and the CBF were on the brink of financial collapse and it was necessary to ask for a formal guarantee of maintenance from anybody wishing to sponsor a relative or friend. In February 1940 the government informed the House of Commons that it was satisfied that the Jewish community had done all it could in fund-raising and agreed to provide match funding of up to £27,000 per month. By the spring of 1940, 60,000 German-speaking Jewish refugees – men, women and children – were in the United Kingdom, constituting 25 per cent of all the Jews who had escaped from Germany, Austria and Czechoslovakia.[17] In October of the same year the government agreed to increase its grant to 100 per cent of each refugee's maintenance cost, as per an assessment by the National Assistance Board, and in addition to pay 75 per cent of the cost of administration and general welfare. By then, the JRC and the CBF employed (either full- or part-time) 600 people and had initiated a bewildering array of sub-committees to deal with the issues and problems of refugees.

The profusion of committees often complicated rather than simplified the work of committee members and the effort by refugees appealing for help to get it. Among those applying for assistance and guidance were young refugees recently arrived on *Kindertransports*. They needed help in order to support the efforts of their parents to leave Germany. Most of the refugees, young and old, had not mastered English and were confounded by the choices of offices to which they were directed. Consider the following:

Hospitality Committee – to find accommodation and homes, particularly for unaccompanied children; also for the collection and distribution of clothing

Domestic Bureau – to find employment in domestic service (one of the few positions for which permits were available) and negotiate labour permits

Immigration Department – working with the Home Office to process the daily flood of applications for entry permits

Emigration Department – to help refugees leave Great Britain for Palestine or the USA and to get appropriate visas

Nursing and Midwives Committee – helping girls and women obtain training and employment in these professions

Medical and Dental Committee – assisting the limited number of professionals to obtain British certification that would allow them to practice

Agricultural Training Committee – placing suitable young people in agricultural and artisan training establishments

Academic Committee – in conjunction with the inter-denominational AAC, placing appropriate people in research and teaching professions

Lord Hailey, chairman of the Inter-denominational Coordinating Committee for Refugees, complained to Harold Laski[18] that the resulting confusion 'did not encourage those who have no affinity with either Jews or Germans to sacrifice time and energy on behalf of these refugees'.[19]

Although accessing information in Britain certainly may have been a difficult and frustrating chore for the British Jews, they were considerably better informed than the American Jews about the situation of their co-religionists in Europe. Not only did the CBF maintain close contact with communities on the Continent, its members also visited Germany, Austria, France, Belgium and Holland and brought back news of conditions and needs. The *Jewish Chronicle* reporters in Europe sent back first-hand accounts of the brutalization of law-abiding citizens, random arrests and imprisonments. Articles reflecting conditions of the endangered Jews appeared every week, setting off a fresh frenzy of activity among Jewish leaders working on behalf of the endangered in Europe.

In contrast, American news agencies were extremely cautious and deliberately low-key in providing information to their readers. Preferring to subdue the news, American Jewish leaders limited the information available to the public. It was not until 26 October 1941 that the *New York Times* printed a small article (on page 6) reporting the massacre of 'thousands of Galician Jews by German Soldiers and Ukrainian bandits'. Eight months later, in June 1942, and buried in the inside pages, a very short article told of the massacre by the Germans of more than 1,000,000 Jews.[20]

American Jewish leaders were worried that a full disclosure of the horrors in Europe would prompt mass demonstrations by Jews and the results would be counter-productive. They preferred to engage in personal diplomacy in an effort to have Roosevelt and his cabinet intervene on behalf of the besieged. But President Roosevelt, preoccupied with his re-election and the economic crisis of the country, had different priorities. He simply did not want to consider the needs of refugees when he was fearing for the safety of Americans. He needed to get America prepared for the war, which he saw as inevitable.

On a visit to the United States in 1936, Sir Herbert Samuel[21] met with the President and asked that American consuls in Germany be instructed to speed the issuance of visas to eligible applicants waiting to go to America. Even this modest request failed, and no such change was effected. Like the rest of the world, America was in the throes of a serious depression and Jews everywhere were blamed for the downturn in the world economy. In the 'Land of the Free' fascist propaganda – from Father Coughlin to the Protocols of Zion and the Brown Shirts – had a certain cache, while news of Nazi atrocities was subdued.

America and, indeed, much of the world seemed to be burying its head in the sand on the issue of the seriously endangered people of central Europe. In contrast, Britain was very much engaged in the problem. Sir Wyndham Deedes, an English Christian deeply concerned about the rampant attacks on innocents in Europe and active particularly on behalf of vulnerable non-Aryan Christians, that is, baptized Jews, joined the effort to secure assistance for the threatened peoples of Europe. Deedes travelled with Norman Bentwich[22] to the dominions of Australia and South Africa to alert the dispersed Jewish communities of deteriorating conditions in Europe. The two hoped (1) to stimulate fund-raising efforts in the dominions on behalf of the persecuted, and (2) to urge the communities to put pressure on their governments so that refugees might secure entry permits. Their efforts produced only limited results. Dominion governments did not respond positively to appeals for allowing besieged immigrants to enter their countries. Landing permits in Australia were issued only on an individual basis to persons sponsored by friends or relatives. South Africa was less cooperative. One country after another found reasons why they could not absorb refugee Jews.[23] A seemingly impenetrable wall of bureaucratic regulations world-wide forbade Jewish entry or severely limited opportunities for Jewish refugees, even as the necessity to speed their immigration to countries of safety became ever more critical. Without their assets, the newly impoverished Jews were not welcome in countries that feared the refugees would be a drain on their economy. Jews in Czechoslovakia, Poland, Italy – in fact, all over Europe – were in a gravely dangerous situation. *Jewish Chronicle* headlines graphically reflected the problems: 'Pogrom in Bratislave: Nazis Lead Looting Mob: Police Arrive Four Hours Late'; 'Tension in Hungary: Half a Million Jews in Peril'; 'Italians Expel Foreign Jews: Vain Attempt to Enter France'.

Unlike most of the rest of Europe, Great Britain contained an established Jewish community and remained free of Nazi control or occupation. But, like the world at large, Britain, too, had its internal tensions and a perceived need to be both politically correct and empowered. Often, its decisions were pragmatic rather than humane. It effectively rejected plans for refugee settlement in colonies or protectorates such as British Guiana, Kenya and Northern Rhodesia.[24] And in its role as policeman to the Middle

East, it restricted entry to most of those Jews seeking to remigrate to Palestine.

Palestine was strictly off-limits beyond specified quotas; its borders were guarded by British soldiers. Those refugees who were able to reach the shores of 'the Promised Land' were either imprisoned or sent back. One report tells of British soldiers patrolling the coast of Palestine; their mission, to keep ships carrying refugees out. They prevented a boatload of starved and weary refugees, stranded off the coast of Tel Aviv, from docking. The half-crazed refugees, who had spent weeks on the boat without proper supplies, water or facilities, jumped into the sea and swam to shore. The soldiers were so affected by the plight of these people, starved, weary to death, and struggling to reach the shore, that they defied the orders of their superiors and rather than arrest the 'illegal refugees' as they staggered on to land, the guards gave them their own rations.

Whilst British soldiers stationed in the Middle East were ordered to prevent people from entering Palestine, Britain allowed people who could support themselves or who had relatives willing to guarantee such support to enter England. It welcomed almost 10,000 unaccompanied and unguaranteed children from Germany, Austria, Czechoslovakia and Poland over the 10-month period between December 1938 and September 1939. Indeed, Parliament streamlined the visa requirements to expedite the children's departure from their European homes and their accommodation in England. But unless their parents could obtain a visa for themselves, they were denied permission to enter the 'island refuge'.

Entry permits were available to adults willing to become farmers or domestics – two occupations for which England needed workers at the time. Movement committee members, having learned how to get around regulations in their efforts to rescue children, spent much time locating jobs for potential refugees and encouraging them to list all their children on their visa applications. If, when the family arrived, a prospective employer could not or did not want to accommodate the child or children with the parents, committee workers would find foster homes for the children. Although the low-paying positions on offer were often beneath the skills of the émigrés, the jobs were eagerly sought and provided a life-line for thousands.[25]

Starting in the spring of 1938 the *Jewish Chronicle* began suggesting to its readers that if their Jewish relatives and friends in Europe were 'prepared to go on the land and remain on the land', then they might be successful in getting the necessary exit visas.[26] In August the *Chronicle* carried a story on an experiment in Stadlau, a suburb of Vienna, where several hundred Jews joined together in a 'back to the land' movement and reclaimed waste land.[27] Thereafter, the *Chronicle* continued reporting on the prospects for farming for new and potential immigrants. A week after Kristallnacht, the *Chronicle* reported plans for the fiftieth anniversary of Mosesville, a Jewish farming community in Argentina. The community was the 'poster-child' of the Jewish Colonization Association (JCA), boasting 3,000 inhabitants, nearly all Jews, who had established two schools, a hospital, a library and sports fields.[28]

Whether the *Chronicle* was trying to shape British Jewry's attitudes towards refugees and farmers or whether it was providing practical assistance by informing its readers and Britain's relief organizations of the options available for émigrés remains a question. But during 1938 and 1939 there was at least a minor theme running through the pages of the *Jewish Chronicle* of farming as a possibility for new refugees, especially for adolescent boys and girls. The newspaper may even have been responsible for the decision of Lord Balfour's nephew to offer Whittinghame, an estate near Edinburgh he had inherited from his famous uncle, as a training farm for refugee boys and girls.

The American Joint Distribution Committee (AJDC), fully advised of events in Europe, joined with the United Palestine Appeal (UPA) and the CBF in forming the Council for German Jewry (CGJ), which sought to raise funds to help adult refugees and their children. But they could not solve the problem of where the refugees could go.

The CGJ in Britain activated a plan to train over a three-year period 80,000 to 100,000 young adults and children and to effect their orderly emigration from Germany to Palestine. Like many plans put forward during this intense time, the plan was totally civilized and completely naïve; as such, it evaporated. Nor was the required money forthcoming from the AJDC. After the Anschluss of Austria in March 1938, the AJDC moved to work more closely with the CBF for the benefit of Austrian Jews.

German students had been a presence in Britain for a long time. However, in 1936 the Home Office ruled that German children would not be admitted for educational purposes unless an approved family in Britain could guarantee they would not become public charges. At about the same time, Sir Wyndham Deedes organized the Inter-Aid Committee (IAC) for children from Germany,[29] that helped all children, especially Christian children of Jewish extraction.[30]

In July 1938 the *Jewish Chronicle* supported Deedes' plea, in the name of the Save the Children Fund, for Great Britain to adopt a more liberal immigration policy. Horrified at the deliberate social policy of the German government, Deedes felt world opinion needed to be mobilized against the barbarity, if it were to be mitigated. He wanted Britain to take an active role in providing more opportunities for asylum for both adults and children.

He further argued that, under proper safeguards, the 'right of work' should be accorded to a limited but substantial number of refugees, especially young people from Germany, who, he claimed, would bring special skills that could enable new industries to give employment to British workers. 'New people should be welcomed and not discouraged', he declared, ending with a statement that not since the Middle Ages has such transgression against human rights been seen.

Deedes focused on the children as being the worst sufferers, having grown up in an atmosphere of hostility kept at white heat by incessant propaganda. Their only hope for survival was migration to countries that would receive and absorb them. The *Chronicle*, in its support of Deedes, wrote: 'The problem of the outcast population of Greater Germany is of such magnitude that every country with a tradition of justice and humanity must contribute something towards its solution.'[31] By then, 60,000 children, from infants to teenagers, were identified as vulnerable.[32]

In the days following Kristallnacht, the British government supported the IAC and the CGJ in their efforts to actively promote transports of children from Germany to England. At the same time, the Home Office made arrangements to streamline the procedure by which foreign children could be admitted. Young refugees were to be re-emigrated before they reached the age of 18 or when their training in England was completed. However, the rapidly changing political situation forced these conditions to be repeatedly renegotiated.

Lord Bearsted[33] led a delegation to Prime Minister Chamberlain to enlist the government's cooperation in funding the rescue work of the voluntary agencies; he also requested that unaccompanied children be granted less restrictive entry to the United Kingdom. When Chamberlain promised to discuss the issues at the forthcoming Evian conference, convened for 6 July 1938 in France, he became a party to the efforts being made to save the children.

For all the anticipation and hope raised by the Evian conference, the results were sorely disappointing and, in fact, counter-productive. Evian confirmed that the free world would do nothing to stop Hitler and instead reinforced the confidence of the Nazis who, concluding they were doing the world's bidding, stepped up their programme of complete annihilation of the Jews. Chamberlain subsequently agreed to support any programme on behalf of children that the Home Office approved.

Another deputation, led by Lord Samuel, executive board member of the CGJ, called on Sir Samuel Hoare, the Home Secretary. The group included representatives from the IAC, the Society of Friends and the JRG. Hoarse ruled that unaccompanied children would no longer need to obtain national passports in Europe or entry visas from British consuls. It was a

major breakthrough. Children were granted entry into Britain on the basis
of identity cards, which the IAC was authorized to issue. The easing of the
required documentation made it possible to process children at a much
faster pace and meant that children who might otherwise not have been
rescued were saved. Hoare further agreed to lift earlier Home Office
restrictions on the accommodation for children, and to allow entry to *all* for
whom maintenance was guaranteed, either by individuals or by voluntary
agencies. In other words, an unlimited number of guaranteed children
would be allowed to enter the country.

To minimize the financial drain on the government and to ensure the
survival of the movement, a system of guarantees was instituted by the
British government in anticipation of the *Kindertransport*; the actual details
of the 'guarantee system' were modified on several later occasions. The
'guarantee' was for any child for whom a British citizen or any foreigner
could make a sufficient cash deposit or sign a promissory note guaranteeing
to pay for the remigration of the child to another country. Such a child was
called a 'guaranteed' case. Whilst the British government limited the
number of 'unguaranteed' children entering without any support to a
maximum of 1,000 per month, it agreed to allow into the country an unlimited number of 'guaranteed' children. The difference between a guaranteed
and an unguaranteed child was £50; to understand what that meant in
1938/39, the sum represented a year's wages for a working–class family.[34] A
guarantor was required to deposit this sum or a signed promissory note
with either the JRC or one of the local Refugee Children's Committees.

By spring 1939 the unprecedented numbers of refugees in Britain
depleted the funds of the CGJ and the services of its constituent agencies
reached breaking point. The executive board had to authorize bank
overdrafts in order for the rescue work to continue. Refugees in the UK
were placing an onerous financial burden on the limited resources of the
Anglo-Jewish community.

Over a hundred voluntary committees (also referred to as 'guardian
committees') had spontaneously formed across Britain to meet the needs of
endangered children from Europe. Eventually, the disparate committees
were grouped into twelve regional committees corresponding to an already
established map drawn for an air-raid warning system. The Movement for
the Care of Children from Germany and Austria was thus launched, with a
central office and regional representatives. In time the name was changed
to the more inclusive and shortened Refugee Children's Movement (RCM).
The local committees became the feelers or the agents for the RCM in
outlying districts. They publicized the distress of children, obtained
guarantees and offers of hospitality from neighbourhood people, and took
a parental interest in the children placed within the individual local juris-

diction. Local committees also raised funds to either establish hostels or to maintain children as necessary once they were placed with families.

The first task confronting the largely volunteer staff of the RCM in November 1938 was to prepare temporary accommodation for the children due to arrive in early December. Two summer camps – Harwich and Lowestoft – both located near the Dover port of entry, were assigned for older children and a third, a children's home at Broadstairs in Kent, was designated for the youngest. Within a fortnight, 500 suitable homes were found from all classes of British society: from artisans to well-known figures of everyday life; from the wealthiest to the unemployed. The RCM set up a new department to investigate the suitability of offered homes and to determine if those who offered to take children could afford to do so. The delay caused by these investigations earned the movement a great deal of criticism. But the organization had pledged that no child's maintenance would fall on public funds. Thus, its financial stability and the welfare of the children were both at stake.

On 21 November 1938 a committee of representatives of a growing number of organizations involved in child rescue work visited the Home Secretary and received promises of government support. Everyone was aware that war was imminent and that fast work was crucial. A day later the first committee meeting of the Movement for the Care of Children from Germany and Austria was held in temporary offices donated by Save the Children Fund. On 28 November the movement issued an appeal for financial and in-kind support, signed by the Earl of Selbourne and Viscount Samuel. Immediately, offers of hospitality and money came pouring in from all parts of the British Isles. They were dealt with as best as possible by a 'scratch' staff of volunteers. Subsequently, the movement's offices moved to Bloomsbury House (see Chapter 1) and extra staff were engaged.

As soon as the RCM office opened in London, English relatives and friends of threatened families in Germany and Austria flocked to it and exerted great pressure on the committees on their behalf. The precarious situation of all Jewish children in Europe was so dire that a policy of rescuing the greatest number possible had to be pursued. On 1 December 1938 the first train-load of children arrived in Harwich. They were spread out across the country, in accordance with the wishes of the Home Office not to have the children concentrated in one area.

Among the RCM's schedule of crucial tasks to be accomplished quickly were securing funds and homes for refugee children and establishing a system for keeping accurate records of their whereabouts and condition. At no time did the movement lose sight of the fact that they were responsible to absent parents for the well-being of their children. Local guardian committees were entrusted with the tasks of identifying potential foster families, supervising the care of children, and helping the movement 'decentralize' its immense efforts. By early December 1938, 26 committees had been formed and 41 more were in the process of formation. By 1939 over 100 local committees were in operation in Great Britain, staffed almost entirely by volunteers.

Whilst all the tasks were complicated, the most difficult was determining how to choose the limited number of children from the more than 60,000 identified as needing refuge in Great Britain. Thousands of letters begging for help were received by the RCM from all parts of Germany and Austria. The dilemma posed by the letters to the volunteers is reflected in the RCM's first annual report.

> Many [letters] were so touchingly written that it required a hard heart to consign them to files and indexes; yet, how were we to know which children to choose since we could not take all? We obviously could not adopt the principle of 'first write, first come', and how were we to be sure that all the details in the letters were absolutely correct?[35]

It was decided to rely entirely on the committees in Germany and Austria to determine priorities in the selection process. An exception was made in the case of those children for whom guarantees were signed in England, generally by relatives or close acquaintances. Which committees the movement worked with in Germany and Austria are difficult to ascertain. The first annual report of the movement, issued in 1940 for the year November 1938 to December 1939, identifies the committees in Germany and Austria as 'large central organizations to look after the interests of the Jewish communities and to facilitate emigration'. They are identified as the 'Reichsvertretung der Juden in Deutschland [Reich Representation of the Jews in Germany]' and the 'Israelitische Kultusgemeinde [Jewish Synagogue Association]' in Austria. In Berlin, the Reichsvertretung der Juden in Deutschland coordinated the work of all the community committees throughout the old Reich. Up until early March 1938 these were recognized by the German government and correspondence between them and England was, on the whole, 'unmolested'. In Austria, where the Jewish community was somewhat more concentrated – 95 per cent of Austria's Jews lived in Vienna – the central Jewish communal organization, the Israelitische Kultusgemeinde, was more easily accessible to the community.

On 12 March 1938, eight months before Kristallnacht, the Nazis took over the offices of the Israelitische Kultusgemeinde. Less than one week later, Adolf Eichmann, director of the Department of Jewish Affairs in the Reich Security Office, took charge of Jewish emigration. He summoned the

Jews, stripped them of their jobs and property, and issued passports stamped with a letter 'J', which was good for two weeks. If the Jews could not find a country willing to issue them a visa within that time, then they were subject to imprisonment. The Jewish community was in total chaos. Eventually, the Kultusgemeinde, with the help of an emissary from the West London Synagogue, secured permission from the Gestapo to restore the services of the Jewish social agency.[36] The Kultusgemeinde provided a necessary link with English groups and facilitated some parts of the emigration plan. They lost no time in trying to identify and process the Austrian children for the *Kindertransports*.

In Germany the Reichsvertretung der Juden in Deutschland was organized in 1935 when leaders of the German Jewish community in Berlin voluntarily established it with no interference from the Nazi authorities.[37] During the first years of its existence, it was a kind of forum or federation whose powers were limited by the needs and desires of its members. Although the Reichsvertretung had no legal standing in the Reich, the Jewish communities of Germany were functioning democratically within the totalitarian regime until Kristallnacht. Immediately the Reichsvertretung in Berlin was disbanded and the offices of all Jewish communities and organizations were closed. Given the acute need of the Jews for both community and cooperation, it is reasonable to assume its activities continued underground. The offices were reopened, with the same staff, at the command of the Gestapo.[38]

Towards the end of November 1938 the Gestapo set up the Reichsvereinigung für judische Auswanderungsforsorge (the National Union in Charge of the Migration of the Jews). The RCM's annual report refers to this time when it says there was much interaction between it and what must have been the phantom Reichsvertretung.[39] It is likely that the movement had no knowledge of the change within the structure of the so-called Jewish communal organization.

A copy of a letter dated 17 November 1938 by Hilda Sturge, a Quaker, in the file of the CRCC states: 'We are now receiving excellent cooperation from the Selbsthilfe (self-help) Deutscher Ausgewanderter and they are now helping us with the case of a Ph.D. in Cambridge.'[40] What Sturge understands to be a Jewish self-help organization was actually established by the Nazis to promote emigration. Nevertheless, there appears to have been some cooperation between the Cambridge committee and the Selbsthilfe Deutscher Ausgewanderter. In return for helping the CRC with the Ph.D. case, the German organization cited in the letter wanted information about four people who had been identified as 'urgent cases'. Sturge asks a Miss Banyard to make enquiries in the House of Commons of Dr Kenneth Pickthorne. The names listed in the letter are not children, but the mechanism of identifying urgent cases seems to be laid out here.

On 4 July 1939 the Nazi-imposed Reichsvereinigung der Juden in Deutschland (National Association of the Jews of Germany) replaced the Reichsvertretung, although it retained its staff. The Reichsvereinigung was conceived as the general, and compulsory, organization for all Jews n Nazi Germany (excepting Austria and the protectorate of Bohemia-Moravia). Yehuda Reshef summarizes its function and duties:

> The [Reichsvereinigung] was established by Nazi law and not by consensus of the Jewish organizations ... Its duties, as fixed by law, were to promote Jewish emigration from Germany and to support the Jewish school system and Jewish welfare. A special provision empowered the Minister of the Interior to assign additional tasks to [it]. The main advantage [was that the Nazis could deal with] a single Jewish organiza-tion subject to [Nazi] supervision. The existence of the Reichsvereinigung enabled the Nazis to implement many of their deadliest orders without much publicity and to play off the Jewish leadership against the Jewish population, who naturally blamed their own leaders ... Rabbi Leo Baeck, Otto Hirsch, Paul Epstein and their colleagues continued at their posts until their arrest and deportation ... The local activities of the Reichsverinigung were executed by the Jewish communities, compulsorily called Judische Kultusvereinigung (Jewish synagogue association) ... [which] dealt with small communities or with single Jewish families. In the course of time the Jewish communities were dissolved and their property transferred to the Reichsvereinigung. All Jewish publications were suspended and only the publication of the bulletin of the Reichsvereinigung, *Judisches Nachrichtenblatt*, was permitted. It served as a channel for the Gestapo to inform the Jews of new restrictions and confiscations without stirring up too much dissent from the outside ... Only two ... leaders [of the Reichsvereinigung], Leo Baeck and Moritz Henschel, survived the Holocaust.[41]

The Reichsvereinigung employed Jews to accomplish and carry out Nazi plans affecting the Jewish community. It served very much as the *Judenrat* did in the far-flung cities and villages of Poland and the Ukraine.

While the Reichsvertretung/Reichsvereinigung and the Kultus-gemeinde responded, as best they could, to the needs of their members, the numbers of endangered children extended beyond the parameters of the two organizations. Excluded from the shelter of Jewish communal support were (1) Jewish children whose parents belonged to neither the Reichsvertretung nor the Kultusgemeinde (these were largely from the orthodox Jewish community, who typically did not participate in secular Jewish organizations), (2) children of non-Aryan Christians (that is, the children of baptized Jews), and (3) Christian children whose parents opposed the political ideology of the National Socialists and were therefore vulnerable to arrest. All were in serious jeopardy.

The non-Aryan Christians and political refugees were the target rescue population of Christian church groups, particularly those that had branches in Germany and Austria. Especially notable was the work of the Quaker organization the Society of Friends, which had offices in Berlin and Vienna. The Friends maintained contact with individual families, forwarded particulars to England and gave whatever assistance they could to facilitate emigration. In addition to the Friends, there was a newly formed Confessional Church, associated with the Paulusbund in Berlin. Two individual confessional pastors, Pastor Gruber and Father Spiro, identified with the Paulusbund in Berlin, are cited in the first annual report of the RCM as deserving of special merit because of their active participation in the rescue work that helped Christian children and those of mixed marriages escape.

The case of children from Czechoslovakia was more difficult. Not only was there no established Jewish social agency, but also, the German take-over of the country was so sudden that there was no time to set up a central organization or to work out the details of a child rescue operation. Nicholas Winton, a young London banker working with Tad Chadwick, an English educator in charge of a school in Czechoslovakia, and assisted by a Mr Creighton and a Mrs Guthrie, set up the Czech Children's Refugee Committee. According to the RCM's first report, their 'devoted work equalled that of the Quakers in Austria'. Nicholas Winton himself personally secured guarantees for 664 children to come to England.

Upon learning of the accute need to rescue children first, Winton single-handedly proceeded to find guarantors by, in his words, 'writing articles, putting ads in the various papers, and knocking on doors'.[42] The Barbican Mission in London provided guarantees for 100 of the Czech children Winton rescued and personally escorted to England. The Mission, founded by a Jewish convert, openly acknowledged its programme of converting Jews to Christianity. Winton came under severe criticism from the rabbinic authorities and the Jewish community for accepting the guarantees of this Christian mission. In response, he asked a question for which there was no answer: 'Which would you prefer, a proselytized Jewish child or a dead one?' Winton claims he would have accepted guarantees from the Devil if he knew he could thereby save children.[43] Unfortunately, the last transport of 184 children from Czechoslovakia was bombed on its way to Britain, leaving no survivors.

By January 1939 it became clear that only a small number of children would be rescued if the operation were limited to only the urgent or the guaranteed cases. In that the guarantee system gave preference to children whose cases were not necessarily urgent, it was not in all cases fair. The RCM was concerned that many of those guaranteed children were from richer families who had relatives or acquaintances prosperous enough to support them.

Because of Britain's severe unemployment problem, a condition was imposed on all rescue efforts: children landing in the UK as refugees would leave the country by the time they were 18 years old. But the start of the war, in September 1939, precluded the enforcement of that condition. The Home Office then announced it was prepared to think about permanent unofficial adoption and residence of younger children and girls who entered domestic service or married British citizens.

The first transports were composed almost entirely of boys over the age of 14 who were either in concentration camps or in danger of being interned. According to the first report of the RCM, community organizations in Germany made up the lists of emergency or urgent cases for whom no guarantees had been secured but who needed to be shipped out fast. On landing at Harwich or Southampton, these unguaranteed children were placed in camps and arrangements were made to send them to private homes or to schools.

Each of the transports carrying groups of children arrived in Britain accompanied by designated Jewish community leaders, who had pledged to return to Germany. Berlin and Vienna were the central points of departure. From each of the large towns of the Altreich, a few children would set in separate compartments or coaches, to join the larger group in Berlin or Frankfurt-on-Main. The most used route to the UK was via the Hook of Holland. The other and longer route took the children to Hamburg or Bremen; there they boarded an ocean liner whose final destination was America with a stop at Southampton, where the children bound for England left the ship. The RCM's first report gives the following description.

The size of the transports varied considerably. Some were no larger than thirty or forty, others approached five hundred in number. Some came from Prague, some from Vienna, some were composed entirely of the pupils of one orphanage or school. Procedure at Point of Entry: When the ship docked at Harwich or Southampton, the representatives of the Movement would go aboard and proceed to place labels [abbreviated visas] around the necks of the children, bearing the name and number of each one. The Immigration authorities would take the children one by one, assisted by the Movement's transport officer, and would stamp the Home Office permits. The children would then go before the port medical officer who would place a stamp on the label around the neck

... The children would disembark and when their luggage was taken off, then appear before the Customs. Usually, the luggage was not searched ... The unguaranteed children then left the harbour by train or bus for the reception camps, while the guaranteed cases proceeded to London accompanied by the transport officers and leaders in a special train.

In London, the guarantors would have been informed of the arrival of the transport and would be waiting for their assigned child. After appropriate forms had been signed, foster parents and children departed for new destinations anywhere in the United Kingdom. In the process siblings were often separated, sometimes for years, sometimes forever.

The local press paid much attention to the arrival of these newcomers. Some of the coverage was quite sentimental. The picture of a sad child clutching a doll was juxtaposed with a happy, smiling group being led off by an equally happy young man holding a child by one hand and ringing an uplifted bell with the other. At the same time, pictures of healthy and prosperous-looking refugee children arriving wearing good clothes, bringing luggage, and hardly appearing emaciated, penniless or destitute produced some criticism or a mild form of expressed anti-Semitism, which was levelled at the RCM.

In fact, many of the children came from middle-class homes whose parents were either from the professional or business worlds. Into the limited luggage the children were permitted to take went the best clothing they owned or which had been purchased by their parents under conditions that could only be guessed. Included also were what few other treasured possessions were allowed them: a toy, a book, a musical instrument, some special food delicacy, a gift of gratitude to the prospective foster parent. The pictures the world saw did not betray the fear, anxiety and trauma of children abruptly separated from their parents. But their clothing, their language and their names set them apart from the British children, among whom they were forced to live.

Whilst a certain number of children from the early transports were sent to private homes, where their maintenance was 'guaranteed' by the host family, the majority of the children arriving were 'unguaranteed' urgent cases, most too old to go to school or even to be sent to private homes. Large summer holiday camps, empty in December, were rented to house the new arrivals. Dovercourt Holiday Camp, near the port at Harwich, was the first to be established; the second was Pakefield in Lowestoft. Neither accommodation was heated, and brutal December weather forced an overnight evacuation of the children to hotels and schools empty during the holidays. A *Manchester Guardian* article of 3 January 1939 gives a succinct, if idealized, picture of what a child experienced at camp:

As the sheltering taxi is nervously dismissed outside the great hall of the German refugee children's camp the visitor fears that knowledge of German may be the only link between herself, the children, and the resident helpers. There are English Christians and English Jews here, social workers, undergraduates – all sorts of people who come and go; above all, there is a band of trained and devoted German Jewish workers, both men and women, under the direction of a German Jewish headmistress whose understanding of children, coupled with her power of organization, amounts to something like genius ... Some of the older children are talking round one of the stoves, a few of the younger ones have toys to play with, and there are always groups round the ping-pong tables. Very few are reading, partly because it is difficult for these children to concentrate after all the excitement of their journey and arrival in a strange country, and partly because the books which have been presented to the camp are nearly all English. But there is one occupation which is unfailingly popular among them all, no matter what their age, and that is writing letters.[44]

The volunteer committees knew very well that they were in a grim race against time to save as many children as they could. The realization extended to the Home Office, the customs authorities, the railway and shipping companies and the hundreds of volunteer workers and paid staff, all of whom cooperated in the rescue operation.

After England was drawn into the war the transports effectively stopped, but not necessarily the flow of refugees, some of whom were able to make their way into the country by circuitous routes.[45] With the cessation of transport activity, the purpose and function of the regional committees changed from immigration to 'managed' after-care. An after-care department of the RCM supervised volunteers who tackled such basic tasks as ensuring adequate custodial care, including medical care as needed, education, and training for older children. Eventually, the local committees became entirely responsible for all the children in their individual areas, regardless of whether they came under the aegis of the RCM or another specific committee, or were sponsored by private guarantors.

Local committee volunteers were expected to visit each child at least twice a year and forward reports concerning the child's education, health and foster home conditions to the after-care department of the RCM. But the war forced new conditions on to the local committees, as new factors had to be taken into consideration: (1) the danger of losing communication between London and the provinces; (2) the difficulty of maintaining visits to individual children in wartime; and (3) the need to economize as much as possible. As a result, twelve regional committees were set up with the same areas under their charge as those of the Regional Defence. Each committee was required to have an organizer and an office, and to be able to provide the necessary care for the children in its own region should communication with the head office be cut off. The regional committees were granted the power to make their own decisions, and the mandate to continue keeping records of the children under their jurisdiction. It was of vital importance to know where the children were and what they were doing at all times. Each regional committee organized local branches and undertook supervisory visits to foster families or hostels to monitor the children's well-being and progress. Local committees were responsible for keeping their offices and records of the children under their care up to date. The twelve regional committees supervised and coordinated the work of 163 local committees. By the time war broke out, the RCM had processed 9,354 of the 10,000 children, which was their target.

The war added to the burdens of both RCM workers and the young refugees in Britain, even as it heightened anxiety about Jewish parents left behind on the Continent. Because the children came from hostile countries, they were regarded as potential enemies. It did not seem of consequence that they were refugees, Jewish children of innocent parents branded 'enemies of the state' in their native lands. In the free country of Great Britain, all those aged 16 or older born in Germany or Austria had to appear before tribunals to be judged innocent and free or potentially dangerous and subject to internment. Without much ceremony or prior notice, the potentially dangerous were sent to places such as the Isle of Man or shipped to Canada or Australia.

Committee members attended the tribunals to help plead refugees' cases; many who were asked to testify did not know English and had no understanding of exactly what was happening. The lives of young refugees, already traumatized, were further disrupted and the work of the committees increased. Some of the new internees had started school or taken jobs; the committees wanted to ensure that upon release they still had a future and could continue on the path they had started. Some of the internees had a few possessions that required looking after; some had families that depended upon them; most needed to be supported emotionally. Committee members wrote letters to cheer up the troubled young people; on occasion, committee women travelled all day to visit internees and to bring them gifts.

Many of the internees felt they had been apprehended like criminals and treated worse. A notorious case of abuse occurred on the ship *Dunera*, which eventually landed in Australia after a brutal journey lasting many months. The hapless refugees, taken directly from work or home to a dock without prior notice, had endured months of confinement in the hold of the ship, without proper facilities or ventilation. Before the ship reached its destination several had died and had been interred at sea, while others incurred permanent injuries from beatings. Two ships carrying young boys for internment in Canada were torpedoed *en-route* with the loss of all on board.

The people of Britain and the refugees were to experience further problems. The blitz of London and other English cities made it imperative to evacuate from endangered areas all British children less than 15 years of age. The newly arrived refugee children in common with their British counterparts had to make another quick adjustment as all schoolchildren from vulnerable areas were evacuated together to the interior of the country. The regional committees in each of the evacuation areas were asked to assume responsibility for placing the children in local homes. There was little time to plan and everyone was under enormous pressure. In addition to assuring the safety of the children, workers in each of the districts also had the awesome responsibility of making sure that records of all the children were safe; they owed that much to the parents who had entrusted their young to the hearts and hands of strangers.[46]

Whole school populations from areas of London and along the coast were dispersed to safer areas throughout England. Overnight, for example, the local Cambridge Refugee Committee (CRC) had to deal with 800 additional children, among whom were also newly arrived refugee children, all evacuated to region 4 and needing supervision. A number were absorbed in larger units, such as hostels and camps, where they were looked after by trained people, but most were placed with families, who were forced to be responsible for their care.

By law, all families in the evacuation areas who had one or more spare rooms in their homes were required to take in children. Thus, the potential of child abuse existed from host families who did not want to have children imposed upon them. Cases have been reported of children not being allowed into their assigned homes when they returned from school – no matter what the weather, children had to wait outdoors until dinner and retire to bed immediately afterwards. Some were beaten for wetting their beds; one was hit over the head with a board and subsequently died of brain injury. These were isolated cases. However, the committees were aware of the potential for abuse and had a responsibility to be especially watchful. On the whole the RCM acquitted itself magnificently in its responsibility to see that the children were as well cared for as could be managed.

Inevitably, a certain percentage of the refugee children were profoundly sad. Nor could they grasp what was happening to them. In its attempt to put the best face possible on an untenable situation, the RCM's first report notes,

The strangeness of the customs, language, food and people, and the absence of all they have been used to and all they have loved have affected refugees generally. By and large children have adapted themselves to their new homes, and once they have settled into a routine of school-going and weekends they lose their homesickness and live their new life happily ... Only about 50 children have had to be removed as a result of incompatibility.

Indeed, most of the refugee children, unhappy as they were, were well behaved and grew to maturity as intact individuals. Some did very well for themselves, and for the wider society. Most married and established stable families, although there were those who suffered serious long-term trauma. Some where damaged beyond repair.

SOCIAL CLUB, 55 HILLS ROAD

The leaders and the volunteers of the CRC and the CRCC were remarkably responsive to the needs of both the refugee children and their parents. Many parents, perhaps not as vulnerable as their children, needed to have a social outlet for their own sanity. In Cambridge, the idea of a social centre for refugees to congregate and socialize was first discussed at a Cambridge Refugee Committee meeting on 9 February 1940. It met with immediate enthusiasm. The London-based Central Council for Refugees agreed that a social centre would enhance the lives of most refugees and contributed £300 towards its establishment.[47] Additional funds and labour were donated by the Cambridge refugees themselves. At the club's organizing meeting, they formulated a set of rules and a statement of purpose for the '55 Club' – named after the address of the CRC, 55 Hills Road.

> The '55' Club exists for the purpose of giving refugees from Nazi oppression an opportunity of meeting one another and of coming into contact with English people. The government of the club is in the hands of a sub-committee of the Cambridge Refugee Committee and of the officials appointed by that Committee.

In his report of the activities of the CRC in 1941, J.H. Clapham, the chairman, identifies the above-mentioned sub-committee as the Cambridge Refugee Children's Committee (CRCC). The two committees worked closely together in sponsoring the 55 Club, whose members included both refugee families with children and adolescents without families in England. Within weeks of its opening, the membership exceeded 200 new immigrants, all of whom appreciated a social atmosphere they could meet compatriots and communicate in their own language. Clapham's report ends on a note of pride, as he urges his readers to come to 55 Hills Road and see the club for themselves:

> They will find here a canteen, a reading room in which are newspapers and periodicals and in which our general library is to be found, a table-tennis room in the annexe, a room for lectures and a small music room. The club rooms open at 11.30, the canteen at 3.30. The preparing and serving of tea and supper is undertaken each day by one or other of a group of Christian congregations, and members of it who are also members of the Club are responsible for the service on their day. Several refugee members are now sharing this responsibility. The services of our voluntary helpers have been a distinctive feature in the life of the Club and we are very grateful for them. Moreover, helpers have not remained on one side of the counter, and friendships have grown which it was the aim of the Club to foster. We look forward, therefore to even greater usefulness in the second year of our existence.[48]

The club opened with 100 members on 1 April 1940 in a three-storey building belonging to Jesus College, who offered it to the CRC at very low rent. Subsequently the CRC and the CRCC moved their offices to the top floor of the same building. By 17 May the social club was fully operational, with double its initial membership. On the premises was a food canteen for which appropriate equipment had been donated. The canteen became a source of significant income for the club; in three years its profits almost quadrupled, going from £391 in 1940/41 to £1,250 in 1943/44. In the same building the club also organized classes for refugees; the first was an English-language course, followed by a reading group whose participants chose for their first assignment a play by Shakespeare. Discussion groups as well as special interest groups – in music and history – were subsequently organized.

Dr Hans Schlossman, a pharmacologist who had emigrated to Cambridge from Germany with his family just before Kristallnacht, was especially helpful to the CRC, both in the formation of the social club and in addressing some of the refugees' problems. Almost all of the refugees in Cambridge, who were active in the social club, were German in origin, Jewish by birth, and secular by design. Dr Schlossman could reason with all of them. But life in wartime England was uncertain at best. Schlossman and other German refugees in Cambridge were interned in May 1940 by a government apprehensive about spies within its midst in wartime. In fact, 281 refugees who were under the care of the CRC were sent to temporary internment until their cases could be heard and decided.

CRC members who visited the refugees found the living conditions in the internment camp onerous and offensive. They complained to the proper authorities and three days later the living conditions were considerably improved. To deal with problems, the interned refugees organized a committee that consisted of Dr Schlossman, Rabbi Ehrentreu and Pastor Hildebrand Lipstein.

In its first social action, the 55 Club successfully petitioned the appropriate government agency to have Schlossman released from the internment camp on the Isle of Man. By October 1944 Schlossman was released and was back at the social club. The club minutes of 20 October 1944 indicate he is active in promoting a Christmas exhibition and sale of handicrafts made by refugees. At its meeting of 14 December 1944 the members, almost all of whom were Jewish, agreed to close the social club on 24 and 25 December and on Boxing Day.

The club managed its affairs democratically, if at times defensively. A problem which found its way into the committee's report of 10 May 1940 concerns what may appear to be a trivial formality, a matter of introducing guests. In the historical context of a time when England tried to differentiate between friendly and enemy aliens, the matter of knowing with whom one was associating was of prime importance, especially for German Jewish refugees. Their anxiety underlies the following incident reported in the record book of the social club:

> One of our refugees, not a member himself, had brought two guests and had not had the courtesy to introduce them. This caused some unpleasantness. The rule that guests must be introduced by members was reaffirmed by the committee as essential.[49]

Early in the club's history, friction developed around the issue of Jewish identification. In spite of the fact that the German refugees, born to Jewish parents, were driven from their homes because of the religion of their birth parents, they did not necessarily wish to be identified as Jews and instead remained secular in their orientation. Their 'identity crisis' is revealed in the positions members took at the social club, and recorded in the minutes:

> The Committee felt it could not approve the running of Jewish lectures and socials at the Club, but would be pleased to try to arrange them outside. As a matter of general policy, it was felt there should be no religious propaganda at the Club.[50]

The social club rejected a gift subscription to the English-language weekly *Jewish Chronicle* on the grounds of 'religious propaganda'. Eventually, they agreed to allow a one-month subscription but not to renew it.[51] When some members suggested social events to coincide with Jewish holidays or lectures on Jewish topics, the majority also vetoed them as 'propaganda'. However, members participated with some enthusiasm in preparations for an annual Christmas party, for which they decorated the room and prepared traditional Christmas cakes.

Student members of the Cambridge University Jewish Society (CUJS), anxious to establish close cooperation with the CRC and to do voluntary work with the refugees, notified the newly hired warden of the social club of their wish to be useful. In fact, they helped organize English lessons and events for younger refugees who were of their own generation. Like young people everywhere, they enjoyed socializing; but, some of the adult refugees in the club found that the behaviour of 'certain' students 'left much to be desired', and reported as much to the warden. When a student challenged the warden to be more specific, the student became *persona non-grata*. The enthusiasm of the CUJS and their open affirmation of their Jewishness apparently made a number of the assimilated German Jewish refugees at the 55 Club in Cambridge uneasy, as did the suggestion of Jewish-related activities.

Refusing Jewish lectures and newspapers, hiding their own Jewish backgrounds, celebrating Christmas with their Christian hosts and hostesses, the new refugees seemed a breed apart. Yet, for all that, the 55 Club at Hills Road was an outstanding success and a proud achievement of both the Cambridge refugees and their sponsors in the CRC.

NOTES

1. Aubrey Newman, *Patterns of Migration: 1850–1914*, Jewish Historical Society of England and the Institute of Jewish Studies (London, 1996), pp. 119–26.
2. Otto Schiff was well known in government circles for his work on behalf of Belgian refugees, for which he was awarded the Order of the British Empire.
3. It exists to this day and is now known as the Central British Fund for World Jewish Relief. For a full account of the JRC and the CBF, see Amy Zahl Gottlieb's authoritative history, *Men of Vision: Anglo-Jewry's Aid to Victims of the Nazi Regime, 1933–1945* (London, 1998).
4. Ronald Stent, 'Jewish Refugee Organizations', in W.E. Mosse (ed.), *Second Chance: Two Centuries of German-Speaking Jews in the United Kingdom* (Tubingen, 1991), p. 581.
5. Louise London, *Whitehall and the Jews, 1933–1948* (Cambridge, 2000), pp. 58–96 and Amy Zahl Gottlieb, *Men of Vision: Anglo-Jewry's Aid to Victims of the Nazi Regime* (London, 1998), pp. 13–19.
6. London, *Whitehall and the Jews*, pp. 58–96.
7. Ibid., p. 59.
8. Gottlieb, *Men of Vision*, pp. 16ff.
9. Ibid., p. 120, quoting Baldwin. The appeal raised more than £522,000 and was sufficient to maintain adults and a large number of children until October 1941.
10. Ibid., pp. 14ff.
11. For a thorough discussion of British policy *vis-à-vis* Jewish refugees during this time, see London, *Whitehall and the Jews*.

12. Gottlieb, *Men of Vision*, p. 13.
13. 'The Jewish People from Holocaust to Nationhood – Series One', Archives of the Central British Fund for World Jewish Relief 1933–1960 (hereafter CBF Archives), reel 32.
14. Transcript of Dubrovsky interview with J. Stiebel, 24 June 1993, Dubrovsky Collection.
15. CBF Archives, microfilm. Reel 28 concerns the Refugee Children's Movement; reel 32 contains papers of the Jewish Refugee Committee.
16. The AAC broadened its parameters to include doctors, teachers, librarians and others and changed its name to the more inclusive Society for the Protection of Science and Learning (SPSL). The records of the AAC and the SPSL are held at the Bodelian Library, Oxford.
17. Stent, 'Jewish Refugee Organizations', p. 581.
18. Harold Laski was a political theorist and a socialist from a Manchester family which was prominent in English intellectual and public life.
19. Stent, 'Jewish Refugee Organizations', p. 586.
20. *New York Times*, 30 June 1942, p. 7.
21. Sir Herbert Samuel was a member of the House of Commons and the House of Lords. As Home Secretary, he played a leading role in efforts to help German refugees in England, and to admit German-Jewish children to Britain before the Second World War broke out.
22. Norman Bentwich was an English Zionist, lawyer and scholar. He was on the executive committee of the Refugee Children's Movement.
23. See Gottlieb, *Men of Vision*, p. 15.
24. See Herbert A. Strauss, 'Jewish Emigration from Germany: Nazi Policies and Jewish Responses (II)', *Yearbook, 1981*, Leo Baeck Institute, pp. 343–409.
25. See Lore Segal, *Other People's Houses* (New York, 1958). The author describes her experiences as the child of a refugee 'domestic worker' in England.
26. *Jewish Chronicle*, 25 March 1938, p. 42; see also Chapter 8 of this book.
27. *Jewish Chronicle*, 5 August 1938, p. 16.
28. Ibid., 24 November 1939, p. 13.
29. Although the IAC started with an initial grant from the Save the Children Fund, its subsequent financial backing was provided in large measure by the CBF.
30. See Gottlieb, *Men of Vision*, p. 100.
31. *Jewish Chronicle*, 1 July 1938, p. 29.
32. First annual report of the Movement for the Care of Children from Germany and Austria, November 1938–December 1939.
33. Lord Bearstead was the son of Marcus Samuel Bearsted whose family founded the Shell Oil Company and the Bearsted Memorial Hospital in London.
34. Amy Gottlieb, who provides the historical framework in a documentary film about *Kindertransport* (*The Children Who Cheated the Nazis*, BBC), estimates that the pound was worth thirty-five times more in 1939 than it is today. It was a substantial sum of money.
35. First annual report, Movement for the Care of Children from Germany and Austria, November 1938–December 1939.
36. Two British citizens, Captain B.M. Woolf, secretary of the West London Synagogue, and Ruth Fellner, a Jewish Refugee Committee staff member, helped restore some of its communal activities. See Gottlieb, *Men of Vision*, pp. 79–80.
37. Frederick Brodnitz, in a memoir of the Reichsvertretung (*Encyclopaedia Judaica*, Vol. 14) (New York, 1972)), claims that the Reichsvertretung der deutschen Juden started in 1933. See Frederick Brodnitz, 'Memories of the Reichsvertretung: A Personal Report', *Yearbook, 1986*, Leo Baeck Institute. Yehuda Reshef (*Jewish Encyclopaedia*) says the plan was first proposed in 1933, but it was not realized as an organization until 1935. A Jewish organization for social services in Germany was originally proposed by the Germans in April 1933, to be called specifically *Judenrat*. The main function envisioned for this organization was the implementation of directives and orders of the Nazi regimes, as it later did.
38. As reported by Shaul Esh, 'The Establishment of the Reichsvereinigung der Juden in Deutschland and its Main Activities', Yad Vashem Studies on the European Jewish Catastrophe and Resistance (*Jewish Agency Yearbook, 1957*), p. 24.
39. The Jewish communities of Germany and Austria had their own central organizations to look after the interests of their members and to facilitate emigration. It is not clear with which committees on the Continent the movement worked.

40. Manuscripts, Add. MSS 8433, Cambridge University Library.
41. 'Reichsvereinigung', *Encyclopaedia Judaica*, vol. 14, pp. 50–1.
42. Dubrovsky interview with N. Winton, 21 May 1995, transcript, p. 3, private collection, Gertrude Dubrovsky.
43. Winton interview, 21 May 1995, transcript in Dubrovsky Collection.
44. Movement for the Care of Children from Germany, Ltd, First Annual Report, November 1938–December 1939, p. 9. The text refers to an article in the *Manchester Guardian*, 31 December 1938.
45. This is an aspect of the rescue operation that has not yet received adequate attention.
46. A large house was rented in Hindhead at which the aftercare department with a staff of 15 maintained the records.
47. Of that sum, £200 was for capital improvements and £100 for running expenses.
48. 'Cambridge Refugee Committee', Add. MS 7974, Cambridge University Library.
49. Ibid., ADD. MS 8433.
50. Minute Book, Social Centre, 1 April 1940–29 November 1940, Add. MS 7974, Cambridge University Library.
51. Ibid., item no. 184, 6 September 1940.

CHAPTER THREE

Six from Leipzig Arrive in England

There was one thing that was perfectly clear to the rescue workers in 1938 and 1939, and to the hunted and the hounded as well. All knew for a fact that endangered families had better odds of surviving if parents and children separated. Survival depended upon maximum mobility. With the safety of their children assured, the parents could and often did go separate ways towards a prearranged meeting-place. In Leipzig, three sisters, parents of six cousins, parted with their children in the hope that both they and their children would live and be reunited. The children eventually came under the protective wing of the CRCC, and did in fact survive. Their parents were not so fortunate.

Leo Schmulewitz, the uncle of the six children, was the agent responsible for registering his nieces and nephews for passage on the *Kindertransports*, and for deciding in which order the children would leave. The oldest, Paula Grünbaum, says her Uncle Leo worked for a Jewish social agency in Leipzig, 'something like a Jewish federation, maybe the Israelitische Religionsgemeinde [Jewish communal organization]'. He had advance notice that the *Kindertransports* were being organized to remove children from harm's way.

Fourteen-year-old Paula Grünbaum would have been the obvious choice of first child to be sent to England. The family needed advocates to help them get entry permits for England; Paula might have been able to pave the way for the parents to follow. But the first transport was intended for those considered to be in serious jeopardy – older boys subject to arrest for work-camps and orphans (any child with one or no parents). Vera Ribetski's father had died when she was two; without a father she was considered an orphan and thus eligible to be put on the first train bound for Liverpool Street, London.

At nearly 13, Vera was the second oldest of the cousins from Leipzig, all of whom eventually arrived in England during the ten-month period between *kristallnacht* – 10 November 1938 – and England's declaration of

war on Germany on 3 September 1939. The organized transports stopped
when the war started, although a trickle of people continued to come into
England by circuitous overland and North Sea routes.[1] In common with
other children who were brought to Britain on Kindertransports, Vera
knows very little about how the transports were organized or what agencies
were involved in identifying endangered children and getting them ready to
leave. Of her family history, she knows the bits and pieces learned in childhood and later put together by the six cousins.

The three generations of the Schmulewitz family of Leipzig had their
roots in Warsaw, Poland, birthplace of Shmuel and Rose Schmulewitz. Two
of their four surviving children – their son Leo and their older daughter
Yetta – were born in Poland. At the end of the nineteenth century Germany
had opened its schools to Jewish children, and the Schmulewitz parents,
along with other Jews, saw much potential for themselves and their families
in Germany. Joining a general migration from Galicia and Poland in 1900,
the Schmulewitzes relocated their young family to cosmopolitan Berlin,
where they anticipated giving their children better life opportunities. Their
daughter Truda was born in Berlin. In 1905, the elder Schmulewitz
accepted an offer from the Broder Shul [synagogue] in Leipzig to be its
cantor, and the family moved. A year later, on 5 July 1906, their youngest
child, Clara, was born in Leipzig.

There had been Jews in Leipzig since the twelfth century. By the first
half of the thirteenth century, an organized community with a school and a
synagogue was in place. But it was not until the eighteenth century that
restrictive laws regarding Jewish living-space were relaxed enough to
permit official rights of residence to a limited number of Jews. In 1837
Saxony, the district to which Leipzig belongs, formally permitted the
establishment of a Jewish community but withheld from it the right to build
a synagogue. Instead, a prayer house with Reform tendencies was opened
in 1855 in Leipzig. At the end of the nineteenth century rules were further
relaxed, and the community of Jews built a grand Moorish-style Reform
temple, the very façade of which proclaimed not only the presence of Jews
but their prosperity as well. Thus Leipzig entered the twentieth century
with two synagogues: the new temple and the Broder Shul built about the
same time as the temple, but on a much smaller scale. It served the traditionally observant (orthodox) Jews, many of whom traced their beginnings
to the city of Brody in Ukraine, then part of Poland. Coincident with the
new tolerance, the number of Jews in the Leipzig region greatly increased
after 1868/69. All anti-Jewish restrictions were abolished in 1905 and the
community continued to grow. From less than 8,000 Jews, there were more
than 13,000 by 1925 in the city of Leipzig, making it the largest community
in Saxony.

The Schmulevitz family did well there, rising up the economic ladder to attain a middle-class life-style and becoming active members of the Israelitische Religionsgemeinde of Leipzig. By 1931 all their children were married, and four of their six grandchildren were already born. The extended family lived in apartments within walking distance of each other and spent most major holidays together. Paula Grünbaum, the oldest grandchild, describes her family life-style:

> We lived in a good size apartment in Leipzig. Our grandparents lived on the third floor and we lived on the fourth. Needless to say, we were always in each other's place. Vera's mother, my aunt, was often with us. Vera and I went to school together, exchanged lunches and so forth. My aunt was my confidante. When I had a fight with my mother, my aunt would say, 'Let's go for a walk so we can talk about everything.' She did not hesitate to tell me that I was wrong. Vera ... spent a lot of time in our house. When we went on vacation, Vera came along.

Paul's father was a printer and compositor. He was also an ardent Zionist and an avid reader. The family enjoyed music, had a gramophone and a grand piano. Each of the two daughters had her own bedroom and shared a bathroom. Their Uncle Leo and his wife lived close by and were in close contact with the family and the nieces and nephews. He was a soccer player, and Paula recalls going to soccer matches to watch him. That was in a happier time. In 1938 most of Leo's time, especially during the period Paula remembered, was devoted to his work at the 'Jewish Federation'; above all else, his efforts were to get as many children out as possible.

Shmuel Schmulevitz, the patriarch, died of natural causes about 1934, when he was just past his sixtieth birthday. After his death, his wife Rose supported herself by dressmaking and eventually lived with her daughter Yetta and granddaughter Vera. By that time the political situation was getting darker by the day, and as it worsened the family drew closer together.

Both social and school situations became increasingly difficult for Jewish children in Leipzig. In school and in the playground, they endured anti-Semitic remarks and physical harassment. Nazi signs and symbols were everywhere, declaring that Jews were forbidden from sitting on the park benches or swimming in the municipal pool. In schools, the Jewish children were segregated and forced to sit or stand in the back of the room. They became targets for verbal and other kinds of abuse. Paula, the oldest of the Schmulevitz grandchildren, did not allow anti-Jewish remarks to pass without challenge. She responded to an insult by hitting the girl who delivered it in the face and breaking her glasses. Paul's mother replaced the glasses and both she and her cousin Vera were transferred to the Karlbach Academy, a Hebrew day-school in Leipzig.

Makeshift schools, staffed by dismissed Jewish academics and professionals, were established for Jewish children. In some way, the segregation of Jewish children made it easier for the Jewish network and social agencies to contact the parents with crucial information they needed to have. News of the imminent *Kindertransports* and applications with instructions for registering the children were distributed through the Jewish schools to families and to others who wanted them.

Through his work with a Jewish agency Leo Schmulewitz knew of transports being organized to send children to England. No doubt he helped distribute application forms to the community. According to the testimony of the two older cousins, not only did their Uncle Leo register all the cousins, he also decided in which order they were to leave. Vera was destined to be the first because her orphan status gave her priority on the first transport.

The six Leipzig children arrived in England on four different transports during a nine-month period. Three came alone – one by one: Vera Ribetski, who was 13, left first; followed by Paula Grünbaum, 14; and her sister, Edith Grünbaum, 7. Three infant Koppold siblings – Harold, 6, Siegmar, 3 and Zilla, 8 months – arrived together, escorted by a young Christian woman, just days before England declared war on Germany and the transports effectively stopped. The parents of the children parted with their 'precious ones' in the hope that they all would survive.

In common with the other refugee children of the time, these six were separated from their parents without understanding why; they were taken to a country whose language they did not know and cared for by people they had never seen. Soon the older two were regarded as enemy aliens. And like the other refugee children, they did not know what had happened to their parents until long after the war ended. At one point the cousins all ended up in Cambridge or East Anglia. They were just six of the 2,000 refugee children for whom the CRCC assumed some responsibility during the seven years of its existence from 1938 to 1945.

On 1 December 1938, three weeks after *Kristallnacht*, the first transport of children arrived in Harwich from the Hook of Holland. It was composed primarily of orphans and older boys, children aged between 12 and 17, who were vulnerable to arrest and detention in labour camps. The Refugee Children's Movement (see Chapter 2) and its various branches in England, had received hundreds, if not thousands, of appeals from desperate parents wanting to send their children to safety. But the working committees found it impossible to determine the most urgent cases. In the end, the first report indicates, it was left to the committees on the Continent to choose the children to be sent on transports.[2]

According to Vera's testimony, the whole extended family accompanied her on the short walk from her home to the station on the memorable day she left Leipzig on a *Kindertransport*. With her were her grandmother, her mother, her mother's two sisters, their husbands and their children, her Uncle Leo and his wife Eva. The family gathered in a tight group at the arched and decorous turn-of-the-century railroad station in Leipzig on the first day of December in 1938 to see this only child of the widowed Yetta Schmulevitz Ribetski off on a train bound for the Hook of Holland and from there on a boat to Harwich, England. All reassured the 13-year-old that soon they would be together in England. Vera's strongest memory of the farewell is that nobody cried. In telling the story, she twice repeats, 'nobody cried', and tears run down her cheeks. She only remembers her mother telling her that in approximately five weeks time the whole family would be together. Everything else is a blur. What remains with her is the unkept promise and the pain of the separation from her mother. 'My mother was everything; my whole emotional stability', she says. A woman now in her late seventies, and with children and grandchildren of her own, she cannot put that pain behind her.

Vera, not yet five feet tall, boarded the first *Kindertransport* train with other children at the Leipzig station, and bravely waved to her family assembled on the platform. Traumatized by her reluctant departure, she was hardly up to the task of family ambassador in England. After the train left, the extended family comforted, as best they could, the bereaved mother, who in her heart knew that she might never see her daughter again.

Vera cannot recall many of the details, but she does remember the children crying on the train and Nazis walking in the aisles laughing. Like all events remembered 60 years later, the details may or may not be accurate, but the emotion is very much alive and real. The train stopped in Berlin overnight; the children were taken off and escorted by waiting Jewish personnel to a building 'something like a YMHA' where cots had been set up for them to sleep. In the morning more children boarded the train, and when they crossed the border into Holland, the transport had hundreds of children on it – 500 according to Vera. She remembers the Dutch women coming onto the train in Holland and distributing hot chocolate and biscuits.

When they reached the Hook of Holland, the children transferred to a boat for Dovercourt, an adult summer holiday camp near Harwich. As the boat pulled into the harbour, Vera was standing with a group of children on the deck, smiling and waving to the gathered crowd. The child refugees were instant celebrities; photographers and journalists were everywhere, and English newspapers made much of the arrival of this first transport. The description of Dovercourt, where Vera landed, is somewhat idealized:

> The place was originally intended for summer holiday visitors, with rows of bungalows for sleeping quarters – 'our own little private houses', the children call them – and a vast central hall ... Here the visitor spends her first evening watching the children, hundreds of them, ranging in age from six to eighteen. Watching a small, fair-haired girl with a cross hanging from a silver chain round her neck, the *visitor wonders whether the little non-Aryan Christians in these surroundings are not even more to be pitied than their Jewish playfellows, who already take persecution for granted as the burden of their race.*[3]

The well-intentioned writer quoted in the first report apparently has no sense of how readily accepted clichés influence perception. What is implied is that Jewish children, regardless of their age, are so used to persecution that they can accept it as the norm. In fact, few of the older and none of the very young children understood why they were in the intolerable situation in which they found themselves. The 'non-Aryan Christians' to whom the writer refers are children of baptized Jews who had hoped that conversion to Christianity would ensure their family's safety. But Hitler's racial laws did not give them the longed-for security. The visitor's report continues in the same romantic and rather sentimental vein:

> Ten days in the camp pass like a dream. It is bitterly cold and there is much sorrow, but there is happiness as well. There are little presents and treats, the children have their friendships and their secrets and their games, the irrepressible child life is wholesome and sweet in spite of everything.[4]

Whilst the first annual report[5] gives an almost idyllic picture of the refugee children in their reception centre, it also reacts to inaccurate assumptions made by the press about 'affluent' child refugees:

> Criticism has been levelled at the Refugees on the grounds that they arrived with large amounts of luggage and were therefore not penniless and destitute. It must be remembered that clothes were all that the children could bring out of Germany and that the clothes were purchased in more fortunate days, and that it saved the expense of repurchasing the clothes in this country at public expense.[6]

It is true that the children – clean, well-dressed and healthy – hardly looked like refugees. They were vastly different from the sick emaciated children who arrived in England dressed in rags during and after the Balkan wars. Whilst the German child refugees of the 1930s had experienced much trauma, they had not yet been abandoned as nobody's responsibility. They were dearly loved children, tenderly cared for by parents whose hearts were broken by their departure. What the journalists did not see was the distress and despair that lay behind and underneath the children's smiles. Nor could they understand then what sacrifices the parents might have made to provide their children with new clothes for their new country. Almost pathetically, some of the children were dressed as if they were miniature lords or ladies.

A Jewish family from London were among those who had assembled on the dock when the boat Vera was on arrived in Dover. They provided a guarantee for a refugee boy and were there to meet their foster son. Upon seeing the boy for the first time, the family knew they had a job to do. A member of the family, who requested anonymity, recalls the event: 'The boy came off the boat wearing funny shoes, and a funny hat, and had a funny name. My mother had to make a proper British gentleman out of him. She changed his shoes, she changed his hat, and she changed his name.' Fifty-five years later, the woman reporting the incident had no sense at all that by attempting to make the child over, her mother might have taken something valuable away from him. She continued to be indignant that the child left their household when he learned his mother had survived, with hardly a 'thank you' for all his foster family had done for him.

Vera was not looking for any family to meet her, and indeed none did. All she could think of at Dovercourt was how lonely she was, and how cold it was in December. She and another child were assigned to a small unheated bungalow with two beds and given hot-water bottles. Neither of the children had ever seen these before and did not know what to do with them. Vera opened her bottle and was scalded. Amid her pain and confusion, she was hardly aware that the hopes for survival of the whole family left behind were invested in her.

On hand to greet the children in Harwich were volunteers from the RCM and a staff of professional people who could speak German with the foreign children. Anna Essinger, head of Bunce Court, recently had moved her progressive school from Germany to Kent, England. She had been invited by the RCM to supervise the children's carers at Dovercourt, the first absorption centre.

Vera spent a week in Dovercourt whilst volunteers from all over England were there to help settle the children. Prospective foster parents arrived daily to pick out children they would take home with them. Vera's foster-mother was among a small group of people from Norwich (a city northeast of London in East Anglia) who had come to claim children. Recalling that time, Vera says:

> One night, a woman stopped at my table and said, 'May I take this child?' I couldn't understand her, I couldn't speak English. But the counsellors who were helping told me in German that 'this lady wants to take you to her house'. I thought I was being sold; I was very frightened. I was homesick and scared. The woman counsellor said, 'No. She is not buying you. You are just supposed to go there till your mother picks you up.' I said, 'Okay. But could I stay just one more day?' Because the next day they were going to show *Snow White and the Seven Dwarfs*. They were opening the local cinema just for the children. The woman said yes. I took a train the next day.

Vera travelled to Norwich to join the family of Bertha and Arthur Staff and their two children, Lottie, 12, and Joe, 16. Bertha was Jewish, married to a Christian. Although the family was very kind, Vera could do nothing but cry and her foster-mother cried with her. Finally, Arthur Staff told his wife that if she could not stop weeping, they would have to send Vera away. Woman and child stopped crying and Vera remained with the family for eight years. She says they were wonderful to her; they all bonded as a family. Eventually, Vera got over her initial apprehension and nervousness, but before she did she went through much distress and anxiety:

> I couldn't speak any English. I was so nervous, I would break dishes all the time. They asked me to help dry dishes. Due to my nervousness, I would drop everything. And I was afraid to tell them because I thought I would be out on the street. I had my suitcase under the bed and I would wrap up all the broken pieces and put them into my suitcase. This poor lady didn't know what was happening to her dishes. They were just disappearing.

Vera claims to have survived emotionally because of her orthodox religious background. She never lost faith, although the Messiah she avidly hoped for did not come.

> I had terrible nightmares. I was a child. I needed my mother. But I grew up. You know, you cry and you cry and you gradually stop. I got a few communications from my mother and then the war broke out. She knew

where I was. My mother was sent back to Poland from Germany, because all the Poles were sent back, and she got caught in the bombing. And then she went back to Germany after Poland was captured by Germany. She was with her mother and her sister. Then they all went to a camp. My cousin Paula said it was Terezin [Theresienstadt]. I don't know. I'm not sure. Nobody ever confirmed it. But they all died.[7]

Vera's foster-mother, a patient and compassionate woman, could never fill the void. But the child understood that Bertha Staff wanted to do for her that which Vera's mother would approve. She taught Vera English by using objects – an apple, teapot, spoon, etc. As Vera became more fluent in English, she was less comfortable in German; in fact, the language faded. She began to worry that when she and her mother would meet again, they would not be able to communicate – a thought that frightened her. With tears in her eyes, she says, 'I didn't have to worry. I never saw anyone again.' Today she still understands simple German, but she says she speaks it like a 'foreigner'.

In spite of the pain that would not go away, Vera found Norwich a charming and delightful town. Its Jewish community, always small, dates back to the twelfth century. Early in the town's history, the Jews of Norwich enjoyed protection from the king. Their special status might have been responsible for the slanderous blood libel that has been associated with Norwich and plagued Jews for centuries. Popularized by Chaucer's 'Prioress's Tale', the myth accused the Norwich Jews of killing a Christian child so they could drink his blood on Passover. No doubt the small Jewish community never lost the sense of 'otherness' and insecurity engendered by such ancient and calumnious stories.

Bertha Staff had grown up in Norwich and was aware of its latent anti-Semitism. Perhaps that was behind her insistence that Vera and Lottie, her foster-sister, attend the synagogue every Saturday. In fact, Bertha instructed Vera to stand up for herself: 'If anyone calls you a bloody Jew, spit right into their face. You don't have to take any garbage from anyone. It's a free country.' But Bertha Staff didn't tell Vera what to do about school prayers: she had to decide for herself what course of action to take. In English schools the day started with a prayer. Vera always left the room because, in her words, 'I was raised far too orthodox to accept anything else.'

Under English law at that time children could leave school at the age of 14. Vera had no illusions about higher education, but she was permitted to attend a secretarial school so that she might be able to work. When war broke out she was considered an enemy alien and no longer had the same privileges as others. As it was difficult for her to find work, she helped the

Staffs in their general store. Eventually, she worked a switchboard in an iron factory for five years, until she was 21.

Norwich was under the jurisdiction of the CRCC, administrative head of region 4. Vera believed that the local Norwich committee was composed primarily of Jewish people, and presumed that only Jews went to Dovercourt to take children home with them. But both assumptions seem highly unlikely. Although Vera estimates that Norwich's Jewish population included only about 25 Jewish families, the *Jewish Encyclopaedia* (1948) indicates a Jewish population of about 200 people.

Vera was fortunate in her placement with the Staff family. Not only was Bertha Staff a foster-mother to her but she later became a foster-aunt to Vera's cousin Paula Grünbaum, who arrived in Southampton almost exactly seven months after Vera came to England. Edith, Paula's sister, followed a month later, and the Koppold children soon after that.

Vera arrived at Harwich on 2 December 1938, two months before her youngest cousin Zilla Koppold was born, and about nine months before Paula and Edith left Leipzig on *Kindertransports* to England. With each child's subsequent leave-taking from Leipzig, the group accompanying the children to the railroad station grew smaller and the emotions less controlled. When Paula Grünbaum left Leipzig, the family group still displayed a brave face, except for her father, who cried and clutched his daughter to him. It was the first time she had ever seen her father cry.

The oldest of six cousins, Paula was the first in many ways: the first child of Abraham and Trude (Gertrude) Grünbaum; the first Schmulewitz grandchild; and the first niece of two aunts and an uncle. But at 14 she was the second of the six cousins to leave Leipzig on a *Kindertransport*.

Paula left from the same railroad station as Vera did, and her journey also took her from Leipzig to Berlin. But she travelled from Berlin to Hamburg where she boarded a boat bound for America with a stopover in Southampton, England. There she met her English relatives whom she had previously only heard about.

Trude's mother helped her pack in preparation for her journey and in the privacy of the bedroom the mother told her older daughter that Edith would soon be following her to England, and that the two sisters must stay as close as two loaves of bread baked together. Paula was further instructed to keep an eye on the other children who also would join them in England. And in almost the same words used to reassure Vera, Paula was told that her parents would be joining them as soon as they could make the arrangements. Before boarding the train, Paula promised her Aunt Clara Koppold, the youngest of the three sisters, that she would make it her business always to know where the Koppold children were.

To Paula her promise was a sacred oath. For the whole time she was in England she kept track of her sister and cousins, spending all her spare time and meagre earnings from her job in a mattress factory discharging her duty. With only a slim knowledge of the British rail and bus systems, and her limited command of English, she periodically made the rounds visiting the children. Later, she consulted with Greta Burkill of the CRCC about their welfare. And she never stopped making enquiries on behalf of her relatives in Germany.

Paula, Edith and the three Koppold children all travelled the same route: by train from Leipzig to Berlin where they changed for a train whose final destination was the sea-port of Hamburg; from there they sailed to Southampton, England. Paula arrived in England on 30 June 1939; her sister Edith arrived at the same terminal on 5 July 1939, and the three infant Koppold children arrived together on 26 August 1939.

Within three months time (and nine months after Vera left) the five cousins all were greeted at the Southampton boat terminal by their distant cousin Dora Binke[8] and her husband Isadore. Although the Binke and Schmulewitz families had never met, they had established contact and affirmed their relationship after Vera left Leipzig.

The Binkes were working-class Jews living in London's crowded, poor and very Jewish East End. Nevertheless, they responded to the plight of their relatives in Germany. By providing guarantees to the British government that they would absorb the cost of eventual remigration of the five children, they expedited their arrival in England.

Paula does not know how the guarantee money was secured by the family. She remembers that at one time the Binke hardware business had gone bankrupt and that 'the family was poor and could not speak proper English'. But she knows for a fact that the Binkes agreed to deposit the required fees and/or sign the required papers so that five of the six cousins from Leipzig could come to England on *Kindertransports*. Families and children without sponsors or guarantors had to wait their turn in a queue to get on a *Kindertransport*. The generosity of the Binkes in providing guarantees relieved the family in Leipzig of considerable anxiety. Before they could do anything to ensure their own safety, they had to be certain that the children were safe.

A week or ten days after she arrived, Paula returned to the same dock with the Binkes to wait for her sister Edith to disembark. As soon as the sisters were reunited, Edith reported that she had never seen a man cry as hard as her father did when he kissed her goodbye. He did not want her to go, but he knew she could not stay. Nor was he able to reassure the child that soon the family would be together again. On 26 August 1939 Paula accompanied the Binkes on a third trip to Southampton to meet the

Koppold children and the young Christian woman hired in Leipzig to escort the children to England.

The Binkes took the children to their small London apartment where they were given a meal and then parcelled out to the families of the two Binke daughters who lived nearby in London: Yetta Teff and Rose Jacobson. Edith went to the home of Rose Jacobson who had two small daughters about the same age as Edith. A few days later, Rose took Edith to the office of the JRC and left both the child and her suitcase there. The same experience was repeated when a second family, with whom the child was placed, also returned her to the committee. Neither Edith nor Paula wish to discuss that period; Edith says the Jacobsons were a different class of people, and she has no recollection of the other family. Paula, by way of explanations, says that Edith arrived with a selection of very beautiful dresses made for her by her grandmother. Each day she would put on a different dress, and the Jacobson daughters – whose family suffered all sorts of deprivations – were envious. Paula observes that the homes of the London relatives were crowded with other relatives from the Continent, and there was great tension and strain between Dora Binke and her husband.

Paula did not have an appropriate place for her eight-year-old sister, nor did she know how to begin looking for one. Indeed, she hardly could think of anything but her parents who needed help to leave Germany. Because she was the oldest, all letters begging for assistance were directed to her. How the 14-year-old child was able to cope with them is a matter for speculation. Paula's mother wrote of her concern for the welfare of her younger daughter, and the urgency for Paula to secure the necessary papers so that they, the parents, could leave Germany. 'Has my Paula made the right enquiries?' is a question repeatedly asked. In another letter, dated 23 August 1939, Paula's mother writes from Poland, where she was forced to go after being declared stateless in Germany, enquiring whether the children received items and money sent for them with people they knew who were emigrating to England. Today, Paula says she did not receive anything, but was reluctant, in 1939, to give her mother this distressing news. At the same time that Paula's mother was pressing the family's needs upon her older daughter, Paula's Aunt Clara Koppold implored her in a letter to keep tabs on the three Koppold children who would shortly arrive.

The children arrived on 24 August 1939. Once more, Paula travelled with the Binkes to the dock at Southampton to await their arrival. The three infant children of Clara and Adolf Koppold were due to arrive in the care of a young Christian woman from Leipzig. Among those waiting in the huge reception area for incoming ships were representatives from the Refugee Children's Movement and the JRC, the agencies responsible for seeing that the children were delivered to those expecting them.

Sometime during the third week of August 1939 Clara Koppold, her three children and a young Christian woman boarded a train at the Leipzig railroad station for Berlin, less than a three-hour journey from Leipzig. The children, aged 6, 3 and 8 months, were the infants of Clara and Adolf Koppold; they were the last of the Schmulewitz family to leave from the elegant Leipzig station.

Of the original family grouping, only the grandmother, Rose Schmulewitz, was there to say goodbye to her three youngest grandchildren leaving Leipzig. When the five boarded the train bound for Berlin, the grandmother was left alone at the station. She returned to her empty apartment. Adolf Koppold, the children's father, was doing forced labour in a camp from which he returned each night – a privilege that would soon end when he was sent to Sachsenhausen. Clara's sister Yetta, her brother Leo and his wife Eva, all born in Poland, were declared stateless and exiled from Germany; her other sister Trude and brother-in-law Abraham were searching for an escape route to Palestine via Budapest and Salonika.

Clara Koppold and her children needed to change trains in Berlin. She might well have stayed overnight in Berlin with the children before continuing the trip to Hamburg. The largest Jewish community in Germany was in Berlin, as were the offices of Jewish social agencies. The Hilfsverein der deutschen Juden, for instance, was still functioning in August of 1939.

Originally founded in 1901 to assist Eastern European Jews, after 1933 it took on the responsibility of helping *émigrés* from Germany to get to all countries except Palestine and Eastern Europe. Jews were not permitted to enter Palestine, nor could they leave Eastern Europe. The agency obtained immigration permits, found transportation, and provided a wide range of financial assistance: travel money, expenses for visas, overseas passage, transportation of household goods, etc. It cooperated with the Jewish Colonization Association to settle several thousand immigrants as farmers in South America.[9] Given Leo Schmulewitz's position in the Kultusgemeinde (Jewish social agency) in Leipzig, it is likely that he and his family knew about the Berlin Hilfsverein and the assistance it provided German Jews in Berlin. Clara Koppold conceivably could have visited the Hilfsverein office while she was in the city, but, to date, records are not available.

There is neither witness nor record of the series of events that occurred on Clara Koppold's journey to engage a young woman to accompany her children to England. A few hours after leaving Leipzig, the small group arrived in the crowded Berlin station near the central zoo. Clara needed current identification photos for her children in order for them to get the pass that would allow them into England. The pictures taken in Berlin are intact and still survive. The two little boys sit by themselves looking into the camera. The baby could not or would not sit alone, so Clara Koppold put her infant daughter on her lap and the two of them were photographed together. The picture outlived the mother and remains as a witness of the time: a thin woman with sad eyes, wearing a simple black dress, holding a baby.

After Berlin, Clara Koppold, her three children and a young Christian woman whom she hired boarded a train for Hamburg. The mother pushed the baby in a pram that also held food parcels for everyone and later arrived in Southampton with the children. Only six-year-old Harold could carry a suitcase, so the young woman who accompanied the children to England probably carried the other cases, each marked with the name of a child. In the cases were new clothes which the children's father, a dressmaker and a tailor, had made for them: warm coats for all three, new suits for the boys, dresses for the baby, a few toys, some family photographs and copies of the photographs taken in Berlin.[10]

At the last train stop, before they reached the dock in Hamburg, the mother kissed each of the children goodbye and quickly left them to take the return train to Berlin and Leipzig. She had no permission and no papers to enter England; nor could she risk what would happen to the children or to her mother in Leipzig if she did not return as promised. Of the three infant children who boarded the boat for Southampton, only the oldest, Harold, has any memory of parting from his mother. As an adult, he understands that, for the sake of her children, Clara Koppold had to leave as calmly as she could. He says he clearly remembers her kiss, her pale face and her look. About his father, he remembers that he was a good tailor and that he made all the clothes his mother packed into their suitcases. And he has another memory that haunts him, and will not go away. He took it with him to England, and later to Israel. It follows him wherever he goes.

Sometime in 1939, six-year-old Harold was sitting in his father's tailor shop, playing on the floor with a box of buttons. An SS officer appeared, his black boots directly in line with the child's eyes. The officer told his father that he was doing an inventory of the merchandise in his shop. When the inventory was completed, he asked Adolf Koppold if there was anything else, to which Adolf responded, 'No, just what you see in the shop.' Harold, sitting on the floor counting buttons, then spoke: 'But Papa, you forgot the merchandise in the basement next door.' The black boots moved towards his father, and two pairs of feet left the room. When his father returned from the police station, he was a different person. Harold is haunted by the memory and still carries it with him.

The three Koppold children arrived in England just days before England declared war on Germany and the transports effectively stopped. At the Southampton dock, an anxious Paula waited in the visitors' area with her London relatives for a young woman with three small children, a pram and three suitcases. Also on the dock were agents from the JRC in London, checking off the children whom they expected and helping those that needed it. A woman soon came down the passageway pushing a pram and escorting two other children each holding on to one side of the carriage. Paula walked towards them, received the children and their belongings and thanked the young woman, who then returned to Leipzig. The Binkes escorted the three infants and Paula back to London.

Clara Koppold knew the children would go to the Binkes. She also knew that Harold would soon be placed by the JRC with a different family, but she had no details concerning his placement. In fact, two days after his arrival, Harold was assigned to a Christian couple, Mr and Mrs Dorrington, living on a farm in Peterborough near Cambridge. Although Clara Koppold knew that Harold was to go to a farm, as soon as she returned to Leipzig, she sent Paula a short, sad note begging to know the exact whereabouts of her oldest son:

> Where actually is our big Harold? Who is taking care of him? Does he ever ask about his parents? About the little ones, I know you are with them, and they are in good hands. O how I would love to see the children. Perhaps it is possible for you to send a picture. It costs me a great deal to overcome – to write a few lines. I have much pain and longing. I can't write anymore. Do stay well and be brave, my dear Paula. Regards and kisses untold times.
>
> Your Aunt Clarchen and Mutti

Clara Koppold was totally bereft without her children. She needed to hear that her children were alright; she wanted to know exactly where her first son was and why the children were separated. In her anxiety, she wrote again to her niece to get answers to questions that Paula could not possibly answer: 'Why is Harold not with his brother and sister? I like to be able to understand everything clearer. The worry about everything is hard to take … Can't write anymore now; too much grief!'

This is followed by another note to Paula, and another plea: 'Dear Paula, please always write to me a very detailed letter, as this is the only thing that I have left from my life.' And to her six-year-old son Harold, she writes: 'My dear big son, Harold, … Papa has gone away; hope he will be home soon. Do you think about your Mutti and Papa sometime? … Be brave and stay well.'

Adolf Koppold was no longer in Leipzig. His wife Clara was now living with her mother in a small apartment on Humbolt Strasse. Before Clara and her mother were deported to Auschwitz, the Humbolt apartment into which she and her mother had to move, was occupied by more than a dozen people.[11] In April of 1940 Adolf Koppold was taken as a forced labourer to Sachsenhausen camp, where he died a month later.

The children had no sooner arrived in London when, on 1 September 1939, their lives were further disrupted by the English evacuation plan. Germany invaded Poland on 31 August. British intelligence learned that a German attack on London was imminent, so on 1 September 1939, all schoolchildren were evacuated from London and the coast to safer inland places. England declared war on Germany on 3 September. Over a four-day period all the children were removed from what the English authorities considered the danger zones. Among those evacuated were the newly arrived refugee children.

The Koppold children went directly to Cambridge where on the whole they had exemplary placements. Their progress was closely watched by the CRCC who wanted very much to keep the siblings together. Paula and Edith had a more difficult time, until they too arrived in Cambridge to stay. That was to make all the difference to all of the children.

NOTES

1. This is a part of the refugee flight experience that has not yet received adequate attention.
2. Many documents of the period were lost or deliberately destroyed. To date, I have not yet been able to identify positively the committees in Germany with whom the English committees worked. One of the Jewish social agencies in Germany was the Hilfsverein der deutschen Juden, founded originally in 1901 (see p. 6).
3. *Manchester Guardian*, 3 January 1939. First annual report, Movement for the Care of Children from Germany and Austria, November 1938–December 1939, p. 9 (my italics).
4. Ibid.
5. Ibid.
6. Ibid., p. 8.
7. Vera's aunt, Clara Koppold, and her grandmother, Rosa Asman Schmulewitz, were together when they were deported to Auschwitz. Deportation book, 1942/45, Bundes Archiv, Berlin.
8. Dora Binke was the great niece of the children's grandmother, Rosa Asman Schmulewitz.
9. See Herbert Strauss, 'Jewish Emigration from Germany: Nazi Policies and Jewish Responses (II)', *Yearbook* 26 (London: Baeck Institute, 1981), pp. 396–7.
10. Some of these details were supplied by Tsvi, the oldest of the three Koppold children, who changed his name from Harold when he emigrated to Israel. The interview with Dubrovsky took place at Nir Oz, in June 1944, the kibbutz on the Gaza border where he lives.
11. Deportation book, 1942/45, Bundes Archiv, Berlin.

CHAPTER FOUR

Greta Burkill and the CRCC

Greta Burkill was committed, passionate, dogmatic, determined, and – in the estimation of some who knew and worked with her – she was difficult. She was neither saint nor sinner, yet at times a bit of both. For English society she was an oddity with a Russian accent. Born Margreta Braun in Berlin on 1 December 1896, she was the third child of two secular Jewish parents whom she described as cultured, middle-class and ethnically mixed – Polish, Russian, German.[1] Her father, Adolph Browne or Braun (1862–1929), was Austrian: her mother, Bertha Nathansohn Braun, was half Russian and half Polish. The young Margreta, or Greta,[2] absorbed the various cultural and social differences which come with such a diversified background. As a child she understood her parental home to be a place of refuge for people forced from their native homes because of their unpopular political views. Probably because of this she made her own adult home a haven for refugees.

Adolph Braun, Greta's father, was one of six siblings (five boys and one girl) all born in different cities in Austria. Her grandfather, Ignasz Braun, an engineer, worked on the first railway system in the Austro-Hungarian empire. Because his position required him to follow the eastward expansion of the railway, he and his family moved a great deal. Yet, all of the Braun children were educated and entered various professions. Adolph studied economics at Basle and Freiburg Universities, receiving his doctorate from the latter. In 1888 he attended the foundation conference of the Socialist Party in Vienna. An ardent socialist and a journalist for *Vorwarts*, he campaigned for the rights of the working classes and was politically active in the cause of giving the masses more power and a better living standard. In his obituary,[3] he is remembered for his efforts on behalf of workers.

Greta's mother was born Bertha Nathansohn and brought up in Russia. As a young woman aspiring to be an actress, she ran away from her provincial parental home to Odessa, and needing money, took a position as a governess to young children. But, full of energy and optimism, she did not find child-care entirely satisfying and moved west. In Berlin, she entered a university, enrolled in a programme of Russian studies, and subsequently developed a world-view that encompassed both socialism and feminism. She too obtained a position writing for the journal *Vorwarts*, where she met Adolph Braun. They married and had three children, a son and two daughters: Greta was the youngest. The Braun's stay in Berlin was cut short when Adolph learned that his liberal political views did not coincide with those of the editor. The family moved to Stuttgart, and from there to Nuremberg where Braun became chief editor of the *Frankische Tagespost*, a newspaper with some political clout in Franken.

The social and political life of the Brauns left them little time for their family. They hired a mother's help for the two older children and a Russian nursemaid for their baby Greta. The nursemaid was a young ideological anarchist who only spoke Russian; hence Russian was Greta's first language. Greta remembers her mother as not being particularly interested in child-minding. It was her father who supervised the carers and enforced such discipline as the children not being allowed to eat sweets and only being allowed books. Eventually the three Braun children were sent to what must have been a progressive boarding school, judging by Burkill's account of the freedom they enjoyed there. At home, Adolph Braun continued his political involvement and activities, which included teaching workers their rights.

When Greta was 8 years old, her parents divorced. Two years later she moved with her mother to St Petersburg, Russia, while her siblings remained in Germany with their father. Bertha Braun started a language school in St Petersburg, hiring one Guy Pritchard, an Englishman, to teach English. Their professional relationship blossomed into romance and marriage. Pritchard, a serious and involved stepfather, was to exert an important influence on Greta's life, and especially on her education.

During her schooling in Russia, Greta became fluent in German, English and Russian. She was tutored in French, Latin and Greek and took ballet lessons. She seems to have been happy, in spite of the political situation in the country and rigorous education in a school where 'all schoolchildren, all students, all officials had to wear uniforms'.

When she came to England Greta retained her affinity with Russian culture; indeed, she never lost her Russian accent, nor, for that matter, her confidence in the abilities and strength of the Russian people. Empathizing with the limitations on the freedom of the Russians, she respected their stamina and creative abilities. Indeed, she tried in her later years to promote a greater understanding of all that the Russian people had suffered during the 200-year occupation by the Tartars who oppressed the general population and treated them as slaves. Nonetheless, as a young girl in her mother's native country, Greta witnessed discrimination against Jews and surveillance of the general population by secret police. Young as she was, she was not indifferent to what was happening. Later she was to write: 'There were lots of difficulties and horrors in Russia at the time, if you were on the unlucky side of life. There were parts of Russia where no Jews were allowed to live. There were universities where no Jews could study. Secret police were well placed to watch the passers-by' (Memoir, p. 7).

Although Greta Burkill was by any definition Jewish and certainly aware of injustices perpetrated against Jews, neither she nor her parents identified themselves particularly with Judaism. She simultaneously sympathized with the plight of the Jews, yet in her adult life absorbed and retained negative stereotypes about them. These came out at odd moments when her best efforts at saving Jewish children failed, or when she was provoked by the inflexible beliefs of religious dogmatics.[4]

Greta reached an age of awareness early in the century which found Russia in a period of serious and destabilizing transition. Uncertainty was everywhere. Determining that his stepdaughter, aged 14 and growing into womanhood, needed the security and experience of an English boarding school, Greta's stepfather, Guy Pritchard, sent her in 1910 to London's Harrowgate Ladies' College. Greta recalls that the school 'found her strange and she found their relaxed easy way astonishing. The teaching was archaic by Russian standards, all languages were taught as grammatical exercise ... It was an elegant school, easygoing, outstanding at games, but not academic' (Memoir, p. 13).

In 1912 Greta's mother and stepfather left Russia and settled in London, together with Greta's sister Ida, who had joined the Pritchard family and later joined Greta at Harrowgate College. Ida finished her schooling and became a junior secretary, while Greta prepared for entrance to university. While her enlightened stepfather thought that 'nice girls' did not need advanced education, Greta thought otherwise. In her memoir, she notes that after Harrowgate, she started 'a new and independent life' in the autumn of 1917 by entering Newnham College, Cambridge. At that time women graduates of Cambridge were awarded certificates but no formal degrees. Already a strong feminist, Greta saw a battle to be fought and won. 'Women were conscious of the needs of the world and were well able to improve the life of their fellow men and women', she declared (Memoir, pp. 14–15).

In 1920, aged 24, Greta became engaged and married during the 'long vacation'. She confides in her memoir that her marriage was 'not a good idea'. Nevertheless, she moved to Liverpool with her husband and did private teaching. For three years, she conducted a weekly class for imprisoned women – work which she considered both interesting and worthwhile.

By her account, in 1925, tired of her husband's infidelities, she started divorce proceedings, and left Liverpool to join her mother in London. Short-lived as her first marriage was, nevertheless she appears to have grown and matured during the course of it.

In 1928 Greta met and married Charles Burkill, a mathematics professor at Liverpool, and for the second time she set up house in the city. They had barely settled in when, after a year, Peterhouse, Cambridge, offered Charles Burkill a position that he accepted. Eventually he became the Master of Peterhouse and a Fellow of the Royal Society.

In the early days of their marriage the Burkills lived the typical academic life, surrounded by interesting friends and busy with absorbing schedules which included caring for their three infant children and managing the home. They especially enjoyed inviting undergraduates to lunch twice a week, and they became surrogate parents for some students who used to drop in to visit at odd times. By 1932 the Burkills and their children were established in a well-functioning if somewhat insular household. Greta wrote: 'Life was peaceful ... There was no involvement with the outside world. Summer holidays were at the sea with the children, skiing on our own in winter and sometimes at Easter' (Memoir, p. 23).

Life changed for the Burkills, and almost everyone else, after 1933 and Hitler's rise to power. In Germany Jews became an endangered species: Jewish academics were dismissed from their university positions and Jewish professionals – doctors, dentists, lawyers, teachers, academics – were forbidden to practise. The idyllic existence Burkill describes in Cambridge was 'rudely broken ... [and] the free countries became conscious that something must be done'. Like their counterparts worldwide, the academic community in Cambridge was acutely aware of the need to stand up and be counted.

The university had always had a fair number of German students. From 1933 those students became increasingly concerned about their parents. In response to their distress a small committee of university-affiliated personnel formed to support their efforts to help their families leave Germany. One day in the mid-1930s, a German student who used to visit the Burkill home on a regular basis appeared in their living room carrying a box of jewellery which he put into Greta's hand. He explained, 'My mother asked me to keep this for her until a time when it was needed. That time is now. Please help me get my parents out of Germany.' Years later, Greta Burkill remembered the incident as a decisive moment for her. Advising the boy to keep his mother's jewellery for another time, nevertheless she said she would try to help.[5]

Along with others in Cambridge, both Charles and Greta became associated in 1933 with the newly formed Academic Assistance Council

(AAC), which had its headquarters in London. The AAC, later more inclusively renamed the Society for the Protection of Science and Learning (SPSL), identified institutions worldwide which offered positions to vulnerable scientists and academics (if they accepted, they were allowed to emigrate from Germany and Austria). Indeed, in the early 1930s, Germany permitted exit to all who had visas to enter another country. To their shame, at that crucial time, few countries in the world opened their gates to political exiles that needed a safe haven. However, an exception was made for academics.

In England and elsewhere, professional colleagues successfully encouraged their own institutions to offer teaching and research positions to dismissed scholars. Both Oxford and Cambridge led all other English institutions in the number of invitations they sent to the best and the brightest in the world, who were then in danger of their lives. Although their numbers were painfully small, intellectual giants of Europe were thus spared the fate of colleagues, friends and family members left behind. They immeasurably enriched their new academic communities.

Charles and Greta Burkill were both supportive of the efforts being made on behalf of refugees and their children. But Greta dedicated herself to the work with increasing energy and commitment. Understanding the vulnerability of the endangered children in Nazi Germany, she focused exclusively on their needs and devoted all her energies to saving them. She enlisted her mother and sister (then living in England) in refugee work, and they in turn tapped into a network of relatives and extended family on the Continent. All joined the clandestine and sacred mission of helping the uncomprehending and the desperate make their way across the Channel. When the refugees arrived in the country, Greta's mother, who was fluent in many languages, dealt with the German, Polish, Italian and Spanish refugees. 'When they decided to come to Cambridge, they became my responsibility', wrote Greta (Memoir, p. 26). 'The trick was to keep within the laws of the country while stretching them to the limit.' She was to develop a particular facility in stretching the rules to the limit.

Greta Burkill understood both the language of the refugees and the language of bureaucracy. Not only did she communicate with people from many different places, but she also developed creative ways of getting around bureaucratic regulations, of softening 'the rules by which we were bound', as she put it. She was indefatigable in the way she could and did exploit every loophole in British law to further her efforts on behalf of refugees. For example, during a short period of time when there was no restriction on the number of foreign dentists allowed into England, she arranged with her cousin in Brussels to send to Cambridge Malli Meyer, a dentist whose husband had been shot in front of her just after his release from a concentration camp.[6] As soon as Malli Meyer arrived in England, Greta and the CRCC were able to arrange for her young son to come to Cambridge where he was enrolled in the Leys School. 'More and more people came to Cambridge: academics and others from all walks of life, and each one had his or her painful problem with which one tried to deal while keeping within the laws of this country', she wrote (Memoir, p. 25).

In short, Greta Burkill did whatever was necessary to attain her immediate goal of saving the greatest number in the shortest time. The frenzied pace of the times, the uncertainty of dealing with emergencies without an established organizational structure or model and the stark needs of displaced people stripped of everything but their lives demanded courage, resiliency, persistence and money. Burkill forged ahead, with or without money. Because finances were crucial and always in short supply she developed fund-raising skills. Interestingly, she does not dwell upon the difficulty of financial shortfalls, except in the odd phrases such as 'Finance had to be found at times, which was not easy' (p. 26).

Greta Burkill was always keenly aware of the distress of hounded people and the needless loss of lives because others did not take appropriate action quickly enough. She cites the desperate case of a medical specialist who had once attended the Munich family of the Duchess of Kent. When the CRC learned that the doctor in Germany was in danger of his life, Burkill wrote to the comptroller of the Duchess's household asking for a guarantee on behalf of the medical man. It was refused. Burkill records that because of the refusal the doctor and his family perished in a concentration camp (Memoir, p. 26).

The failures of her best efforts haunted Greta Burkill into her old age, although to the outside world she seemed totally fearless and indomitable. Given the pressures of the times, one could not dwell on disappointments. Events moved too quickly:

> All the time one tried to be a step in front of Adolf Hitler's next move of destruction, and this was a great strain and produced a lot of heartache ... Matters did not run smooth and one's mind was always working on how one could help another innocent person out of the inflamed hell which was central Europe. To be quicker-witted than Hitler was not an easy task. (Memoir, p. 27)

Everyone working on behalf of refugees knew they were in a race against time, but no one knew when the inevitable axe would fall. It finally fell on 10 November 1938, with '*kristallnacht*'. Cambridge, Britain – indeed the whole world – were all in shock at the unexpected violence and wanton cruelty. Burkill gives her impression of how the news was received in Britain:

> The Nazis ran amok, killing, destroying and rounding people up for concentration camps ... *kristallnacht*, a night of terror and murder ... The whole of Great Britain was aghast – the horror of it all went like an electric current through every town and village. The feeling was 'we must save the children'. Committees were formed and information collected. A Cambridge Children's Committee [the CRCC] was formed – Mrs Hartree was Chairman, Sybil Hutton and I [Greta Burkill] as Hon. Secretary, Mrs Pope as Treasurer. (Memoir, pp. 27–8)

GRETA BURKILL'S PERSONAL INVOLVEMENT IN LIVES OF REFUGEES

Successful rescue operations in England in 1938 depended upon volunteers making critical decisions quickly and efficiently. When Greta Burkill and the CRCC became aware of the plight of Ernst Reuter, a prominent left-wing politician and a former mayor of Berlin who had been arrested and thrown into a concentration camp in Germany, they helped obtain his release and transfer to England. Only after Reuter arrived, did the CRCC arrange for his young son also to come to England. The 13-year-old Harry Reuter was taken into the Burkill household immediately upon his arrival in Cambridge and enrolled in the Leys School. He was the first of three German refugee boys, sons of academic parents, whom the school admitted. Subsequently, the elder Reuter, with the help of the CRCC, secured two concurrent positions in Turkey: as a professor of economics, and as an administrator of the new Turkish railway system. Reuter left for Turkey, while his son Harry remained with the Burkill family. Like many of the children in whom Greta Burkill invested so much energy, he repaid her efforts years later by retiring, at the end of a long professional career, from a professorship at Imperial College, London.

Greta Burkill and other members of the two refugee committees in Cambridge – the CRC (which helped refugee adults and families) and the CRCC (which focused on the needs of the refugee children) – worked cooperatively in response to emerging situations. By mutual agreement (or assumption), the CRC handled most of the financial matters. Greta was somehow involved in all of the activities, taking place at the committees' headquarters at 55 Hills Road, Cambridge, particularly those concerning the children.

The records of the two Cambridge committees indicate Burkill's steady presence at most of the meetings, although she was generally a subdued participant. She did not make waves; her battleground was not in the office but in the field. When the government put a cap of 1,000 unguaranteed refugee children allowed into the UK in any given month, but left open-ended the number of guaranteed children, she immediately set out to secure as many guarantors as possible. Arming herself with pictures of appealing children, she knocked on the doors of Cambridge citizens, and picture in hand, tried to convince the householders to assure the safety of the child by a pledge of £50 and an offer of hospitality for that same child. In this way, Cambridge families assumed responsibility for some 70-plus children. How many of those placements were the results of Burkill's persuasive tactics is not known. She and Charles Burkill took two refugee children into their own home.

Working with the CRCC in their newly acquired headquarters at 55 Hills Road, Greta Burkill organized a group of women into a quasi-Red Cross group. They knitted blankets for the hospitals, collected warm clothing to distribute to those who needed them, and organized volunteers to work at the local military hospital. Burkill says that her day consisted of 'Red Cross work in the morning and refugee work in the afternoon and other duties ... somehow'. Her 'other duties' included managing the lives of her three children and the two refugee children now living in her home.

There was no let-up in the intense work of the committees, who coordinated their jobs in order to deal with the demands of events. On 31 August 1939 Hitler invaded Poland. Knowing an attack from Germany was imminent, the British government ordered an immediate evacuation of children, nursing mothers and elderly from London and cities on the eastern coast vulnerable to strikes from the Continent. The CRCC's regional offices were requested by the government to assume additional responsibility for the supervision of evacuated children in their areas.[7]

If the situation was chaotic for volunteer workers trying to keep tabs on thousands of children evacuated from London and other cities on the coast, it was extremely frightening for the children themselves. They were issued gas masks, instructed on how and when to use them, and sent away from the security of their homes. For the very young newly arrived foreign refugee children the evacuation was not only frightening, it was totally baffling. They had only recently arrived in England, still traumatized by the separation from their parents, and had not yet adjusted to the foreign-ness of the country. Nor did they have sufficient language skills to understand what was happening or to communicate their feelings. Once more they had to take their belongings and leave a home in which they only recently had been accepted for an unknown destination.

By law, every home-owner or dweller in the evacuation area with a spare room was required to take children unless there was a good reason to excuse them. Most of the villagers and country people cooperated, but some home-owners in evacuation sites were hostile to the idea of foreign children entering their homes and resented the law that compelled them to accept the children. Thus the committee members' oversight was crucial to the well-being of the children. Needless to say, the work of the committee members expanded dramatically.

According to Burkill, the Orthodox refugee children 'spoke Yiddish and did not want to speak English. Dr Loewe, [Cambridge University] Reader in Rabbinics and a member of the Cambridge Refugee Committee, went round the region trying to weld them together and give them confidence' (Memoir, p. 31). Burkill accompanied Dr Loewe on his rounds, dealing with the administrative issues concerning the children. The region, spanning all of East Anglia, included such cities as Norwich, Ely, Bury St Edmunds, Bedford and a number of other towns.

Volunteers worked everywhere, doing what they could for refugee families, refugee children and evacuees. The hard-pressed committees never lost sight of the fact that they were responsible to the absent parents for the well-being of their children. They were scrupulous in their record-keeping, especially in keeping track of the whereabouts of the children. It was not always easy. Blitz or no blitz, the older children determined to return to London often did. Yet Cambridge acquitted itself splendidly. Burkill estimated that '2,000 [children] went through our files, the steadfast number [for whom the CRCC was responsible] being 800' (Memoir, p. 32).

In trying to do everything she felt had to be done, Greta Burkill overextended herself and finally had to take some leave. She records that she 'collapsed with pneumonia and pleurisy'. The illness led to an enforced period of rest in Wales with her children, away from all distractions.

In May 1940, while Burkill was in Wales, the government, concerned about the possibility of German espionage in England, enacted security measures which were to have a considerable effect on the lives of refugees. Refugees in England were already sensitive to the xenophobic anti-immigrant mood in the country. They were careful in what they said and how they behaved. When the government initiated a plan to separate all who might be spies from the population at large, and 120 'Alien tribunals' were inaugurated to conduct 'hearings', the refugees' lives became yet more difficult. The tribunals began operating in October 1939. Educated British from a wide range of backgrounds – academics, lawyers, judges, senior police officers, ordinary and distinguished citizens – were appointed to act as judges. According to the historian Amy Gottlieb, the JRC in London prepared reports for approximately 48,000 refugees who had registered with its office and were still in the country.[8] All non-citizens aged 16 and over from German-speaking countries were required to appear. Most of those called to testify were newly arrived refugees. At the tribunals they received rating of A (to be interned); B (to remain at liberty, but subject to some restrictions); or C (friendly aliens, to be certified 'refugees from Nazi oppression', with no restrictions). Those deemed to be threatening, or potentially threatening, were removed from the community to a secure and remote facility. By the end of March 1940 some 73,800 refugees had been examined in the tribunals and 75 per cent were classified as refugees from Nazi oppression. Twenty per cent of the men and 17 per cent of the women were professionals: doctors, dentists, psychologists, teachers, architects, etc. Women who came to England as domestics represented 25 per cent of all the women called before the tribunals.[9]

Frightened, and not yet fully understanding English, the refugees called to testify at the tribunals needed support. Members of the CRC and the CRCC accompanied those from region 4 (the Cambridge district) and stood by them during their ordeal of testifying. Between October 1939 and May 1940, all refugees deemed to be a potential danger to the state, the educated and non-educated alike, were interned in what seemed to many an irrational and poorly thought-out scheme. An unknown number of the Cambridge refugees – generally older boys and men but also some women – were thus interned for varying periods of time. They had no advance notice as to when or where they were to go: a knock came on the door, a policeman or other official was there, and the soon-to-be internee was taken away. Nor did the family left behind have any information as to where the son, husband or father was to be detained. Many were taken from their workplace without any advance notice, nor did they have the right of appeal.

Once more, young people had to leave at short notice without any clear idea of where they were going. Once more, parents and children were parting and nobody knew where they would be or how they could contact each other. The CRC and the CRCC had the burden of taking care of both the distraught families left behind and the distraught young people forcibly led away. A practical detail was that the committees immediately acquired another job: that of storing the belongings of those who had few possessions and no families.

A number of the 16-year-old interned boys were shipped out to Canada and Australia and an indefinite number of both girls and boys were interned on the Isle of Man (midway between the Northern Irish and English coasts). Even though it took at least ten or 12 hours to get to the internment camp on the Isle of Man, the Cambridge committee volunteers made periodic visits to their internees, raising their spirits by gifts of food, books and warm clothing. Others organized systematic letter-writing to the internees, even while the Refugee Children's Movement petitioned for the release of those internees who had been under the charge of the CRC and the CRCC. In her Memoir, Burkill records that she considered the experience to be 'catastrophic, a bureaucratic miscalculation' (p. 33).

Max Perutz, newly launched on his scientific career as a microbiologist at Cambridge University, was one of those arrested in May 1940 and interned on the Isle of Man. By his own account, he was in the erudite company of 'hundreds of German and Austria refugee scholars, mostly Jewish and all anti-Nazi, who had been rounded up in the official panic created by the German attack on the Low Countries and the imminent threat of an invasion of Britain'.[10] His 63-year-old father, a recent *émigré* to Cambridge, was also interned on the Isle of Man, but father and son were in different places. The elder Perutz was released in January 1941. Because Max Perutz's scientific training was useful to the British, he was retained but given assignments while interned to help in the development of anti-personnel weapons. Eventually he too was released, and in September 1943 was granted British citizenship.

Rabbi David Margules, a Hebrew scholar and teacher educated in Vienna, distinguished rabbi of Czechoslovakia and Austria and a Cambridge refugee who taught Hebrew to the town's Jewish children, was also interned on the Isle of Man in July 1940. On 15 November 1940 he sent a letter to the medical officer of the Onchan internment camp at the Isle of Man asking for release on medical grounds. He wrote:

> I am 56 years of age, a refugee from Nazi oppression and was classified by the Aliens Tribunal in category 'C' [the most benign classification]. Before I came to this country, I was kept by the Nazis at Dachau Concentration Camp. Having been Chief Rabbi of Salzburg (Austria) I was treated there even worse than other Jews, and the after-effects have surely affected my health … The state of my health has seriously deteriorated since I was interned in spite of the careful medical treatment received at this camp … I desire to proceed to … Cambridge where my wife with two daughters live, and where I shall receive treatment.[11]

By September 1941, Rabbi Margules was released. He returned to Cambridge, where he resumed his position as rabbi and Hebrew teacher and accommodated in his home visiting rabbis and Jewish scholars. In July 1948 he became a naturalized British subject.[12]

Greta Burkill and her co-workers in the CRC office actively worked for the release 'of university scholars, undergraduates, and schoolchildren from Canada … The War Office did not let them go, though the Committee

ultimately succeeded in obtaining the release of a number of internees.'
According to Burkill, 'the 16-year and older [children] should never have
been rounded up' (Memoir, pp. 33–4). The committee may have prevailed
in having some internees released, but in too many cases the lives of 16- and
17-year-olds were seriously disrupted when they were sent to internment
camps. Perhaps though they were the lucky ones. Several hundred were
sent away to Canada, in spite of the risk of being torpedoed on the high
seas. One boat, the *Arandora Star*, was actually hit and sunk, and half the
ship's young passengers were lost.[13] Others, young and old refugees,
deemed by the specially created tribunals to be a danger to British society,
were shipped off to Australia on substandard boats. The *Dunera* is notorious for the way its British crew members brutalized the refugees *en route*.
They were later convicted of cruel and inhumane treatment of passengers.[14]

A CRC report reflects that during the period June 1940–June 1941 the
major preoccupation of the committee had been the problem of internment
and the condition of the internment camps. At the end of a year, very few
of the Cambridge refugees remained in the camps, and some had actually
returned to Cambridge from Canada and Australia. According to the
report: 'A great deal of work has been done and much correspondence
carried on to help in securing this large measure of release.'[15] The report
also notes that the committee offices continue to occupy the house at 55
Hills Road which had 'recently become the headquarters for the newly
formed East Anglian Regional Council for Refugees'.[16]

GRETA BURKILL ON EDUCATION

Of all the responsibilities assumed by Greta Burkill and the CRCC, none
were as demanding and crucial as the education of refugee children. It is
clear from her memoir that she considered her major contribution to the
children lay in her efforts to ensure that the capable and the talented were
educated to the limit of their abilities. She had what could be called a
missionary zeal in her determination that the natural gifts and talents of
refugee children should be encouraged and developed.

According to British policy, refugee children were to be schooled up
until the age of 14 at which point they would either get vocational training
and go to work, or get jobs that did not require further training. On the
other hand, British children who demonstrated promise and ability were
helped by the government to advance to progressively higher levels of
education. Thus talented refugee children did not have the same opportunity for advanced education.

Greta Burkill saw a serious problem in government funding policies which differentiated unfairly between gifted British schoolchildren and equally gifted refugee children living in Britain. However, most of the leadership of the Refugee Children's Movement in England did not agree with her on this. The majority of the regional committees thought their responsibility was to provide minimum rather than maximum education, and so it was deemed sufficient for refugee children to finish their formal schooling at the age of 14. But in region 4, Burkill fought a fierce battle for talented refugee children to advance in the educational system in the same manner as their British counterparts.

Education is a leitmotif in the story of the challenges both Burkill and the CRCC faced in their efforts to serve in *loco parentis* for the children entrusted to their care. Over and over, in her memoir, Burkill repeats words to the following effect: 'I gave to others the responsibility for finding clothes for the children, for their medical supervision, for finding work opportunities for them. But when it came to their education, I was in charge. I wanted to make sure that each child was educated to its potential.'

The technical education offered in England to refugee children from Germany, Austria and Czechoslovakia was not of the same kind or calibre as they would have received in their native countries. According to Max Perutz, Burkill stood up at Cambridge University meetings and, shaking her fist in the direction of erudite but uncomprehending scholars, she insisted that qualified young refugees living in England be granted the same privileges and opportunities as other equally qualified students, no matter where they were born. She would not accept a negative response.[17] She won in some cases and lost in others, but the fight was passionate, just and, in the end, justified. Impressive contributions were made by young refugees who ultimately received government assistance for their education and subsequently became noted in the arts, humanities and sciences. Ironically, many of them never learned of the fight Burkill put up for them. To her credit, she sought neither recognition nor acclaim for the subsequent accomplishments of her 'children'. Yet, their successes resulted, at least in part, from her hard-fought battles on behalf of those who had no one else to fight for them.

In 1939 Cambridge students were funded by a bursary which granted £175 a year to each qualifying student and in addition paid all the college and university tuition and laboratory fees. A British student could also apply for a county scholarship on the strength of his or her school certificate results. The young refugee students had more limited opportunities. While some did in fact obtain scholarships, the procedure was not uniform; in many districts, refugee students in particular were not informed as to their options. They had missed at least a full school year and they had had to adjust to a new language, new life-style and completely different school methods and ways of teaching. Yet, no matter what ability many of these young students exhibited, they were not eligible for state scholarships or state bursaries and had to give up all hopes of university or higher technical education.

On 21 February 1945 Greta Burkill presented to the monthly meeting of the regional representatives at Bloomsbury House, London, a memorandum on behalf of the Cambridge region. It recommended that qualified refugee children receive the same maintenance as other British children during the two years required to gain a 'higher school certificate or a university entrance scholarship standard'. In the name of the Cambridge committee, Burkill asked the Ministry of Education to grant young refugees the same government support that it granted other British students: for example, a government-aided teacher training course of three years at a university and one year's professional training.[18]

Burkill was passionate about redressing the injustice and hardship the system imposed on otherwise deserving young people by denying them equal opportunities. She was also aware of the potential loss of talents to the community and the world. She writes:

> With Higher School Certificates only to their credit [refugee children] are debarred from those forms of service which would, with this further education, make them of maximum use to the State ... High intellectual ability is not a personal possession but an asset which the community ought to develop for the general benefit. There is no greater social danger than the thwarting and frustration of such outstanding abilities.[19]

To prove her point, she documents the cases of three refugee boys who did very well in their respective schools and examinations but needed financial assistance. For these boys, either their college tutors or one of the many refugee committees were able to come to their assistance. She then presents the case of one unfortunate young man who was prevented by lack of funding from continuing at school. In his four terms at school he did 'outstandingly well', earning four distinctions and five credits and attaining a school certificate. Nevertheless, he had to support himself by working in a toy factory. When London was bombed, the factory disappeared. He then worked for an estate agent, but was unhappy at the job. To its credit, the International Students' Service intervened and the young man was given a free place in a northern polytechnic. The Refugee Children's Movement maintained him in one of its hostels for a year. After gaining his intermediate BSc, he supported himself by washing dishes in a restaurant and studied at night. He finally gained a scholarship to Imperial College,

London, and support was guaranteed by the International Students' Service. But the delay in his education, the uncertainty of his future and the previous strain of his experiences as an adolescent Jew in Vienna caused a breakdown in his health. He was hospitalized and ultimately committed suicide. The history of this young refugee student who started life with much promise and ended it in despair affected Burkill deeply. She understood all too clearly that those children who had no guarantors or sponsors were in the greatest danger and thus the Refugee Children's Movement had to assume more responsibility for them. She tried to exploit every possible opportunity to help those she considered the most vulnerable.

On behalf of the CRCC, Burkill submitted proposals to the Central Committee asking it to grant funds allowing those refugee students who attained a high standard in their higher school certificate exam, to remain at school until the age of 18. The Central Committee was a government agency set up in 1940 to provide government supplements to various classifications of refugees.[20] Burkill further argued that where financial necessity was proved those needy refugee students should be given maintenance grants. 'In the event the grant was insufficient ... the Central Committee could make grants supplementing their awards according to the needs of the individuals ... in consultation with the university authority.'[21]

Like all social reformers who often need to fight the very people and agencies they want to improve, Burkill was at odds not only with the government but also sometimes with her own committee. Not everyone agreed that refugee children should be given the same opportunities as British children. She summarizes her struggle for equal educational opportunities thus:

[The fight] was long and bitter – I felt all the gifted refugee children should have a chance to go to the University, whilst the Movement thought they should earn their living and be of use in the war effort. I felt there should be no difference between the British and the refugee boy or girl. Ultimately, I won and the doors were open. This produced a crop of outstanding researchers, people in business and all fields ... To get the money for their University education, one had to use all sorts of means, but we always made it ... They [refugee children] all did very well in their different Universities and many of them are now well known in the wider world. (Memoir, p. 34)

A CASE HISTORY: FREDERIC BETTELHEIM

When Greta Burkill recognized extraordinary talent in a refugee child, she felt she had a mission and the movement had an obligation to encourage and develop it. One of her protégés, as she called these special children, was young Frederic (Freddy) Bettelheim. It is worth looking at the case of Frederic Bettelheim in some detail as by doing so we are able to get considerable insight into the influence which Greta Burkill exerted.

Freddy and his sister Frances were placed on a *Kindertransport* leaving Vienna for England. Their parents then made their way to Caracas, Venezuela, where they maintained themselves as best they could: Mrs Bettelheim took in sewing while her husband worked as a waiter. At the end of the war, the Bettelheims initiated efforts to reunite with their children from whom they had been separated for nine years. On 18 June 1947, Dorothy Hardisty, general secretary of the RCM, sent a letter to Mr and Mrs Bettelheim in Caracas. The correspondence set in motion the eventual reunion of Hedwig and Fritz Bettelheim with their children Frederic and Frances. But it took more than a year for a meeting between the parents and their son to take place, and even longer for them to be reunited with their daughter.

On 9 August 1947 the Bettelheims wrote to Mrs Hardisty to say that, anxious as they were for a meeting, they had to wait because of lack of finance. Mrs Hardisty sent a copy of the letter to Greta Burkill with a note saying, 'These parents seem to me to be wonderfully patient and unselfish.'[22] In their letter to Mrs Hardisty the Bettelheims wrote:

> We *are* longing to see our children, and we have suffered a lot by being parted from them for so many years already. We do realize most painfully that we have lost – forever lost – a part of the intimate, natural relationship between parents and children who are living together. We renounced these relations quite consciously, for the sake of *their good*, for *their* better future. That meant a terrible loss for ourselves, and has cost us a lot of struggling and longing and grieving. It was a most dangerous experiment, too – but Heaven was merciful to us, and preserved our children from bombs and other dangers during the war. [They found] kind and helpful friends [who] guided and assisted them, and helped them to their highest aims: Cambridge University … Our gratitude to the English people … who helped and supported our children is too great, too deep to be expressed in poor words.

The Bettelheim children had been guaranteed by Norwich citizens: Frances, aged 11, by Mrs E.C. Evans of 50 Franksome Road; and Freddy,

9, by Mr Braham, 23 Castle Street. Neither of the sponsors sought financial support from the movement. In fact, according to a report from Greta Burkill to Mrs Hardisty, the children 'never had any financial help from our Committee whatsoever'.[23] The parents actually supported their children by sending money directly to the guarantors of the children, but, according to Burkill, neither Mr Braham, Freddy's guarantor, nor Mr Jevons, his headmaster into whose home the boy moved, used the money. They both 'put it into a Post Office account for the boy so that he did have something to start off when he came to Cambridge'.[24]

Clearly the Bettelheims must have arrived in Venezuela with some financial resources, which they carefully managed and used to support their children. In 1947, anxious to see their children, they contacted the CRCC. According to their letter to Mrs Hardisty (9 August 1947) most of their disposable funds had gone to pay for their son's and daughter's education in England. Both were then at different stages in their university careers. Frances was at London University and Frederic at Cambridge. They were both brilliant students who depended, at least partly, on scholarship aid.

The Bettelheims could not afford the fare to travel to England or to have both of their children travel to Venezuela immediately. Furthermore, they understood that their gifted children's futures depended upon success in their respective courses of study and they had no desire to compromise in any way their educational opportunities. They wrote to Mrs Hardisty:

> We cannot, we must not spoil the careers they have so promisingly begun, for which they have worked so hard. And besides this, it is also a money-matter, and we are not yet in a position to pay for such a luxury as a trip from England to Venezuela ... Through all these years, we have gladly, and proudly done our utmost to help support them financially, in their effort to get the best of the world-famous English education, and we do not at all regret it.

But by mid-December 1947 they had saved up enough money for their son to visit them. Although the Bettelheims wanted their son to travel to Venezuela during the next long vacation, Greta Burkill told them that it would be difficult for him to do so, as Fred had to prepare for important exams the following year. The outcome would have a direct bearing on his career. Burkill assured the parents that the following year, after Freddy graduated, he would be free for the whole of the long vacation.

One can only imagine the feelings of the parents who had not seen their son in nine years and who were being asked to think not of themselves but of their son's future career. Burkill sounds either naïve or manipulative when she writes 'It is asking a great deal from you to wait again, but I know that you will want the best for Freddy, who is very anxious to give you all the happiness he can, and I am sure would put his future aside for your wishes.' Burkill did not seem to understand why the parents, who had waited so long to be reunited with their children, could not wait another year. So absorbed was she in the career of her star refugee child that she discouraged an immediate visit to his parents on the assumption that a break in the boy's studies could compromise his future. In her next letter to the parents, she suggested that instead of Freddy visiting them in Venezuela they could come to England to visit both their children and to meet the people who have given them 'such generosity and kindness during their time [in England]'. Certainly, she said, there were people in Cambridge who would be happy to give them hospitality during their stay. Burkill misses entirely the parents' need: (1) to take care of themselves and their children with their own resources; and (2) to become reacquainted with their children in their own home, on their own territory. Nor does she appreciate the Bettelheim's deep longing for their fractured family to start a process of bonding.

Burkill was by no means malicious or coldly calculating. But by assuming the parental role over their son, she upstaged the parents without even realizing it. No doubt she understood how crucial finances were to the displaced survivors of Hitler. But she went beyond propriety when she told the Bettelheims, who had taken some pride in the fact that they had been supporting their two children to the best of their ability, that they would be relieved of any financial responsibility if their son, a scholar of King's College, qualifies for a full grant from the Ministry of Education. She implied it was for the Bettelheim's own good not to pressure Freddy to visit before his scholarship grant is assured and went on to suggest that the senior Bettelheims should consider putting in a claim for the property they lost in Austria. How the proud Bettelheims reacted to these suggestions is a matter for conjecture.

The Bettelheims were deferential in their response to Greta Burkill's letter (28 December 1947). Politely and carefully, they repeatedly thanked her while, at the same time, expressing their strong and natural desire for a speedy reunion. Being told of their son's intellectual gifts, the parents assured Greta that they would never stand in the way of his future. Yet, for all that, they wished to see Freddy as soon as possible, while Greta, for her part, wanted them to wait until he had finished his undergraduate work. The parents tried to reconcile their desires with Greta's apparent wisdom:

Before we learned better from you, we thought the visit would be first this summer (1948), his last opportunity for a long holiday ... Through your [letters] we see things quite differently now. What you told us

about Freddy's possible career, the high aim you believe him to be qualified for, has quite overwhelmed us ... We understand quite well ... it
would be much more convenient ... for him to spend the whole of the
1949 long vacation for a trip to Venezuela ... after having accomplished
– we will hope successfully – his 3rd year at College.

Apologetically, they explained to Burkill that when Freddy wrote to tell
them that he could not come for the whole of the long vacation time, they
immediately suggested that he come 'for the remaining five weeks'. They
explained:

> We were, however, perfectly aware that such a precipitated and hurried
> visit could not be the ideal solution of our meeting again, to which we
> had looked forward for so long. But we have put up with the idea of
> having the boy with us for a few, short weeks, since we thought there
> would be no opportunity for him, for years to come, to have longer
> holidays. We know better now, by your kind information, and therefore
> we wrote to Freddy yesterday, leaving the decision up to him: whether
> he would prefer to come over for a few weeks, this autumn, or – as you
> suggested – for the whole of the Long Vacation in 1949.

Their daughter Frances wrote to her parents that she could not take the
time off from her school commitments to visit them until 1949. In their
letter to Greta Burkill, the parents explained their circumstances:

> We are looking forward to her visit very, very much, just as anxiously as
> to Freddy's. We beg you to understand that we cannot offer the boy to
> come over in 1948 and 1949 since we could not afford to pay 3 fares
> within the next 2 years. He has, therefore, to decide for one or the other
> possibility.

Although the Bettelheims took pride in their children's brilliant school
performance, their disappointment in the delay of a family reunion was
evident:

> Though both our children are writing us very satisfactorily, frequently,
> and affectionately, quite naturally there remains [*sic*] always many
> important matters we do not hear through them, or which we do not
> understand clearly enough ... We have also been a little worried, for
> quite a while, that our memory is falling slowly into oblivion – more
> with the boy than with the girl. In this respect, too, your ... reassuring,
> and comforting [words make it] easier for us to wait another year before

we can see and speak with our son, who was a mere little child when we had to part with him.

They shared with Burkill their pleasure that their daughter will be a British subject in 1949. But underneath was the realization that it represented another step away from them, the parents, to whom their children no longer can relate: 'We cannot imagine a better luck for our children, than to get naturalized in *the* country which has been so kind and generous to them, and where they naturally must belong with their hearts and minds.' What was left for them was the pride that at the very least they had been able to support their children and themselves. Therefore, they bristled a bit at Burkill's suggestion that they may be relieved soon of Freddy's school expenses:

> You were also kind enough to mention our financial situation; we dare, therefore, speak to you quite frankly about it. We are working both of us, and earning together a trifle more than £1,000 a year. But in this most expensive country this apparently high amount does not correspond, not even with the half of its purchasing power in England. Our prospects for the future are not too encouraging, either, since we are growing older and more tired ... We will consider ourselves very lucky if we will be able to maintain our present standard of income ... All we were able to do for our children, in all these last years, had to be very limited, unfortunately.
>
> We feel deeply indebted to ... so many kind-hearted people in England ... such loving care, kindness, and helpful understanding, as was allowed our children, can never be paid back in cash. We are ... sorry that we have not done better as regards money matters in a country where many people gained a little fortune within a few years.
>
> But you must not think that we are living in misery, or that we have to do without the necessary little comforts of life. We live in a nice flat and we have plenty of good food, all for a reasonable price. This is made possible by the fact that we live in a common household with our brother-in-law's family ... which makes everything more convenient – and much cheaper ... We beg you, when you speak next with Freddy – and the boy is sure to come to you for advice – do set him at ease as regards our situation ... This boy who is working so hard in order to achieve his great aim *shall not be worried about us parents. We would be very thankful for this particular kindness.* We do realize, however, that the boy's further care largely depends on his ability ... So far, and as long as we are able to help the boy to go on with his studies, we will always gladly do it ...

You mentioned also the possibility of *our* going to England, next summer. We also have often considered it, and it sounds rather tempting to visit this blessed and beautiful green England, to see our children in their background and to make thank-you visits to the many most dear people who have given them loving care and kindness for so many years. But ... we have, for the time being, abandoned this idea. It was also extremely nice of you to advise us about our property, lost in Austria. Our house in Vienna has already been restored to us, but it is rather damaged, and a financial advantage, whatsoever, is not yet within sight.

    Fritz Bettelheim, Hedwig Bettelheim (signature)

In 1948, almost three years after the Second World War had ended and many letters had been exchanged between Greta Burkill and the Bettelheims,[25] the parents were finally reunited with their son. It was Freddy himself who decided that he wished to see his parents as soon as possible and was able to set in motion hurried arrangements for his visit in the spring of 1948.

Alas. The more things change, the more they remain the same. The Bettelheims, in being driven from their birthplace and home, had experienced the difficulties of all Jews in Austria and Germany in the years following Hitler's rise to power. In 1948, in Venezuela, where they had sought and received sanctuary in 1939, they ran into problems trying to get a visa for their son: 'Venezuela is not readily prepared to admit, even on a visitor's visa, anyone who is Jewish' they wrote to Greta. She, with her customary resourcefulness asked a senior tutor who taught Freddy at Cambridge to write a letter on his behalf, because 'the Minister of the Interior in Venezuela would be more impressed by tutorial paper with plenty of crests than with anything on refugee paper which will conjure up in his mind a row of long beards!'[26] At the request of the parents Greta secured a return ticket for Freddy via New York, so that he would have an opportunity to meet surviving relatives living there.

In getting Freddy ready to leave for his trip to Venezuela, Greta did everything a mother would do: she made sure he was vaccinated against tropical diseases, that he had his return papers and tickets in order and had extra passport photos with him in case they were needed. She sent all the details concerning his arrival to his parents. Finally, there was one last thing she had to do before he left: she needed to prepare the Bettelheims psychologically for a reunion that might be 'a bitter experience' for all concerned. Drawing on her experiences of parent–child reunions, she warned the Bettelheims of possible consequences. There had been instances when neither parents nor child could recognize or relate to each other. The parents would remember the small trusting clinging child of nine years ago who had known only the home he had to leave under great stress. Burkill wrote of their son: 'In the nine years, the child has come under new influences, has grown up in a different country ... where he, a stranger, first had to become acclimatized and ... with time ... part of that atmosphere.'[27] For their part, she continued, the parents too have probably changed 'in a way ... which they never would have ... had they stayed in their own country under normal conditions and had grown with the growing child'.

As the reunion with their son drew nearer, both parents were anxious about the outcome. Fritz Bettelheim, in a letter to Burkill, tells her of a refugee in Caracas who was from Vienna. Her son (the same age as Freddy) was placed in a home in Scotland. He and his mother met, after many years, in Paris. When the mother returned to Venezuela, she said of her son, 'He was very considerate, very tender; but he spoke only reluctantly of his foster parents of whom he is naturally very fond. We have to realize that we have lost our children.'[28]

The Bettelheims were quite aware of the nature of the problem confronting them. They and the children lived entirely different lives during the nine years since they last saw each other. Fritz Bettelheim wrote to Greta Burkill:

> We know that Freddie is attached to people we do not know personally, but who have been *with* him in decisive and dark days. When [he] comes here, he will soon notice that we are *not* jealous – and we *don't* think we have lost anything when he is deeply attached to other people, too. In fact, we would not understand it otherwise ... We are bold enough to think that problems will be resolved, not created, by our reunion with our little 'Friedel'.[29]

Fritz Bettelheim ended his letter by again thanking Greta Burkill:

> It was very very kind of you to think of these problems and to prepare us mentally for Freddie's arrival. You have indeed succeeded in making us reconsider the whole matter. Many ardent thanks for your kind thoughtfulness. (Letter to Greta Burkill, 27 May 1948)

A day after Fritz Bettelheim posted his letter to Greta Burkill, Hedwig Bettelheim felt the need to write her own letter expressing her realistic expectations that child and parents will feel like strangers to each other after an absence of nine years. She wrote: 'You may be sure that we will ... try to understand our newly found grown-up boy, and to respect his *different* way of living, behaving, and thinking. We do hope our ... love for our children will help us to bridge these past 9 years with their ... most unlike experiences.' Helga Bettelheim felt the world has somehow been redeemed because of the 'many kind-hearted people who have taken care so generously ... of the homeless refugee children, when they needed it most'. As for Burkill's fears that the parents would be jealous of their children's foster-parents, Helga assured her: 'We are not jealous of them, really not, and we also hope that we have not lost the whole of our children's heart, in spite of their being truly, and affectionately – and lastingly, I dare say – attached to other, quite different people.'

Yet Helga Bettelheim was still coping with a loss that could never really be restored. She expressed the regret that many parents must have felt as they pondered what they had lost in the long separation from their children:

> What I most wished for, and longed for during all those years of separation, is most simple and primitive. I wanted to be near [my children] when they were ill, or worried, or in anxiety, to nurse them, and to soothe and comfort them. And quite particularly of Freddy, I wanted so very much to have him sit at a table, across from me, and to serve him good 'old-fashioned' hearty meals, and to look at him while he eats with appetite. This latter I've wished for years, and now I mean to indulge in it to my heart's content. I also want, so very much, to hear my boy's voice, his laughter, to see him smiling, to talk to him – and to pamper him a tiny little bit.
>
> But, I do not intend – nor wish – to 'chain' him once more to his parents. On the contrary, I mean to leave him as loose and independent as the circumstances will permit, and I am honestly proud that he will be allowed to go back to Cambridge, and go on with his education there.

For all her wisdom and bravado, Hedwig Bettelheim was worried about the meeting with her son after such a long time. She expressed some of her anxiety to Greta Burkill in a long and frank letter:

> How will the boy find *us* after these long, and oh so trying, years? I am afraid we have changed a lot, and for the worse: worn, harassed and old as we *are* and *look*. What a difference to the comparatively young, high-spirited, and fairly representative couple he knew, and probably still remembers! For *this* reason, I am so particularly grateful for your respective 'little talk' with Freddy, for your preparing him gently for what he can expect from us, and thus spare him the first shock and disappointment.
>
> Maybe we will also appear somewhat 'queer' to him, and certainly we're mentally unbalanced – the most unaccustomed matter for him.

Let me hope that by means of our ... love we will find the right way and words to one another.

As to the 'Permisa' affair ... we owe its final granting ... to the generous ... intervention of the British Institute here, whose director and sub-director are both Cambridge men and who made it *their* concern because [of] the recommendation letter of Mr Wilkinson ... Once more, our most heartfelt thanks for your kindness and under-standing, and help. Please do forgive me this 'effusion' in very poor English. Hedwig Bettelheim (signature)

Freddy arrived in Venezuela early in July 1948. A letter from Greta Burkill to his parents went before him. It informed them that their son had gained a first in his natural science tripos, news she also had cabled to Freddy while he was *en route* to Venezuela. Freddy wrote to Greta on 8 July 1948 to thank her for informing the family of the good news. He did not go into his feelings at all, except to say:

My parents have, of course, aged, especially my father, but I found no difficulty in recognizing them. My aunt and uncle have not changed so much either. We all share a very nice new house in a good residential district 5 miles from the centre of the town. Not all Caracas is so nice. So far, practically all the people I have seen are from Vienna ... My German is still not at all good, but the language difficulty is not acute.

In July 1948 Fritz Bettelheim wrote to thank Greta Burkill yet again for keeping them informed of Freddy's success. He reported that the family meeting went very well; they and the boy recognized each other immedi-ately. He went on:

In the first days we kept your ... sensible remarks in mind – but now we are no more cautious at all ... There are no 'problems' between him and us. And we never expected that he would tell us *everything*! He speaks quite frankly about people and things in England.

Once more, we beg you to accept our deepest thanks for all your kindness and help. Fritz Bettelheim (signature)

Helga Bettelheim also wrote to Greta Burkill to express genuine grati-tude for all her help in the family's reuniting in Caracas.[30] The reunion was, she said,

a thoroughly heart-warming and happy one. The boy is still the good, good-humoured, and easy-to-be-handled child he used to be, and our house is echoing with his laughter, and reflecting in everyone's face his always smiling, radiant eyes. We can only now realize in its full extent how ... much we owe the boy's English friends and patrons, especially the Jevons family ... and ... Cambridge ... The boy is very happy there, genuinely happy and at home. This circumstance reconciles us in a high degree with the bitter fate which drew us apart in his early childhood. We feel he has found in England, not only refuge when he most needed it, but also a house and country where he feels he belongs to, with his heart and soul, brain and body ... To your kindness, dearest Mrs Burkill, and [your] efforts, we owe, to a great extent, the realization of this happy reunion. May a kind fate reward you for it, with undisturbed happiness in your family.

Most sincerely and gratefully yours, Hedwig Bettelheim (signature)

Frederick Bettelheim returned to England and finished his university work, gaining high honours and distinctions. He never lived with his parents, although they did visit each other. He changed his surname to Jevons as a compliment to the family with whom he lived during those crucial years in England. He is married with two grown-up sons, and is Emeritus Professor of Science and Technology Policy at Murdoch University, Australia.

NOTES

1. Margreta Burkill's undated memoir is in typescript form and is held at the M.G. Burkill Archive, Cambridge University Library. It is written chronologically and starts with her early childhood experiences. (References are given here as Memoir.) A transcript of a 1980 interview with Greta Burkill is held at the South Archives of the Imperial War Museum, London.
2. I use the informal name 'Greta' throughout. It was how she was known.
3. *Der Abend*, Berlin, 13 May 1929, p. 1.
4. See chapter 5. I met Greta Burkill at her home in May 1984; it was to be our first and only meeting. It was not until I started research and looked at personal and private papers now in the possession of Harry Burkill, her adopted son and executor of her estate, did I realize that she was Jewish. That is, she was born to a Jewish mother and father. There is no evidence that she officially converted. For Judaism (and, ironically, for the Nazis too) her lineage was enough to establish her as a member of the Tribe.
5. Greta Burkill reported this incident to me when we met in 1984.
6. Because of the fear within the English medical profession of foreign competition, the government imposed a quota on the number of dentists and doctors allowed into the country.
7. See chapter 5 for problems of evacuated refugee children.
8. See Amy Zahl Gottlieb, *Men of Vision: Anglo-Jewry's Aid to Victims of the Nazi Regime, 1933–1945* (London, 1998), pp. 168–9.
9. Ibid.
10. Max Perutz, 'The War That Was: Enemy Aliens' (typescript given to Dubrovsky by Perutz), p. 7. The account was published in the *New Yorker*, 12 August 1985, pp. 35–6.

11. Nina Lieberman, *He Came to Cambridge: Rabbi David Samuel Margules* (London, 1982), back cover.
12. In April 1951 the minutes of the CRC (18 April 1951) reported Rabbi Margules' death.
13. See Peter and Leni Gillman, *Collar the Lot: How Britain Interned and Expelled its Wartime Refugees* (London, 1980), pp. 190–201.
14. See Miriam Kochan, *Britain's Internees in the Second World War* (London, 1983).
15. J.H. Clapham, CRCC report, August 1941, Cambridge University Library.
16. The CRCC had been asked if they would assume the administrative responsibilities for region 4 of the Refugee Children's Movement. According to the report by J.H. Clapham, chairman of the CRC, the regional office was presided over by Mr B.J. Matthew. The region consisted of the towns of Bedford, Letchworth, Luton, Bishop's Stortford, Welwyn Garden City, St Albans and Watford, as well as Cambridge.
17. Max Perutz, interview with the author, 5 April 1994, private collection.
18. Memorandum presented to the Central Office for Refugees, Burkill File, Imperial War Museum Archives.
19. 'Education of Young Refugees above the Age of 16', p. 2, Burkill File, Imperial War Museum Archives.
20. See Gottlieb, *Men of Vision*, pp. 160, 162, 164.
21. 'Education of Young Refugees above the Age of 16', p. 6.
22. Information about the Bettelheims comes from correspondence between the RCM, Greta Burkill, Dorothy Hardisty (General Secretary of the RCM) and the parents of Frederick Bettelheim. It includes one letter from Frederic to Greta Burkill. It is difficult to establish whether this was the first contact made between the CRCC and the Bettelheim parents. The letters are dated from 9 August 1947 to 15 July 1948. If the Bettelheims had correspondence with the RCM before 1947, it has not survived. The correspondence is held at the manuscript room, Add. MS 7974, Cambridge University Library.
23. Letter to Mrs Hardisty from Greta Burkill, 13 January 1948, Add. MS 7974, Cambridge University Library.
24. Ibid.
25. See correspondence in the Burkill file, MS 7585, Cambridge University Library, which dates from 9 August 1947 to 8 July 1948. Most of the letters are from the Bettelheims to Greta Burkill, but also included are letters from Cambridge tutors and other correspondence related to the education of Frederick Bettelheim.
26. Letter from Greta Burkill to L.P. Wilkinson, senior tutor, King's College, Cambridge, 9 July 1949, Add. MS 8433, Cambridge University Library.
27. Letter from Greta Burkill to Mr and Mrs Bettelheim, 7 May 1948, Add. MS 7974, Cambridge University Library.
28. Letter from Fritz Bettelheim to Greta Burkill, 27 May 1948, p. 3 of four, Add. MS 7185, Cambridge University Library.
29. Letter from Fritz Bettelheim to Greta Burkill, 27 May 1948, p. 3 of four, Add. MS 7974, Cambridge University Library.
30. Letter, Caracas, 15 July 1948, Cambridge University Library, Manuscript Room, Add. 7974.

CHAPTER FIVE

Cambridge and the Jews:
Religious Wars

In the 1930s and early 1940s the *Jewish Chronicle* reported the abysmal situation of desperate refugees, hounded like criminals everywhere, not permitted to leave their country of residence without obtaining proper credentials and not allowed to enter any country in their search for a safe haven. Where the hounded were permitted to purchase a passage by sea, the vessels they boarded were more often than not turned away from the countries for which the passengers were destined. In at least one instance, aboard a ship in the middle of an ocean, starved and half-crazed refugees threatened the crew and each other. *Jewish Chronicle* headlines such as 'Wanderers in the Mediterranean Treated Like Lepers: Ghastly Scenes on Cargo Boats' tell the whole story. Other headlines include: 'Shanghai Refuses to take More'; 'Last Refuge for the Homeless Closed'; 'Strong Measures in Milan'; 'Out of the Frying Pan: Italian Government Plans Abyssinian Settlements'. Jews in Czechoslovakia and Poland and in the Mediterranean countries were in a particularly dangerous situation. More headlines in the *Chronicle* are: 'Pogrom in Bratislava: Nazis Lead Looting Mob: Police Arrive Four Hours Late'; 'Tension in Hungary: Half a Million Jews in Peril'; 'Italians Expel Foreign Jews: Vain Attempts to Enter France'.

The pages of the newspaper read like geography books: far-away places with unfamiliar names are considered as refuge by the desperate, but invariably they are turned away. Spurious reasons are given by governments who claim to honour human life but object to refugees. Palestine is strictly off-limits beyond specified quotas: refugees arriving there after considerable struggle are either imprisoned or sent back by British police protecting Middle Eastern borders, but others in the same British police force are so moved by the plight of the wretched that they do not obey their superiors' orders. Jumping into the water, the police help those struggling to shore, starved and weary to death. Instead of arresting them, they give their own rations away to feed the hungry.

In the midst of the international turmoil *vis-à-vis* the plight of the Jews and Jewish refugees, the Jewish world itself was torn by idealistic Zionists who wanted to affirm their rights in Palestine (and thus provide a legal and safe haven for the refugees) and pragmatists who understood that the immediate need to remove people from danger had to take precedence over everything else. Whilst they fought, the endangered remained endangered.

The most vulnerable were the children. In 1938 in Germany and Austria, with their parents arrested, children were on their own, seeking their own salvation. Some who had been signed up for a *Kindertransport* could not be found. They were wandering alone, running, hiding, searching for food. Others, with distraught parents left behind, managed on their own to find a way to escape. Otto Hutter of Scotland reported years later how he happened to leave Austria on a *Kindertransport*. On his way home through a park in Vienna, he bumped into a former classmate who urgently advised him to go quickly to the Metropole Hotel and register himself for a *Kindertransport*. Otto turned, ran to the hotel, and became the 359th child of 360 to be signed up for the next transport to England.[1]

Some 90 per cent of the refugee children arriving in Great Britain during the ten-month period between 1 December 1938 and 3 September 1939 were Jewish. Already bewildered and traumatized by their experiences, they were further confused when they were taken into the homes of strangers with whom they had no common language, no shared religion, and no understanding of how to bridge the gap. For the most part, they received the patience and kindness they needed. To children from traditional Jewish homes, religious differences added to the personal dislocation and anxiety they felt. Silently they cried in the secrecy of their beds at night and prayed to God to send their parents to them. In spite of the concern of rabbis, the children no longer cared if the food they ate were kosher or not.[2]

The RCM and the CRCC knew very well from their inception that Jewish refugee children should be in Jewish homes, and failing that, that their religious obligations should be respected. Over and over, in its guidelines and in much of its literature, the CRM emphasizes that the religion of each child must be honoured and that 'all children must be able to receive the religious instruction of their own denomination', consistent with the faith of their families. In their deliberations, committees stressed that 'children must not be asked to attend the religious services of any denomination other than their own, nor should the religious status of a child be changed while it is under the guardianship of the Movement'.[3] This, too, is stated innumerable times in correspondence and position papers, and almost always in the same words:

> The right of every child to receive religious instruction according to the faith of its parents must be observed ... no departure from this

procedure can be countenanced without the permission of the parents or unless the child has reached what must be considered as years of discretion in matters of its own religious conviction.[4]

Before the first transport reached England, the CRCC tried to locate Jewish families. In her memoir, Margreta Burkill, a leading member of the CRCC, describes how she armed herself with photographs of appealing babies, pre-adolescents and teenagers and went out on a quest to obtain Jewish host families. Because there were few Jewish families in and around Cambridge who could accommodate the children in need, the CRCC focused on the appropriateness of the homes offered. They visited prospective foster parents and tried to determine, as best they could, the suitability of the environment for the incoming child. Inevitably, mistakes were made. Although the committee workers did their best to judge if the would-be parents were kind and could provide a reasonable environment for the refugee child, the volunteers did not have adequate lead time to properly investigate the offers. With all their good-will and conscientious efforts, the well-intentioned amateurs found the numbers arriving more than they could handle efficiently. In the end, the largest number of refugee children were assigned to those who stepped forward to offer hospitality. These were, on the whole, Christians.

In a brochure published for the benefit of foster parents caring for Jewish children, the Christian Council for Refugees calls for sensitivity and understanding of the difficult position in which the Jewish community finds itself:

> While the religious welfare of the Christian children is being well cared for ... the problem confronting the Jewish community is far more difficult [because] so many of these children have been placed in non-Jewish homes. The situation calls for sympathy and tact on the part of the Christian community. By a right approach to this problem, the latter may contribute much to the removal of those misunderstandings and prejudices which have played so large a part in the rise and development of anti-Semitism in other countries.[5]

The question of why so few Jewish people offered hospitality to the refugee children arriving in England remains. The community certainly must have known of the need for homes. In the months leading up to the *Kindertransports* notices from desperate parents in Germany, Austria and Czechoslovakia appeared regularly in the personal columns of the *Jewish Chronicle*. In short, poignant phrases, German, Austrian and Czech Jews pleaded with readers in England to offer refuge and hospitality to their innocent and vulnerable children. A sampling of these adverts suffices:

'Will charitable family offer hospitality to healthy and refined Jewish girl, motherless, aged 11½, now in Vienna. Very urgent case.' (25 November 1938, p. 2)

'Who will take into their home Jewish boy, 14 years old, of good family, and help him to a future out of the Austrian trouble?' (15 July 1938, p. 2)

'Which noble-minded Jewish family would look after our 7-year-old girl for a few months? Of good merchant's family and healthy. At the same time girl's mother is looking for a position in household. Experienced in all duties.' (15 July 1938, p. 2)

'Orthodox Jewish family urgently required to guarantee and to care for a baby still living with his parents in Berlin.' (7 July 1939, p. 2)

'Will a family accept a refugee girl, 5½ years old, from a good Czech home. All expenses paid.' (7 July 1939, p. 2)

'Would someone please offer guarantees for good and studious boy, 15½ in Prague. Speaks Bohemian, German, English, Hebrew. Parents in desperate straits.' (7 July 1939, p. 2)

'Full adoption sought for baby girl, 6 weeks old, in perfect health.' (28 July 1939, p. 2)

'Two boys (10 and 13) and a girl (15), children of poor printer in Vienna, living in damp basement, implore hospitality.' (4 August 1939, p. 2)

Although Chief Rabbi Joseph Hertz of England knew about the transports of children being organized in Europe, he chose to remain publicly silent both on the imminent arrival of the *Kindertransports* and on the need for homes to care for the young Jewish refugees. In the same issues of the *Jewish Chronicle* that carry appeals from the desperate on the Continent on behalf of their children, Rabbi Hertz published weekly columns instructing his readers on the necessity of observing religious laws and traditional rituals regarding food, holidays and prayers. Nowhere in the widely circulating newspaper does the Chief Rabbi betray any knowledge of children from Germany, Austria and Czechoslovakia arriving in the United Kingdom.[6] Whilst admonishing his readers to observe *kashrut*, the spiritual head of the Jewish community makes no recommendation to his readers about the community's obligation towards Jewish children in need of homes. The Chief Rabbi did not take the initiative to say: 'These are our children. They are our responsibility. Let every family step forward and welcome at least one homeless child into your hearts and your homes.' He failed to exercise moral leadership when he failed to instruct his constituency on a personal duty Jews have to all persecuted human beings, and especially to their own children. It took an ordinary citizen, Nathan Simons of London, to suggest, in a letter to the *Chronicle*, that 'every Jewish family adopt a German-Jewish or Austrian-Jewish child. This would greatly help the authorities who are now engaged in solving the refugee problem.'[7]

On the other hand, Jewish secular organizations in England were involved since the Anschluss in planning for the anticipated needs of potential Jewish refugees and Jewish communal leaders alerted the public to the fact that hospitality for refugee children was 'urgently' needed. In 1933 Otto Schiff of the Shelter in London had called a meeting of influential Jewish leaders to urge the formation of an organization to help the expected flood of refugees. The Jewish Refugee Committee and the Central British Fund grew out of those deliberations (see Chapter 2). Following this initiative the British government took over the care and education of young refugees.

The British branch of the B'nai B'rith set up hostels and took responsibility for hundreds of children. The Women's Appeal Committee for German and Austrian Jewish Women and Children, presided over by Mrs Anthony de Rothschild, raised money for stateless Polish children to be brought to England. Young British Habonim idealists worked directly with refugees and children and helped immigrants in practical and social ways to adjust to their new conditions. However, the Chief Rabbi, who was philosophically not in tune with the Labour Zionism of Habonim, often disparaged both the organization and its young idealists.

In the spring of 1939 efforts were made in Hendon (London) to assist refugee children. Although little had been done to assist adult refugees, a hostel for 70 boys was established in Cliftonville and maintained by the local community.[8] The RCM bore the entire cost of training these children. Teenage boys, subject to arrest in their European countries for forced labour in work camps, had priority on the *Kindertransports*. But ironically, their age made it difficult for them to be placed in private English homes. The urgent need for housing remained. A hostel was established in Ealing, London, for 25 boys aged 15 to 18 and an appeal was posted in the *Jewish Chronicle* for beds, mattresses, linens and funds.[9]

From the early days of the RCM, volunteers were faced with the difficult reality that the English Jewish community, especially the orthodox among them, were not coming forward in any significant numbers to take refugee children into their homes. Orthodox homes were desperately needed. In the spring of 1939 the *Chronicle* printed an appeal from the

Marchioness of Reading, Mrs Norman Laski, and Mr Louis H. Gluckstein, MP:

> The situation in the region for hospitality for refugee children is causing grave anxiety. There are practically no offers of hospitality from Jewish homes left on our records, yet the need is as pressing as it ever was ... There is an especially acute need for Orthodox homes; it is impossible to bring over Orthodox children because of the shortage of hospitality for them.[10]

The statement could not have been more emphatic. A month later another letter in the *Chronicle* from a chairman of a care committee for refugee children expresses disbelief at the reaction of the Jewish community and 'the paucity of Jewish homes offering hospitality. Little would one have believed that the response would be so meagre and that it would have been so difficult a task to persuade a Jewish home to take a Jewish child.'[11] The writer implicates both the Jews of London and those in the provinces for not responding sufficiently 'to the cause of children, who constitute by far the simplest class of refugees who can be helped'.[12]

In this tense period of frantic activity and increasing dread, Chief Rabbi Hertz maintained a public silence concerning the needs of refugee children for homes. But he was outspoken about Jewish religious education for *British children* in Great Britain. On 5 June 1938 he delivered a Shavuot sermon in the Golders Green Synagogue in London. In the course of the sermon he sternly reproached the community for its seeming indifference to the need of support for Jewish education at home, which, he said, was the 'sacred obligation' of the community to provide. He counselled the congregation to make education for British children its priority and demanded that members donate as much as possible for it. He exclaimed that nothing should distract them from their obligation, not even the incessant demands of those across the Channel. In an imperative voice, he commanded:

> Say not, 'We are being drowned by appeals in aid of the hundreds of thousands of victims in Germany, Austria, Poland and Romania' ... We cannot allow the suppression of German and Austrian Jewries to overwhelm English Jewry ... Failure to support the urgent needs of Jewish religious education in *this* [emphasis added] country at this present serious juncture would bring ... inevitable decline of the Anglo-Jewish community on which so much depends for the future of Jewry.[13]

Whilst his parochial concern was not totally out of place, one wishes the Chief Rabbi could have taken a more catholic view. And yet, he and Jews worldwide were sorely tried as they learned of the destruction of European Jewry and of centres of Jewish learning. Not only were the European extended families of British Jews in mortal danger, but Judaism itself seemed to be on the brink of extinction and with it the cherished values that had sustained the Tribe since the beginning. Jewish education had the burden of keeping a small flame alive, even as Christian English women assumed the burden of keeping small Jewish children alive. In those difficult times, priorities kept shifting and, alas, colliding with each other. Nothing was simple; nothing easily divided into black and white. The rescue and relief operations, both in Britain and on the Continent, became compartmentalized into special interest groups, each with its own mission and agenda. The Jewish community, then as now, was divided into the orthodox and the non-orthodox, with their apparent irreconcilable differences.

Jewish social organizations in Germany and in Austria (see Chapter 2) did all they could. They notified parents to register their children for the prospective *Kindertransports* and facilitated the paperwork. Typically, the orthodox did not belong to these secular Jewish groups and were at a disadvantage in the scramble for securing places on the transports for their children. Thus, Rabbi Schonfeld received urgent messages from colleagues in Germany and Austria concerning the fate of their children.[14] In response, Schonfeld organized his own transports specifically for and limited to children from orthodox families. Indeed, two of the earliest transports to arrive in England were organized by him.

In addition, Christian religious organizations were working on behalf of children of parents who were vulnerable because they subscribed to the wrong political ideology. They too needed to be taken to a safer place. The Catholic Committee for Refugees from Germany focused on Catholic children whose politically active parents wanted to secure their safety; the Church of England Committee for non-Aryan Christians and the Quakers targeted for rescue baptized Jews (non-Aryan Christians) who, according to Hitler's racial laws, were as vulnerable as the non-baptized. Quakers helped baptized and intermarried Jews to leave Germany and Austria.

In Britain members of all religious denominations worked responsibly on the numerous local and regional committees across the country. Many Quakers were involved in the CRCC, and a fair percentage were working members of the RCM. Most were sincere about their mission and conscientious in carrying out their assigned work. Among those, however, were some who absorbed, believed and repeated negative propaganda, popularized by the Nazis, about Jews and Jewish wealth.

The serious decline of the world's economy was used by the Nazis as a platform to inflame the general population against Jews, who were blamed for the plight of the dispossessed. Nazi propaganda provided the public with a rationale for hating Jews, who were identified, as a group, with the vulgar new rich and singled out as the villains in the world's failing economy. Unfortunately, too many otherwise good people believed the distortions. In a Quaker report on anti-Semitism in Austria, stereotypes of Jews are used to explain the 'most painful phenomenon in Vienna ... the outcrop of war profiteers, speculators and smugglers'.[15] The report specifically identifies the 'speculators' as Jews:

> Unluckily many of these speculators were Jews. Not by any means all, but the Jews were more conspicuous than the others, and made a noisier display of their ill-gotten gains ... The Rothschilds, for instance, were the financial kings of central Europe. Banks were mostly in the hands of Jews and the expert trade almost entirely. They were good linguists and, because of the dispersion, they had friends and relatives in every country.[16]

The Quaker report confirms for Christians that Jews were all the things the world said about them; for Jews, it confirms their deepest fear, namely that Christians cannot be trusted as friends. Little wonder, then, that Jews were wary of Christian good-will and suspicious of the Quaker involvement in the refugee rescue operation.

The Nazi menace in Germany and Austria forced honest, hard-working Jewish professionals and working-class people to flee their native lands in order to preserve their lives and those of their families. Sadly, there were few countries that granted them permission to enter. Britain was a notable exception in the number to whom they granted entrance permits, even though popular sentiment was largely against allowing new immigrants, particularly impoverished Jews, into the country. Jewish refugees represented at one and the same time an obligation, a responsibility and a threat. Adult refugees were seen as offering unfair competition to the British labour pool and children were considered a drain on the economy. Even British Jewish citizens, especially relative newcomers, were intimidated by the anti-Jewish propaganda and needed to keep a low profile. One refugee woman, who asked not to be identified, said: 'The Jewish community in England was not happy that so many refugees were coming into the country.' Thus, Britain's Chief rabbi, understanding perhaps the temper of the times, was circumspect in his public statements about refugees and silent on the issue of homes for refugee children. To be fair, Hertz's silence regarding refugee children may have resulted from his assessment that it was better to act less publicly, for fear that he awaken even more anti-Jewish and/or anti-refugee feeling than was already in place.

Although for most of its history the British Isles was relatively immune from foreign attack, it was not free from the virus of prejudice that infected Europe and drove it to murderous rage. Great Britain had its share and a long record of anti-Semitism. After all, Jews were expelled in 1290 and it took some 370 years for the British crown to allow their return. British Jews subsequently maintained a relatively low profile. Nevertheless, they did not escape the notice of the likes of Oswald Moseley and his British fascists, who, in the 1930s, would have been happy to have Great Britain rid of its Jews.

As Hitler's power grew, the small British Jewish community, largely a poor community centred in London's East End, became extremely concerned about relatives on the Continent and, at the same time, nervous about an anti-Semitic/anti-alien backlash in Britain. It was a repeat of what they had felt at the end of the nineteenth century, when vicious pogroms against Jews in eastern Europe prompted a migration to Britain. In more modern times, according to Richard Bolchover, as the need for the community to absorb refugees grew, so did a 'well-entrenched fear of arousing anti-Semitism. [Therefore] the community attempted to restrict the number of Jews entering the country ... [and its leaders] tried to exercise considerable selectivity regarding Jewish immigrants to Great Britain'.[17]

Early in the 1930s the British government was heavily involved in efforts to limit immigration. In a Quaker report entitled 'An Account of the Works of the Friends Committee for Refugees and Aliens, 1933–1950', one finds:

> British immigration policy at that time ... put many obstacles in the way of refugees wishing to come to the UK. Permission to stay was ordinarily granted only for a limited period and only to those who could prove that they had adequate means of support, and with the idea of protecting British workers, particularly at a time when there was unemployment ... The effect of this policy was that, up to the beginning of 1937, there were not more than two or three thousand German refugees in the UK at any time, compared with very much larger numbers in France.[18]

The general public, who assumed an attitude of guarded self-isolation from all 'foreigners', were baffled by outsiders. In the early years of the twentieth century few British citizens had travelled extensively in Europe, and those who had were mainly academics or Foreign Office staff. To some people, 'Jewish' and 'foreign' were synonymous.

In the mid-1930s well-meaning English volunteer workers were in charge of refugee children's lives. But not all were free of anti-Jewish sentiments. Some were sincere Christian fundamentalists who saw themselves on a mission to rescue Jews for eternity, some were simply biased. Witness, for example, the case of a Mrs Howe, secretary of a Bromley (Kent) committee, who stated that had she known refugee children could not be brought up as Christians, she would not have brought any from the camp.[19] Another citizen of Kent, an irate RCM employee, hated all Germans. To her, Jews who came from Germany were Germans; they were indistinguishable from each other. Her anger comes almost two years after the arrival of the first transports from Germany. By then, Britain had endured severe German bombing, the destruction of its cities, and a large number of casualties. Judging by her words, the woman's frustration and anger must have been intense:

> I should like to make it quite clear that if the English-paid staff of the movement are to be asked to interview an Alien, however friendly, I should rather as a British woman accept the unemployment benefit of the British government. I consider your request that I should meet Mrs Hahn-Warburg further abuse of the hospitality that England is giving to refugees from Nazi oppression. I am not aware that she is a naturalized British subject and even if she were, where personal matters are concerned, she is still a German.[20]

Lola Hahn-Warburg was a German Jew and a member of the famous Warburg banking family, with branches in America and elsewhere. She was also an active member of the CBF and on the board of the RCM. In 1939 she travelled to Germany and risked her life to confront the bureaucratic German officials in charge of the *Kindertransport*; single-handedly she ensured the safety of hundreds of children.

RCM offices, particularly those in London, were constantly crammed with frantic and frustrated Jews trying to get the cooperation of office workers in order that they might help relatives escape from Germany. The various agencies were staffed primarily by volunteers from the community at large, who worked staggered hours and under a great deal of pressure. Files, handled by different people on different days, were typically muddled and misplaced, resulting in confusion and frustration. Frustration clashed with frustration as office workers and their clients needing assistance confronted each other. They well might have assaulted each other with conventional slurs about Jews and Christians.

Certainly, Jews are not totally innocent of using negative stereotypes in reference to each other or to Christians. Greta Burkill, Jewish by birth and as committed as anyone could be to the right of all people to freedom and life, was guilty of thoughtless anti-Jewish remarks. No one could say that she was anti-Semitic, but her prejudices lived side-by-side with her passion for justice. When provoked or at points of sheer exasperation, she made anti-Jewish remarks and gross generalizations.

Appalled and sickened by the plight of the Jews in Europe, Burkill worked tirelessly for human rights without reference to religion, ethnicity or social-economic class. She understood and empathized with the difficult decisions parents had to make in choosing to send their children away to safety. When Jewish refugee children were discriminated against by the British educational system, Burkill faced up to the authorities and demanded equal opportunities for all British students who demonstrated their ability to succeed in a university or to serve in the Armed Services. At the same time, in the memoirs she left behind, she makes gratuitous and unsupported comparisons between Christian and Jewish host families:

> The despair of the parents drove them to entrust the children to us, who were unknown, of a different religion and with different backgrounds. The fantastic thing was that it worked, that only too often the children found greater humanity in the Christian homes than with their co-religionists, who felt, having saved them, they could use them. I came to the sad conclusion that water was thicker than blood.[21]

The membership of the Cambridge Refugee Committee (concerned primarily with refugee adults and families) and the Cambridge Refugee Children's Committee frequently overlapped. With the exception of Burkill, the two committees in their earliest days were composed almost exclusively of Christian men and women. In an interview for the sound archives of the Imperial War Museum, Burkill was asked about the composition of the CRCC: 'Were they all "Gentile ladies"?'

Obviously made uncomfortable by the question, Burkill laughed nervously as she responded:

> Oh yes. The trouble is we had no damned Jews on the books ... There were no Jews in Cambridge. There were only three academic university teachers who were Jewish at that time – in fact, only two because the other one was a doctor. And therefore the whole thing was run by, let us call, Gentiles.[22]

Her observation is hardly borne out by the facts; Burkill, who was Jewish, was herself completely involved by choice in refugee work. In addition, the committees' own record books report many offers of help from Jewish academics and other Cambridge citizens, among whom are: Dr Salaman, Dr and Mrs Loewe, G. Ellenbogen, Ms L. Levy, H.C. Bergman, H.H.B.

Mosberg, M.O. Lowenstein, E. Nahum, T.H. Epstein, G. Tischler, Joan Freedman, O. Kahn-Freund, H. Lowenstein, W.E. Mosse, Eva Goldman and Esther Simpson.[23] Of this group, only a very few – that is, Dr and Mrs Loewe and Dr Salaman – were on the committee engaged in refugee work. It is quite possible, as has been suggested to me, that Jews volunteered but were not encouraged or invited to come to meetings.

It is also possible that, even in Cambridge, not everyone trusted or liked Jews. And among those who found fault with them were members of the CRCC itself, including Burkill. In the minutes of the CRC for 13 May 1938, while the committee was still in the process of identifying both itself and its work, there is some limited discussion concerning the location for the next meeting. The entry reads: 'The two meetings we have had have just seemed to happen at the Loewe's house, but it might be better from some points of view not to continue there ... I think your room in King's would be a very good place – both central and *neutral*!' (emphasis added). One wonders for whom King's would be more neutral.

Questioned in a taped interview about how funds were acquired for running the committees, Burkill said she had forgotten, adding that she was never interested in money and did not even remember who the treasurer was. She remembered contributions from a Professor Raven, who became Master of Christ College, and from Mr Matthews, who was a city council- lor and had a large grocery shop in Cambridge. 'Worthy citizens of Cambridge contributed,' she concluded. Burkill made no mention of the funds raised by the JRC and its sister organization, the CBF, which initially provided the entire financial support for the RCM and, by extension, to the two Cambridge refugee committees.

Burkill remembers two valuable helpers in 1935, both Jews: Dr Meyer, a lawyer from Munich, and Dr Hans Schlossman, who emigrated in 1935, theoretically to take a Ph.D. in physiology. By way of explanation, she offered: 'But [Schlossman's] primary interest was to get out the maximum number of his family and the maximum amount of his family's wealth. His father was known as the wealthiest doctor in Germany.'

Burkill falls back on the old prevailing stereotype of Jews as oppor- tunistic, wealthy and interested primarily in preserving their assets. Without realizing it, she exposes her bias in interviews. In discussing the difficult decisions committee members had to make in determining which cases were urgent and which could wait, she talks of efforts made to get women out on domestic permits or as ward helpers. These were the only jobs for which women could apply. Men could only come to the UK as agricultural workers or miners. But, says Burkill, 'None of these were Jewish occupations'. As if those desperate Jews, trained in a variety of professions, were not ready and eager to accept any job that would allow them and their families to escape what they understood to be their impending doom. Burkill helped one young man come to Britain as a farm labourer, and then concluded that he was absolutely hopeless as a farmer. It is not clear if she discouraged or helped other applicants from Germany and Austria come to the UK as farmers. She did place in Cambridge a number of well-educated and cultured women as domestics. Later, to her credit, she confides, in a memoir, disgust at the way English women whom she thought she knew treated the German domestics in their employ. The domestics were far better educated than the women for whom they worked.

Burkill's facile acceptance of widespread stereotypes did not prevent her from helping those that needed help. More than anything, she respected intelligence and did what had to be done to advance educational opportunities for all young people in Britain. Not invested in any particular religious education, she was aware and considerate of the special educational needs of orthodox Jewish children.

But her efforts, particularly at the evacuation centre in Ely, to provide children with a secular education in addition to a religious one brought her into conflict with the Chief Rabbi's Religious Emergency Council, which was headed by Rabbi Schonfeld; Schonfeld was, for a while, its sole member. In an unpublished memoir, Burkill mentions unfair and upsetting accusations the CRCC had to endure from the orthodox community.

On the eve of Britain's declaration of war against Germany, an evacuation plan, already in place, was activated. All nursing mothers and young children were moved to the interior of the country (see Chapter 2). Entire schools, including personnel and pupils, were evacuated. By law, all homeowners with spare rooms were required to accept children. Among the children evacuated from London were refugee children, some of whom had only just arrived. Bewildered and frightened, they went wherever they were sent. The two London Jews' Free Schools – for boys and for girls – were evacuated to the cathedral city of Ely in Cambridgeshire; Rabbi Schonfeld's Jewish Secondary School was evacuated to Shefford, a small rural town in East Anglia. Both Ely and Shefford were in region 4 and came under the purview of the CRCC.

Coincident with the declaration of war, the *Kindertransports* to Britain effectively stopped. It was only then that a number of British orthodox rabbis, privately and publicly, seemed to wake up to the fact that Jewish children were in Christian homes in the British countryside, where very few Jews lived. In October 1939, with the first evacuation of children to the countryside barely completed, a letter from a Rabbi M. Spira, of London's Willesden District Synagogue, appears in the *Jewish Chronicle* expressing the concern that the hospitality of the hosts of evacuated Jewish children placed in Christian homes could 'become the cause of disintegration of the religious character of their protégés, a thing abhorrent to the Englishman as it is to the pious Jew'. Rabbi Spira wanted evacuated Jewish children to be placed in special hostels, staffed by qualified Jews and assisted by refugee adults. In such an environment, he claimed, 'religious education in a true Jewish spirit' would result and 'Jewish parents would be able to devote themselves to their war tasks with a mind unburdened by a sense of anxiety as to the spiritual welfare of their children.'[24]

Apparently Rabbi Spira's plan was frustrated because English parents – Jewish and non-Jewish – reacting to a lack of enemy action, took their children back to their homes in London and elsewhere. An angry writer to the *Chronicle* was sharply critical of the action of those parents, because the evacuation 'was done at great expense'. The writer accuses the parents of 'selfishness and disregard of the precautions which the Government has seen fit to arrange … Such a parent is not only endangering the life of the child, but is also seriously prejudicing his educational opportunities.'[25]

One must consider that among the evacuated, Jewish children were a small minority. For the plan to bring Jewish education to dispersed children in many hamlets, villages and towns to be effective, a critical mass was necessary. Thus, to the organizers of the temporary religious educational facilities, English Jewish parents who removed their children from the evacuation centres endangered the fragile plans to give the evacuees continuing Jewish education in far-flung places and to give work to newly arrived refugee rabbis who were then being supported by the Jewish community.

The argument that the education of evacuated children was seriously compromised by the action of their parents is specious, especially when viewed against the lack of overt concern about the welfare of Jewish refugee children among those evacuated. For refugee children, the evacuation was disastrous. It represented yet another adjustment they had to make; and one hard on the heels of having to leave their parents. Unlike their English counterparts, they did not know where their parents were, nor where their new homes were, for that matter. English parents could visit their children at the evacuation centres, and English children knew to whom and where they would be returning. If the homes they left were Jewish homes, they would return to them and participate in whatever way the family observed their holy days. The situation of refugee children was completely different. Not only were familiar religious observances removed from them, but their parents and native homes were beyond their reach.

By January 1940, the expected bombings had not occurred, and 60 per cent of evacuees returned to their homes at the request of their parents. They were followed by others. The children were safe. But the first evacuation served as an important dress rehearsal for the blitz, which started in earnest on 7 September and continued for 76 consecutive nights, wreaking massive destruction and havoc.

The autumn bombing of English cities forced a second evacuation of whole schools of young children to the interior. At the request of the government, regional RCM committees agreed to supervise the evacuated children in each of the regions to which they were evacuated. Because it was mandatory for all citizens in the evacuation areas who had extra rooms in their homes to take in children, some children were in homes of people who resented their presence (see Chapter 2).

The CRCC was responsible for the education and care of the refugee children in region 4, a large area that included all of East Anglia. With the evacuation in place, the committee assumed responsibility for an additional 800 children evacuated to their region. Among these were recently arrived young refugees from the Continent. Overnight, harried volunteers had to review all the files, become familiar with special problems and remember the names of the children. In 1939, before the age of computerized lists permitting instant access to all kinds of pertinent information, volunteers – the majority of whom were women – had to memorize the information and get it right the first time. A child's welfare depended on it.

Into region 4 came evacuated civilian women and children from east and north London – Whitechapel, Swiss Cottage and Hampstead – where a large number of Jewish refugees lived. Entire London schools, complete with children and teachers, as well as London university colleges and institutions were evacuated. The London School of Economics and the Academic Assistance Council were among the institutions relocated to Cambridge.[26]

Life in the 1940s became more complicated both for the RCM and for the CRCC. With the arrival of evacuated refugee children, members had to confront unfair and upsetting accusations and the displeasure of the Chief Rabbi's Religious Emergency Council. The RCM also had to deal with the surreptitious removal of Jewish children from their placements. The 'kidnappers', instigated by rabbis, showed no regard for RCM rules nor consideration for the children's caretakers. Orthodox rabbis over-reacted to the placement of Jewish refugee children in Ely, located in region 4 and under the supervision of the CRCC. In her memoir, Burkill, caught in a complicated position between the CRCC and the orthodox segment of the Jewish community, tersely comments: 'Ely was a real cross to bear.'[27]

Among the London elementary schools arriving in Ely were the Jews' Free School for Boys and the Jews' Free School for Girls, founded in 1817. In the 1930s Anthony de Rothschild was principal of the boys' school; the headmaster was Dr E Bernstein (Ph.D., F.R.G.S.). When the two free schools were evacuated to Ely, Dr Bernstein accompanied the children and continued in his role.

Rabbi Solomon Schonfeld was the principal of the London Jewish Secretary School, founded in 1929 by his late father, Rabbi Victor Schonfeld.[28] Judith Grunfeld, headmistress of the secondary schools, worked under Schonfeld.[29] She and her own infant children accompanied the schoolchildren evacuated to Shefford and resumed her position as headmistress in the new location, also located in region 4 and therefore under the jurisdiction of the CRCC.

Schonfeld, as chair of the CRREC, initiated in the name of the Board of Deputies a major fund-raising drive for his evacuated Jewish secondary school in Shefford.[30] The advertisements for funding stressed that Jewish religious classes would provide traditional education to evacuated Jewish children scattered in the English countryside. That it also would provide an opportunity for the European rabbis, whom Hertz had been instrumental in rescuing from the Continent, to work as teachers was not part of the text, but was very much in Hertz's mind. Hertz hoped the government would provide stipends for teaching rabbis, since religion was a required course in British schools. In fact, the Jews' Free Schools were among the state-aided schools in England. The government's response to extending the aid to Schonfeld's Jewish secondary school was not as Hertz wished it to be. The itinerant rabbis were paid small salaries out of the Religious Emergency Council fund.

On 9 May 1941 a letter written by Rabbi Hertz critical of Jewish education in Great Britain was made public after a serious controversy within the Board of Deputies. Hertz writes that the present position of Jewish education in Great Britain, as well as the difficult problems that will confront it after the war, has given him (the Chief Rabbi), the deepest concern, and he warns of danger ahead: 'The situation is especially grave in that there is danger that Jewish religious education is being deprived of its Jewish and religious character.'[31] Hertz deplores the lack of support by co-religionists, 'the present leaders of Jewish education', for his efforts to provide evacuated Jewish children with kosher and Passover food. He sees 'the most sinister signs of all' as being the emergence of a new liberal religious movement, which, he fears, will give liberals and reformers an overriding vote in all religious questions. Taking both to task, and affirming his belief that the government must assume responsibility for the religious education of children, Hertz writes in his letter that he intends

> to open the eyes of Jews in Great Britain to the deadly peril threatening our traditional Jewish life; to rescue our educational machinery from the hands of men who are inimical to traditional Judaism and its fundamental institutions, like Milah, Sabbath, Passover, and *kashrut*; to reawaken all sections of the community to the vital importance of

greater sacrifice and effort on behalf of the religious future of our children as well as to make use of any new possibilities in the educational field ... One of these possibilities is government support of religious instruction in state schools.[32]

Rabbi Hertz appeared to believe that government support for Jewish religious instruction in all state schools was imminent, and he wanted to ensure that it would not be on liberal Jewish lines. He exclaims: 'Liberals have less than 1 per cent of the child population of Anglo-Jewry', a dubious statistic. The letter closed with Hertz's announcement that he was forming a National Council of Jewish Religious Education to put Jewish education in Great Britain on a satisfactory basis.

Concern about the future of Judaism in the face of the destruction of European Jewish centres of learning and scholarship is entirely understandable. However, the hysteria about Jewish children losing their Judaism as a result of evacuation, or concern about the 'unhealthy' influence of liberals in state schools is ludicrous if not opportunistic and/or hypocritical. Where was the hue and cry about the care and education of refugee children before their arrival? Why did the Jewish establishment not make an overt appeal for homes for these children? Was there no concern then about their Judaism?

In the summer of 1941 the Board of Deputies considered several issues: Zionist unity, fund-raising, the dissension among various Jewish factions, and the question of Jewish refugee children exposed to Christian influences. Rabbi H.A. Goodman of the Union of Orthodox Hebrew Congregations spoke of more than 9,000 Jewish children brought to Britain from Germany under the auspices of the RCM. They had practically no Jewish contacts, were visited by non-Jewish friends, and no effort had been made over a period of years to give them religious education. This issue was particularly contentious. Goodman, claiming that there was considerable feeling in the community about the problem, challenged the RCM to provide statistics on how many of these young people had been baptized.

Professor Selig Brodetsky agreed on the importance of the matter, and noted that he had also sought information of the same issue. But, he added:

The Board of Deputies had never been concerned with the Children's Movement, or with the whole question of dealing with refugees, which was dealt with by other organizations. [Nevertheless] the Executive would do everything possible to see to it that the education of these children was safeguarded (emphasis added).[33]

Bringing some balance and sanity to the discussion, S. Gestetner, a member of the board of the RCM, responded to the hysteria of the Chief Rabbi and the emphasis on religious education. Gestetner, defending the RCM's work, writes:

> I think there is considerable misunderstanding as regards the activities of the Refugee Children's Movement – It should be remembered that it was during a period of not more than eleven months that we were able to bring over to this country nearly 10,000 children. All parents who consented to separate from their children had only one wish at heart, to save them from further Nazi persecution. Thanks to the open-heartedness of people in this country, we were able to bring this large number of children over in such a short time. *The response of Anglo-Jewry was not as great as we anticipated, and we were more than thankful for the hospitality of those true Christians who felt it their duty to save these persecuted Jewish children.* Nevertheless, we felt all along the responsibility to ensure that these children, whose parents were Jews and had been brought up in the Jewish faith, should have religious instruction wherever it was possible. The problem of religious instruction became an even greater one when many hundreds of children had to be evacuated and homes found for them by the billeting officers – We have now formed a special sub-committee to deal with the religious education of Jewish children under our care (emphasis added).[34]

Whilst the controversy raged the quiet city of Ely accommodated itself to the schoolchildren. Into a city where many of its citizens might never even have seen a Jew had come a massive influx of Jewish children – a mixture of evacuees and refugees, most of them orthodox – who could not be accommodated easily in ordinary British homes. The billeting officer, who happened to be a vicar's wife, was 'a very sensible and intelligent woman', according to Burkill's testimony. She commandeered a large country house for the two Jews' free schools; the Cambridge committee found cooks who understood the rules of *kashrut*[35] and made sure that general standards of cleanliness were maintained. Burkill describes Ely thus:

> The really extraordinary thing is that Ely ... had never known the face of a Jew ... A lot of the children were refugees besides evacuees ... from very orthodox orphanages in Czechoslovakia and had never met anyone but Jews. They would not drink the milk, they would not do this, they would not do that. It was really a heart-breaking job ... The Jewish Free School for Girls worked very well because the headmistress was very sensible. She said, 'Well it's wartime and we can't really expect the

children to keep the laws. We can keep the laws, but the children should eat anything that's put before them.' So there was complete friendship and love between the Jewish girls and their teachers and the hostesses. But there was endless quarrel with the others ... We did have a very great deal of trouble with that school ... Ely was a real cross to bear ... Luckily it was near enough for us to interfere frequently.[36]

Initially, Rabbi Hertz was quite pleased with what was happening in Ely. Indeed, he successfully solicited Marks and Spencer to provide the equipment for the school and its playground. Both Hertz and Schonfeld assumed the schools would be under Schonfeld's leadership and that the costs would be absorbed by the British government.

At the same time as children were settling in Ely, Schonfeld was making arrangements for housing his Jewish secondary school. He acquired a large old house in Shefford, a small rural community in East Anglia, and fitted it as a school and a dormitory for 20 students, two teachers and a principal. The school was short-lived; a fire in the kitchen went out of control and the house burned down. The children were then transferred to an abandoned cinema, which was converted to a school facility and dormitory. Part of the money raised in the 1941 fund-raising drive by the Board of Deputies went towards the creation and administration of the strictly orthodox Shefford school.

Schonfeld and Hertz might have hoped that the children from the two Jews' free schools in Ely would be transferred to Shefford when it opened. But the CRCC, which had the responsibility of overseeing its operation, was not about to surrender its role. Burkill and her assistant visited the Shefford school often. The unannounced visits dismayed the administrator who always seemed unprepared for strangers coming in to inspect her kitchen, which Burkill found to be filthy.[37] She also found the emphasis on religious education too narrowly focused and substandard in that it did not prepare the children for independent life in the UK. In addition, she noted that the children had lice and there was no proper welfare worker to supervise it. She did not send any of her children there.[38]

However, it was the substantive difference between the school curricula at Shefford and Ely that worried the orthodox. Whereas Shefford focused almost exclusively on religious teaching and practices, the Jews' free schools in Ely provided a range of subjects including Hebrew language, biblical literature and secular subjects such as art, science and extra-curricular activities. A story in the January 1942 issue of the *Hereward Hall Gazette* spoke of a new pottery kiln being installed at the school, and the value of art in the lives of the boys. In the July 1942 issue the news sheets' lead article concerned a boys' programme of building model planes, which a resident, Mr W.M. Lane, supervised.[39] The programme, which met two evenings a week at the school, included interested non-Jewish local boys, who participated in the craftwork. In working on the models, the boys were required to work out the maths and physics as it applied to certain parts of the models.

The secular subjects to which the young men were exposed, the perceived lax control over ritual requirements, the association with Christian boys, the proximity to a famous cathedral, all mitigated against acquiring any kind of 'seal of approval' from Chief Rabbi Hertz and his future son-in-law, Rabbi Solomon Schonfeld. While the city of Ely carried on rather peacefully, the CRREC was totally displeased if not apoplectic over the religious ramifications of the education the children in Ely were receiving.

The situation also produced a nervous reaction from some in the Jewish community itself, stemming in part from an editorial in the *Jewish Chronicle* (10 November 1939) on the first anniversary of *kristallnacht*. The editorial warned that the evacuation presented a thorny problem for the nation, but serious and special – religious, educational and social – difficulties for Jews. The writer argues that Jewish evacuees are different in experience, attitude and even in looks. Expected to live among people who had never seen a Jew, the children presented 'a first-class risk of mutual misunderstanding'. The editorial asks for adequate measures to be taken, lest the children become the harbingers of new waves of anti-Semitism. 'The situation cannot be permitted to continue', the editorial cautions. 'Further delay means asking for trouble and getting it.'

This was followed by a flurry of letters in the *Jewish Chronicle* in support of Jewish education for evacuated Jewish children who might otherwise be lost to Judaism because of little contact with the traditions of the religion. Every week in June 1941, full-page advertisements in the *Chronicle* announced a new appeal for funds with hysterical large-type headlines. One reads: 'Who will be responsible if they grow up without religion?' In the middle of the page is a drawing of a thoughtful young girl and boy. The answer is: 'YOU – unless you honour your obligation towards them by contributing to the Board of Deputies' Appeal.'[40] Another advert borrows from the well-known Save the Children Fund headline, 'Save the Children'. Among the 'commandments' listed is, 'And thou shalt teach thy children'. This is then elaborated as follows:

> The lives of our children and their Jewish schooling have been ruthlessly disrupted by the war; unless we save the children there is no future for Anglo-Jewry; Anglo-Jewry is the only free great Jewish community left in Europe. It is the symbol of the restored Jewries [*sic*] in a devastated Europe. We must provide more religious education,

more kosher canteens, more communal centres, more play centres, more ministerial and social work, more teachers, more hostels ... QUICKLY! The future of our children is in Your hands.[41]

Richard Bolchover uses the phrase 'politics of fear' to explain the anxiety of British Jews. 'Implicit [in the behaviour of the community] was the fear of a retributive anti-Semitism', which led British Jewry to dread appearing as anything other than a religious community.[42] Given what was happening on the Continent, the anxiety is understandable, even if misplaced.

For Schonfeld, neither the Jews' Free School for Boys nor its personnel pleased him and he determined to get the boys out by any means he could. Years later, a man commented on Schonfeld's commitment by saying, 'If he didn't trust the education a child was getting, he would remove the child by any means, fair or foul.' Fair or foul, both Hertz and Schonfeld were involved in schemes to entice orthodox boys away from Ely and to send them, instead, to one of the yeshivas headed by Agudist rabbis: Rabbi Weingarten, Rabbi Schneider or Rabbi Munk

In September 1941 the *Jewish Chronicle* reported on the removal of a St Ives Jewish evacuee child.[43] The child had gone to Cambridge for religious instruction, probably provided by a liberal rabbi. After his lesson he was taken to Rabbi Munk's hostel in Tyler's Green and not returned to his home placement in St Ives. In a confidential memo to a Member of Parliament, W. Seabourne Davies of Bournemouth, Burkill described the abduction from St Ives; but her concern was about Ely. She feared that in other places 'exactly the same enticing is going on to the detriment of all refugees and the happiness of the children involved'.[44] Burkill presented the history of the problems the CRCC were experiencing by unauthorized and illegal acts of what amounted to 'kidnapping-by-abduction' in Ely.

Children were sent money and instructions on how surreptitiously to leave their school at Ely and go to a yeshiva in London, where more money would be waiting for them. In March 1940 a bilingual questionnaire (in German and English) was sent by Schonfeld's office to Joseph Liebermann and other students at the Jewish Boys' Home in Ely, ostensibly to determine answers to questions such as whether Jews were living in the nearest town and if they were receiving kosher food and religious instruction. However, the questionnaire also solicited from the children the names and addresses of other relatives living in England and the names of other boys at their school.[45] Letters were then sent to boys whose ages ranged from 11 to 13, encouraging them to leave their school without telling anyone, giving them careful instructions, and promising money when they arrived at a specified school or yeshiva. Some letters were actually accompanied by pound notes, and more was promised.

One of the first boys to leave the Ely home as directed was Eugene Lustig, who was 12 years old. Once initiated into the yeshiva, Lustig was busy for months trying to get other students at Ely to leave the school. Harry Stern, who received a letter, was not to be persuaded:

> Sorry to disappoint you but I made up my mind not to come to the *Jeschivah*. I am happy here in Ely as anywhere … I wouldn't let Mr and Mrs Johnson down after they had me for two years. [The Johnsons were probably his foster family.] Also Dr Bernstein. He has done so many good things for me. Brought me out of London air raids. Why should I go back again? There may be any night an air raid. Best greetings, Harry Stern (signature)

Five boys, all under the age of 13, were enticed away from the Jews' Free School for Boys in Ely. Headmaster Bernstein travelled to London on three successive days in an effort to talk to the boys, but in spite of promises and assurances he was not able to see any of them privately. Bernstein emphasized to whomever would listen that the boys needed to return to their school in Ely, and proper steps had to be taken for an orderly transfer to the yeshiva. Frustrated in all his attempts, he filed a detailed report with the RCM that included copies of the letters sent to students at the school.[46] The letters and the report provide dramatic evidence of the 'fair or foul' tactics employed to remove boys.

In the first part of the report, which Bernstein titles 'A Story of Enticement', he relates what he considers to be the facts of the enticement of five boys, and includes copies of the letters sent to them and/or other students at the school. The principal stresses that the programme at the school prepared the boys for life in England, as Jews. As for the Jewish instruction the boys received at Ely, it was as full as that given by the yeshiva. However, in addition to the religious instruction, the children at Ely had full English schooling. The complete absence of secular education in the yeshiva, according to Bernstein, was a serious loss where boys, who will inevitably have to earn their livelihood in England, are concerned.

Bernstein, embroiled in a tug-of-war with fanatics, is hardly an unbiased and impersonal witness. At the time he wrote his report, he was frustrated at his failure to succeed in his mission to return the boys to Ely so that the prescribed steps for transferring them to the yeshiva could be taken. In addition, he is attacking the whole philosophy of yeshiva training, with which he finds serious faults, especially with the strict and unyielding interpretation of religious laws. He sees a real need for young people to have skills that are marketable and satisfying, as well as spiritually uplifting. And he feels that if the boys will be living in England, then they must learn to be Englishmen. He is convinced that the business of enticing people away from their school is both destructive and insidious and that it must be stopped. Here, he is emphatic: 'The enticement ... undermines the moral strength and discipline of the Home, and so fatally hinders the progressive development of the Home's work ... to lure the boys away is mischievous to a grave degree.'

The RCM, aware of the problems in Ely, notified the school's chairman, Dr Rothschild. Rothschild responded that the matter was being 'put in order'.[47] In May 1943 cases of unauthorized removal of boys from their Manchester homes to the talmudic college at Gateshead were reported to the RCM.[48] By October 1943 the Chief Rabbi finally expressed his wish that all children, known to have orthodox Jewish parents, be placed in Jewish homes.[49]

The RCM agreed with Burkill and Bernstein on the necessity for the Home Office to take some action to stop the pernicious 'enticement' of children away from their placements. They had enough solid evidence to convince the civil servants that legal steps had to be taken to safeguard the position of the committees and to stop the abuse of the children. It was understood that, given the absence of their parents, both the refugee children and the committees supervising their care needed a clear, unambiguous and official assignment of 'guardianship'.

A month after Bernstein filed his report with MP Davies, a letter from Cambridge committee member P.J. Hartree to Professor R.S. Hutton gives the first indication that the Cambridge committee was considering legal action to stop the kidnapping. Referring to the incident in St Ives, Hartree writes: 'I hear that the supposed kidnapping of a refugee child is fluttering the dovecotes and may come into the courts.'[50]

By January 1944 the issue of guardianship for refugee children was being debated in Parliament. The Union of Orthodox Hebrew Congregations published an eight-page pamphlet, *The Child-Estranging Movement: An Exposé on the Alienation of Jewish Refugee Children in Great Britain from Judaism*.[51] The pamphlet, an inspiration of Rabbi Solomon Schonfeld, was widely circulated through the synagogues. Schonfeld crusaded to have Jewish refugee children placed in Jewish homes and wanted official guardianship assigned to the Chief Rabbi, his father-in-law. The pamphlet begins with a pitch for legal guardianship of the refugee children to be taken away from the RCM. Schonfeld claims that the movement has failed to appreciate its responsibilities as a 'quasi-guardian', and has not realized its duty to see that 'its charges are brought up in the faith of their parents'. He goes on to say that the RCM was 'formed with the capital donated by Anglo-Jewry', which was essentially true, but when he defines Anglo–Jewry as 'an overwhelmingly orthodox community', he is on a slippery slope. He goes on to berate the movement: 'There has been a persistent though veiled tendency throughout to direct the education of the children away from orthodoxy ... They have been and are tendentious, away from orthodox Judaism.' The pamphlet accuses the RCM of using the children by sending them 'as ambassadors into the homes of Christian foster parents where they could assimilate and create Christian-Jewish good-will'.

Grounds for this policy, says Schonfeld, was first laid when parents, petitioning to send their children out of Europe on transports, were advised to indicate no preference for the type of home to which their child would be sent. The writer makes a telling point when he says that 'any child described on the questionnaire as being other than "orthodox" was and is regarding as outside the responsibility of the general Anglo–Jewish community'.

Does Schonfeld offer this as a way of excusing the Jewish community for not taking refugee children into their homes? Can he really be suggesting that Jewish children of non-orthodox parents are not the responsibility of the general Jewish community? Conceding that parents desperate to send their children to safety might not have insisted on an orthodox or even a Jewish home, Schonfeld subtly blames some authority figure for implying that insistence on an orthodox or Jewish home presented a difficulty that 'might have impeded the emigration of the child. Thus many parents refrained from making stipulations, under the implicit duress of risking the child's rescue.'

Schonfeld excuses the orthodox community in England by saying that children described as 'other than Orthodox' were not the responsibility of the general Anglo–Jewish community, which, he implies, is totally orthodox. At the same time, he says the parents were coerced by the threat of RCM people, who told the parents that if they wanted the child to be placed in an orthodox home, they would have to wait until such homes were available.

THE CASE OF THE SIBLINGS FROM LEIPZIG

To support his claim of the 'estranging of the children from Judaism', Schonfeld gives thumbnail sketches of sample cases. Among the children he cites are the three Koppold children from Leipzig: Harold, Siegmar (spelled incorrectly as Siegmar) and Zilla. Harold was then living with the Sofiers, a traditional Jewish family in Cambridge, who provided him with a stable and warm home and who helped him study for a *Bar Mitzvah*, which was held in the small Cambridge synagogue on Thompson Lane. Harold's siblings, Siegmar and Zilla, were living nearby in Cambridge and they saw each other daily. The children celebrated all the Jewish holidays together at the Sofier home. Together with his foster brother, Norman Sofier, Harold joined a Zionist youth group and ultimately moved to a kibbutz in Israel.

Siegmar lived with the Mansfields, a Christian family consisting of a bachelor, his maiden sister and their niece. The whole family doted on Siegmar and he was completely bonded to them. Elsie Mansfield helped the boy prepare for his *Bar Mitzvah* and accompanied him to the synagogue for his lessons. The Mansfield home was close to the Sofier home and Siegmar enjoyed playing with his brother Harold and participating in family events at the Sofiers. Zilla, the baby of the group, was in the care of her old cousin, Paula, and lived with Paula and her sister Edith in their own apartment in Cambridge, close to the Sofiers.

Among the refugee children, some of whom had no knowledge at all of where their siblings were and had no way of visiting them, these children were fortunate in the care and attention they received, both from the Sofiers and the Mansfields and from the CRCC who continued to follow their activities and their growth.

THE GUARDIANSHIP ISSUE SETTLED

Schonfeld tried very hard to have guardianship of the Jewish children placed under the Chief Rabbi or the CRREC. He did not succeed. But he does provide a rationale as to why so few Jewish families came forward to take children into their homes in 1938 and 1939, when the majority of child refugees arrived in Britain. Although he accurately points out that when an appeal for money was launched in 1938, 'a rush of generous contributions from the entire Jewish community' came through, money is a far cry from taking responsibility for a child.

At a Board of Deputies meeting in December 1943 the guardianship issue was discussed and subsequently reported in the *Jewish Chronicle*. The Chief Rabbi asked the Board of Deputies what steps were being taken to combat the Guardianship Bill, which had as its object the appointment of statutory guardians for refugee children. The *Chronicle* quotes Rabbi Hertz's letter as follows (in part):

A way has been found for removing genuine Orthodox children from non-Orthodox environments. But not *every* Jewish child; and five years after Anglo-Jewry failed to answer the challenge of the refugee children reaching our shores, it seems almost impossible to achieve more. (*Jewish Chronicle*, 24 December 1943, p. 5)

On 31 December 1943 a letter to the *Chronicle* from Dayan I. Grunfeld urges the Jewish community to provide homes for Jewish refugee children: 'The Anglo-Jewish community must come to [the help of the RCM] by providing Jewish homes and establishing as many Jewish hostels as possible.'[52] He is five years too late in his suggestion.

As of September 1943 the Guardianship Bill was discussed in the House of Commons. It came up for a vote in February 1944. Neither the Chief Rabbi nor the CRREC was designated as the ultimate authority for the Jewish children. Parliament voted to vest the guardianship with Lord Gorell, who had been acting in that capacity since 1938; the RCM was officially given the authority to make decisions in regard to the children; and the legal guardian was given the mandate to take 'any steps necessary to safeguard the child's religious education and, moreover, will have a legal duty to take such steps'.[53]

NOTES

1. Otto Hutter, 'Kind 349', *Kindertransport 60th Anniversary* (London, 1999), p. 102.
2. Inge Sadan, 'Memories of Childhood', *Kindertransport 60th Anniversary*, pp. 116–17.
3. See 'The Jewish People from Holocaust to Nationhood – Series One', Archives of the Central British Fund for World Jewish Relief 1933–1960 (hereafter CBF Archives), microfilm reel 28, Refugee Children's Movement, 'Instructions for the Guidance of Regional and Local Committees', p. 17.
4. CBF Archives, reel 28, 161/37.
5. 'Caring for the Child Refugees', Christian Council for Refugees from Germany and Central Europe, Bloomsbury House, London, WC1.
6. Based on a thorough review of the *Jewish Chronicle* from 1937 to 1942. The *Chronicle* is the oldest circulated Jewish publication in England.
7. *Jewish Chronicle*, 25 November 1938, p. 16.
8. *Jewish Chronicle*, 'Helping Refugee Children', 19 May 1939, p. 26.
9. Ibid., p. 19.
10. Ibid., 12 May 1939, p. 35.
11. Ibid., 9 June 1939, p. 23.
12. Ibid.
13. Rabbi Hertz, 'Lessons of Vienna: A Shavuot Sermon', 5 June 1938, Letters and Papers from 1934–1945, Zionist Archives, Jerusalem, A354/19.
14. Schonfeld's late father, Rabbi Victor Schonfeld, had strong connections to *yeshivas* of Europe, other orthodox communities, and to the world Agudah.
15. Francesca M. Wilson, *In the Margins of Chaos: Recollections of Relief Work in and Between Three Wars* (London, 1945), pp. 128–9.
16. Ibid.
17. Richard Bolchover, *British Jewry and the Holocaust* (Cambridge, 1994), p. 49.
18. Lawrence Darnton, 'An Account of the Works of the Friends Committee for Refugees and Aliens, First Known as the German Emergency Committee of the Society of Friends, 1933–1950' (Friends Committee for Refugees and Aliens, 1954), p. 34.
19. CBF Archives, reel 28, 5 May 1943, 166/295.
20. CBF Archives, reel 28, 20 October 1941, 166/136.
21. Margreta Burkill's memoir, p. 29, Add. MS 7974, Cambridge University Library.
22. Mrs M. Burkill, Oral History Program, Sound Library, Imperial War Museum.

23. The names of people offering to help are recorded in the minute book of the Cambridge Refugee Committee. Add. MSS 8433 and 7974, Cambridge University Library.
24. *Jewish Chronicle*, 6 October 1939, p. 19.
25. Ibid., 20 October 1939, p. 17.
26. The Academic Assistance Council was subsequently renamed the Society for the Protection of Science and Learning. It had broadened its scope to help not only world-class intellectuals being expelled from German universities, but also a range of academics including teachers, laboratory assistants, librarians and other professions.
27. Burkill Papers, Cambridge University Library, undated autobiographical piece in typescript, probably written in the 1970s. In a conversation with me in 1984, Burkill stated: 'London Rabbis objected to the education the children were getting. They kidnapped some of the children from their schools and had them placed in Yeshivas.'
28. Schonfeld was also head of college and chair of the Yisroel Yeshiva.
29. *Jewish Year Book* (London, 1939; *Jewish Chronicle* publication).
30. Schonfeld was for a time the CRREC's only member and its chair. He was able to use the authority conferred on him by the position and proximity of the Chief Rabbi to gain privileged access to government officials and MPs. Soon after this, he married the Chief Rabbi's daughter.
31. *Jewish Chronicle*, 9 May 1941, p. 5.
32. Ibid.
33. Ibid., 30 May 1941, p. 1.
34. Ibid., 13 June 1941, p. 24.
35. *Kashrut* are the laws governing the preparation and consumption of foods that observant Jews must obey. They proscribe certain meats and all shellfish, and indicate that there be no mixing of meat and dairy dishes or utensils.
36. 'Oral History Program: Mrs M. Burkill', pp. 16–17. Tapescript MS in the author's collection. On 5 September 1939, Chief Rabbi Hertz sent a letter to Marks and Spencer asking for contributions to provide equipment and supplies for a school in Ely in which refugee children were enrolled. At this time, Rabbi Hertz expressed his pleasure at the reception that the children received in the famous cathedral town. Parkes Library, Archives and Manuscripts, Southampton University, MS 175/66/4.
37. Burkill memoir, Cambridge University Library.
38. Burkill's evaluation is in contrast to that of the headmistress of the school, Judith Rosenbaum, Dayan Grunfeld's wife, who writes of it in the most positive of terms and stresses the values of the Jewish education the children received there.
39. *Hereward Hall Gazette: Incorporating the Evacuation News Sheet of the Jews' Free Boys School*, Ely, January 1942 and July 1942, edited by the Ely Jews Boy's School headmaster, Dr E. Bernstein, and printed at the Evacuation Headquarters of the Jewish Free Boy's School Press. Available at the Cambridge City Library, Cambridgeshire Collection, C457.
40. *Jewish Chronicle*, 20 June 1941, p. 17.
41. Ibid., 27 June 1941, p. 17.
42. Bolchover, *British Jewry and the Holocaust*, p. 103.
43. *Jewish Chronicle*, 19 September 1941, p. 27.
44. Letter to William Seaborne Davies, 25 November 1941, Burkill Archives, Cambridge University Library.
45. The original questionnaires are among the Schonfeld Papers in the Parkes Library and Archives, Southampton University, UK.
46. The report and all the correspondence relating to the incidents described are in the Burkill File, Imperial War Museum Archives.
47. CBF Archives, microfilm reel 28, 166/202 and 166/209. The actual correspondence between the movement and Rothschild are not included in the microfilm archives. They are noted in the minutes of movement committee meetings.
48. Ibid., microfilm reel 28, 166/294.
49. Ibid., microfilm reel 28, 166/355.
50. Hutton Files, Churchill Archive, Churchill College, Cambridge, UK.
51. *The Child-Estranging Movement* (London: Union of Orthodox Hebrew Congregations, January 1944), Imperial War Museum Archives, Burkill file.

52. *Jewish Chronicle*, 31 December 1943, p. 12.
53. Hansard, *Proceedings of the House of Commons 1943–44*, 'Guardianship (Refugee Children) Bill [Lords]', 1576–1582.

CHAPTER SIX

The Rabbis:
Joseph Hertz and Solomon Schonfeld

Out of the Holocaust came a number of memorable, righteous and just people, who, for all their selfless dedication on behalf of the victims, were ordinary men and women with their own strengths and weaknesses, vulnerabilities and prejudices. Neither heroes nor villains, they were, in fact, often a combination of both. Most, like the members of the Cambridge Refugee Children's Committee, worked in groups; a few insisted on working alone. All were committed, strong, courageous, stubborn and often biased human beings, acting out of the highest moral imperatives to do what they considered to be right. They drove themselves to the point of exhaustion to rescue foreign children caught in a devil's web. Sometimes they seemed to work at cross-purposes.

Children sent away from their European homes to places and people unknown to them were like the spoils of war in that people fought over them and their futures. A child's trajectory propelled them from a warm and loving home to refugee camps in a strange country. Their care was managed and supervised by committee members they did not know, speaking a language they did not understand. Young innocents were totally unaware of the efforts being made on their behalf and the controversies inspired by their needs. Most of the children were Jewish by virtue of their birth and their progenitors. Among those involved deeply in their care and education were members of voluntary committees, composed largely, but not exclusively, of Christian women. The volunteers felt a strong responsibility to the absent parents, who had entrusted a sacred treasure – their own children – to strangers. Likewise, ordinary British citizens who welcomed foreign children into their families also felt the same heavy obligation. Quakers and other Christians, some of strong religious faiths, knew little about the Judaism of their foster children. They tried the best they could to make the young refugees feel welcome. In large measure they succeeded in preserving the lives of the young refugees, if not their religious convictions.

The primary agency involved in the placement and supervision of children was the Refugee Children's Movement.[1] Because of the RCM's involvement in the actual lives of the children, it came under severe scrutiny from Chief Rabbi Joseph Hertz and his son-in-law, Rabbi Solomon Schonfeld. Both the RCM and the rabbis were concerned with the refugee children at this time and were committed to their welfare. The problem was that they had different ideas about what that meant. For the Cambridge Refugee Children's Committee, the children's welfare had to do with their physical and emotional well-being and their education, growth and development. The rabbis, not indifferent to the children's health, understood what some others did not: the future of the Jewish civilization depended upon the children – refugee and non-refugee. Thus, the rabbis prioritized the children's spiritual growth.

It is a reasonable assumption that the thoughts of the young refugees at this time were not on their religious inheritance but on the families into which they were born and which were now not available to them. Emotionally, these children needed to preserve their sanity and their lives. Given the fact that most of the children were placed in Christian homes, identity issues became at one and the same time confusing, painful and academic. Chief Rabbi Hertz and Rabbi Schonfeld tried as best they could to protect and preserve both the children and Judaism. No doubt, they made mistakes. But they were sincere in their commitments. That at times they may have been misguided is something else.

CHIEF RABBI JOSEPH H. HERTZ

Joseph H. Hertz (1872–1946), Chief Rabbi of the United Hebrew Congregations of the British Commonwealth, was born in Slovakia. At age 12 he emigrated with his parents to New York. In 1894 he became the first graduate of the new Jewish Theological Seminary of America. After a two-year stint as a rabbi in Syracuse, New York (1894–96) he was appointed rabbi of Johannesburg, South Africa. There, his outspoken opposition to Boer discrimination against aliens and religious minorities resulted in his being deported for two years (1899–1901). At the end of the Boer War he returned to his former post in South Africa, where he served for ten years. In 1911 he returned to America to assume the position as rabbi of a New York orthodox congregation, Orah Hayyim. Two years later, in 1913, he was elected Chief Rabbi of England and spent the rest of his life, until his death in 1946, in that position.

As Chief Rabbi, Hertz enthusiastically embraced his new position with 'courage and energy' and was especially helpful to recently arrived immigrants. His endorsement of the Zionist agenda is credited with influencing the outcome of negotiations leading to the Balfour Declaration in 1917. However, his religious dogmatism often erupted in seemingly irrational outbursts. He deplored the liberal branch of Judaism and railed against it and its supporters even while supporting Zionism on behalf of orthodox Jewry.[2]

Although Hertz served for a long time as Chief Rabbi and received honours for his English translation of the Hebrew Chumash,[3] his tenure was not always smooth sailing. He made as many enemies as he made friends. Often pompous and impressed by his own importance, he was at times both crude and bellicose when addressing adversaries (real or assumed). He attacked them verbally and often irrationally, no matter who they were. For example, in November 1931 – in his eighteenth year in the position – he was invited by Professor Herbert Loewe of Cambridge University to attend a service at the nascent Cambridge University Jewish Society. Upon seeing that the printed programme identified him as 'The Rev. Dr Hertz, United Synagogue' instead of 'Chief Rabbi', his official title, he became quite angry. He regarded the omission as the ultimate insult and subsequently wrote a scathing letter to Loewe, a reader in Rabbinics,[4] accusing him and liberals in the Cambridge synagogue of destroying the service on Saturday morning by turning 'it into a mockery' and 'breaking up an Orthodox Service' by 'introducing parodies of prayers into the Service'.[5] Charging that Loewe could not be taken seriously, the Chief Rabbi wrote: 'Caprice and prejudice seem to blind your judgment in regard to present-day Anglo-Jewry, why not then also in regard to Anglo-Jewry in the past?' He justified his rudeness by saying his speaking-out was a function of his office and that his duty as Chief Rabbi required such honesty in order 'to avoid a total severance of our relations'.[6] That Herbert Loewe worked tirelessly on behalf of Jews in Cambridge and elsewhere eluded the Chief Rabbi, who demanded a respect he did not, necessarily, earn.

After Hitler's ascension to power in January 1933 events in the world changed dramatically. On 31 March 1934 Rabbi Hertz, fearing that German-Jewish communities were in danger of disappearing, issued a 'Moral Challenge to Jews of Great Britain'[7] in which he urged the Jewish community to contribute to the second appeal of the Central British Fund, recently organized in response to the dangerous situation in Europe. Subsequently, Rabbi Hertz was profoundly engaged with the problems of European Jewry.

In the spring of 1934 Hertz and his wife sailed to Alexandria in Egypt. Their trip was marred by the 'seriousness of the news from Palestine'.[8] To his son Leon, living in Palestine, he wrote: 'Is the government unwilling to guarantee safety of life? Is there to be capitulation to bandits simply because they are anti-Jewish?"[9]

By June 1936 Hertz had finished his *magnum opus*, an English translation *of The Pentateuch and Haftorahs* with extensive notes and commentaries. The publication brought the English Chief Rabbi immediate acclaim, and he relished the honours bestowed on him.[10] Subsequent letters to his son are full of pride and excitement at the reception of this translation; notably, there is no mention of the approaching storm about to burst upon the world. On 5 June 1938 Hertz preached what he called 'A Shavous Sermon – Lesson of Vienna' at the Golders Green Synagogue in London, in which he exhorts the community to ensure a viable future for Judaism by supporting Jewish education for the young.[11]

Hertz was a passionate, egocentric man with a splenetic temperament; his public appearances were as remarkable as they were unpredictable.[12] On 25 July 1941 the Chief Rabbi was invited to address a meeting of Jewish communal leaders in Cardiff, Wales. He began with a remark that in Cardiff the youth of the community could grow into better people than their parents. He ended by saying: 'We have heard so much from Cardiff and in the recognized Jewish Press about their unity that I have come to the conclusion that the Community is so united that it were as if frozen to death. I did not come to Cardiff for a vote of thanks.' And with that, he abruptly left the lecture hall and the astonished guests.[13]

In June 1942, with the world at war and Jews behind barbed wire, the Chief Rabbi, presumably concerned about the future of Judaism and the Jews, in a letter to his son expressed regrets to learn that his son and his son's family had attended a Passover *seder* at Givat Brenner, one of the earliest of the kibbutzim established in what is now Israel. According to the Chief Rabbi, the kibbutz members do not guard against *khometz* [leavened dough or bread forbidden during Passover]. 'Passover laws are not to be lightly set aside', he chides.[14]

For Hertz, the laws concerning food were a metaphor for Judaism. He felt a responsibility to supply all the Jewish refugees – children and adults – with kosher food. His determination to do so became a minor theme in his encounters with and behaviour towards the refugee committees. The volunteers, working round the clock to rescue as many children and adults as possible, especially after *kristallnacht*, did not make *kashrut* [dietary laws followed by observant Jews] their priority. But for Rabbi Hertz, Judaic laws governing behaviour and food were emblematic of the whole of Judaism. And he lost no opportunity to impress his beliefs on committee workers: they were rescuing the children, but he was preserving their Judaism for the future.

He employed refugee rabbis, whom he was instrumental in rescuing from the Continent, in the task of providing kosher food and matzos to refugee children living as far away as northern Scotland. One woman retains a painful memory from her childhood of two rabbis coming to visit her on a farm north of Glasgow. Eight years old, she had arrived in Britain on a *Kindertransport* in August 1939 and had been placed in the farm home of Christian fundamentalists in Scotland. From a fairly traditional and observant Jewish home, she was with people who had no knowledge at all of the laws of *kashrut*. She had no option but to learn about a different religion and to live with a set of strict rules governing her personal behaviour. According to her testimony, in the spring a year or two after she had joined the family, two rabbis appeared on the farm. It was the first contact she had had with anyone Jewish. One of the rabbis put a box of matzos into her hands and said: 'Eat these. It is Passover. Do not eat bread.' The two then left without engaging her in any conversation. Disappointed, angry and feeling bereft, she threw away the unopened box of matzos and apparently closed the Jewish chapter of her life. Before she was 20 she married a man belonging to the same fundamentalist sect as that of her foster parents. Together they raised their children as Christians. Sixty years later, in an effort to come to terms with her past, she took her children on a trip to Israel and actually met surviving family there.

Whilst in December 1938 the *Jewish Chronicle* reported an acute need for foster homes in Britain for refugee children, Rabbi Hertz was calling for a conference of UK rabbis and ministers to present a report of the Chief Rabbi's Religious Emergency Fund, whose primary purpose, initially, was to provide kosher food for Jewish orphanages and hospitals in Germany and to provide spiritual care for refugee children. Hertz had been engaged in a successful effort to obtain temporary visas for a large number of German rabbis and teachers of religion in danger of their lives. He placed them in vacancies across the United Kingdom and the United States. He had less success in securing religious Jewish homes for refugee children in Britain, although, according to the *Chronicle*, 'Dr Hertz appealed to Ministers to enlist as many religious homes as possible … prepared to accept a child.'[15] Hertz wanted the ministers to form local 'Friends of the Children' committees, which would arrange proper care, schooling and religious instruction. But few religious Jewish homes were offered.

In their struggle to prioritize the needs of child refugees, various committees were pulled in different directions. But, for those concerned with Jewish religion, the issues were more complicated. They wrestled with what they saw as inextricably related responsibilities: saving lives and saving Judaism. Often there were head-on collisions between those who placed the highest priority on the saving of lives and those who felt the future of Judaism itself was at stake and must be attended to at all costs.

Sir Robert Waley Cohen, on the Council for German Jewry, stressed the necessity of utmost speed in the rescue of children. But Rabbi Hertz insisted that children not ride on the Shabbat and be given only kosher food to eat at the reception centres. Hertz's intractable position resulted in 24-hour delays of some transports of children scheduled to leave Germany and Austria on a Friday evening or Saturday afternoon. One cannot estimate how many more children would have been saved if the transports had left as soon as the children could be boarded. But, thanks to the rabbi's concern, when the children finally arrived in Britain, they were greeted with kosher potato chips and candy. And at Dovercourt, where the first child refugees were taken, the children were, in fact, fed kosher food.

RABBI DR SOLOMON SCHONFELD

Rabbi Dr Solomon Schonfeld was an enigmatic rescuer: a clergyman who marched to the tune of his own drum. He was often at odds with the British establishment, and just as often at odds with the Anglo-Jewish establishment. With the acquiescence of his future father-in-law, Chief Rabbi Dr Joseph Hertz, he created the Chief Rabbi's Religious Emergency Committee, which he headed and, for most of its life, was its only member. His mission, to rescue beleaguered Jews menaced by Hitler's passion for a *Judenrein* world. Among target populations to be rescued, he chose to serve ultra-orthodox Jewry, notably Agudath Israel followers.

Schonfeld started out rescuing rabbis and yeshiva students, then spread his net to include children of Agudath families ignored by the Jewish communal organizations in Austria and Germany, then moved on to rescue other forlorn and abandoned children in Poland. On the way, he provided Jewish men in British service units with ritual objects and kosher food so that they might observe the commandments. For soldiers in the field he devised special ambulances that morphed on the Sabbath into temple arks. He created new schools and yeshivas where none had existed before, and, like the ambulances, which had a double life – during holidays, they were dormitories for refugee children.

A pragmatist and an inspirational genius, Schonfeld understood the need for prompt action to rescue Jews and felt he could accomplish more by acting alone than by subscribing to groups. He reacted quickly when opportunity to meet an urgent need presented itself. For example, when a child scheduled to leave on one of his transports did not show up, he took another child in its place and gave the child the missing person's identity papers. His methods caused no end of trouble to the officially recognized committees in Britain responsible for reporting to the Home Office on the children who arrived. What this misplaced identity did to the children is anybody's guess.

After the defeat of the Nazis, Schonfeld spirited children out of Polish orphanages and away from foster families. The children were presumed to be Jewish, the parents were presumed to be dead. He brought the children to Britain and settled them in his schools, where they received a strict Jewish education. All in all, Schonfeld is credited with saving thousands of individuals who might otherwise have died.

A rescuer of rabbis and children, a vigilante determined to preserve the Judaism he valued, a 'catcher in the rye' poised on the brink to prevent others from falling over the edge, he charmed Members of Parliament, convinced government agencies, raised money, and paid no attention to entangling rules, regulations and paperwork. He bent the rules, shaded the truth, and ignored others working just as conscientiously for the same end. He was a pragmatist, he was a dreamer, he was a vain and conceited man, he was a gentle father-figure to the orphans he brought to England. He was a stern and judgmental defender of Judaism – a fundamentalist branch of Judaism.

At the time of the Anschluss in 1933, Solomon Schonfeld was in his early twenties and ready to assume the mantle of his dead father, Victor Avigdor Schonfeld, the founder of Britain's Agudath Israel Movement.[16] He rescued children from orthodox families in Germany and Austria and assigned them to orthodox families in Britain without investigating the conditions under which the children would be living. He provided financial guarantees to the British government from his own resources where needed, and then instituted major fund-raising drives among British's Jews. And always, he worked alone, making decisions by himself, which others carried out for him. He is described by people who knew him as a 'one-man rescue operation'.[17]

Schonfeld's first foray into rescue work early in 1938 concentrated on rabbis, religious teachers and functionaries. British refugee committees tended to overlook these people because the Anglo-Jewish establishment considered them unproductive and not easily assimilated. But Schonfeld convinced the Home Office to grant entry permits to Jewish scholars on the grounds that there was a shortage of 'Jewish clergy' in Britain. Most of the rabbis admitted were from Vienna. Because of their occupations, they represented no threat or intrusion into the stringent British labour market.

Indeed, Schonfeld used the 'desperate shortage of ecclesiastic officials' to obtain permission from the Home Office for adolescent Jewish boys from Germany and Austria to come to Britain, where they would be trained for the rabbinate. The boys, too old for *Kindertransports*, were in imminent danger of being sent to labour camps. Schonfeld established overnight a rabbinic seminary in Britain and the young men were admitted as students immediately. The teaching staff was drawn from newly arrived immigrant rabbis.

In March 1938, after Hitler had marched into Austria and made it part of his Third Reich, Solomon Schonfeld received desperate calls for help from Agudath Israel leaders. The *Kultusgemeinde*, the official Jewish communal organization in Vienna, was organizing children's transports to Britain but was excluding the ultra-orthodox. Appeals were made to Schonfeld to start transports for those children who had 'no other means of leaving Austria'. He went directly to the British Home Office asking for entry permits for several hundred Jewish children from Austria and personally provided guarantees of support.

By December 1938 he had organized two transports of 125 children each, all from Agudist families. Children of the religious Zionists were not included because Schonfeld regarded a 'religious Zionist' to be a contradiction of terms.[18] He received permission from the Foreign Office to have all the children of each transport put on a *zamel* or combined passport. Knowing how impressed the Germans were by uniforms, Schonfeld, who intended to accompany the children back to Britain, had a military-looking uniform designed for himself, complete with brass buttons that bore the insignia SS. The first transport left Vienna on 20 December, the second a few days later; each was accompanied by two teachers who were committed to return to Austria after the children were deposited in Britain.

Although Rabbi Schonfeld was willing to assume financial responsibility for the care of his charges, he realized he could not do this indefinitely without some kind of official sanction, particularly from the Anglo-Jewish establishment. In 1938 he approached Chief Rabbi Hertz, who was not an Agudist but orthodox in his religious observance and orientation, and suggested the formation of a Chief Rabbi's Religious Emergency Council for German and Austrian Jews, later shortened to Chief Rabbi's Religious Emergency Council (CRREC), nominally under the auspices of the Chief Rabbi.

The new CRREC rescue organization became the vehicle for the manifold activities of Solomon Schonfeld, who continued to work as a loner. The difference now was that when he approached government agencies with requests for entry permits or individuals for financial and other assistance, he could cite the authority of the Chief Rabbi of the British Empire. Under the signature of the CRREC Schonfeld expanded the sphere of his activities, including bringing vulnerable children from Germany and Austria to Britain. He personally organized several *Kindertransports* and was in charge of them from beginning to end. He directed his efforts to orthodox and Agudath families.

Among the young orthodox refugee children Schonfeld brought to Britain was a new crop of yeshiva students. He had expected they would be taken into the homes of various members of the orthodox community.

Evidently that did not happen. When the Home Office asked Schonfeld for proof that there were funds and facilities to feed and house refugee children, Schonfeld invited an inspector to his Jewish secondary school, closed at that time for a holiday break. He had replaced the desks with cots and had turned the school into a dormitory for 250 children. When the space proved insufficient, he cleared out his own house (which he shared with his mother) and filled it with cots, retaining only a small attic room for himself, while his mother moved to the home of a relative. Schonfeld subsequently put out word among his own community that families were needed to take in children and eventually all the children were placed in private homes.

As a young man of 27, he committed all his time in 1939 to rescuing children and adults. Direct personal approaches to the Home Office resulted in his cutting through bureaucratic red tape in a manner unimaginable to the staid Anglo-Jewish establishment, which kept its distance from him considering him to be irresponsible and un-English.

The RCM demanded that its local committee do home inspections of prospective foster parents. Because Schonfeld preferred working as a lone agent, he did not feel he was bound by the rules of the movement in his rescue work. He simply did not have the time to examine the home, nor interview the prospective foster parents for the new crop of refugee children he brought into the country. Both he and Chief Rabbi Hertz were satisfied that they had done the best they could if the children were placed in orthodox homes. Unfortunately, orthodox religious practices do not, necessarily, guarantee children a healthy or safe environment or protection from abuse. There are those who continue to suffer in their adult lives from the exploitation they endured as refugee children in the Jewish orthodox foster homes in which they were placed.

Jill Carper (a real person, but not her real name) was 8 years old when she and her 15-year-old sister were put on Schonfeld's transport by their father and an aunt.

'My mother could not face it,' says Jill, now a highly skilled professional woman. 'She packed our best clothes, clutched us to her, and then ran next door while my father shepherded us out.'[19]

Jill Carper speaks slowly about 'Rabbi Doctor Schonfeld', her voice so low that it is almost inaudible. 'Thank God for Rabbi Dr Schonfeld. He saved my life.' There is a long pause, during which Jill keeps turning a pen in her hand. Then, almost as an afterthought, she adds, 'Of course, I was not put into the best home for me.'

Asked what was wrong with the placement, she demurs, obviously uncomfortable, looked carefully at her pen, and then changes the subject.

'My husband and I have raised five children and they are all totally observant in their Jewish lives.'

'But what was wrong with the home in which you were placed? Was it not a Jewish home?' She is torn between wanting and not wanting to tell all.

'Oh, it was totally Jewish. Strictly kosher. Shomer Shabbos. It was just not the right place for me.'

'Why?'

'I was a big kid for 8 years old. My sister was sent to another family and I rarely saw her. It was hard to get to where she was living. And she had no place for me to stay. She married when she was 17, then she could take me into her home.'

'What was wrong with your placement?' It is clear she needs to answer the question. It is just as clear that she wants to avoid the answer.

Finally, she draws a deep breath and hurried phrases come out of her.

'Every night, the man of the house came into my bed, on top of me. Every night. I could not leave. I did not know where to go and to whom to talk. He had a wife and a daughter my age, and I could not tell either one of them. On the day my sister married, I left and never went back there.'

The effort she exerted in her confession makes her limp, like a balloon from which the air has escaped. Then, marshalling her resources, she turns, almost in anger, and blurts out: 'If you write anything about this, I will deny every word.'

How did the Agudist, the upright patriarch of the home to which an 8-year-old child was sent, justify his behaviour? Did he compare himself to Abraham, whose wife's handmaiden bore him a child? Or to Jacob, or any of the other patriarchs who bedded with handmaidens? Did he compare notes with other religious Jewish men who also had refugee children in their care?

Jill Carper's painful memory is real. Repeatedly raped as a child, she yet gives thanks to God for having spared her the horrors of the Holocaust. At the same time, she is exhausted by the shame of revealing her childhood secret and feels guilty to have shared it. So she repeats her homage to the man who saved her life. And blesses Rabbi Doctor Schonfeld.

Remembered pain upon pain of all kinds is a subtext in the lives of all refugee children/adults. Rationally, they understand that unusual situations grow out of unusual times. But their wounds are still raw, indeed, they will never heal. Although they are now grandparents and far removed from that time, when they speak of the unspeakable they become once more the children they once were. Sexual exploitation was just one of the abuses that some children endured.

In 1940 Schonfeld married the Chief Rabbi's daughter, Judith. Despite the sanction of the Chief Rabbi, the Board of Deputies of British Jews and the Anglo-Jewish establishment did not accept Solomon Schonfeld and did not approve of his vigilante rescue operations. When they pointed out to Rabbi Hertz that 'This is not an activity in which the Chief Rabbi should engage', Dr Hertz responded:

As Chief Rabbi I am supposed to care for the needs of Jewish religious teachers, scholars and clergy. Dr Schonfeld's activities come under this heading. This is not a communal matter but a religious matter, and when it comes to religious matters, no communal organization has the right to dictate to the Chief Rabbi. And remember, Chief Rabbis seldom die and never retire![20]

NOTES

1. Initially named the Movement for the Care of Children from Germany and Austria.
2. 'Hertz, Joseph Herman', *Encyclopaedia Judaica* (Jerusalem, 1971) vol. 8, pp. 397–8. He is cited as being 'no respecter of persons', a title he earned because of his pugnaciousness.
3. J.H. Hertz (ed.), *The Pentateuch and Haftorahs*, 2nd edn (1937; London, 1987). Translation of the Torah and commentaries in the form of Haftorot. The Torah consists of five books: Genesis, Exodus, Leviticus, Numbers and Deuteronomy. The entire Torah with designated Haftorot – readings from the Prophets – is read in the synagogue over the course of a year. The selections from the Prophets expand or illuminate the portions of the Torah to which they are appended. Hertz translated into English both the Torah and the Haftorot, and provided his own commentaries in the form of footnotes. His translation is widely used, especially by Conservative synagogues.
4. Loewe was a Reader in Rabbinics at Cambridge University and served occasionally as an acting Rabbi for the Cambridge Jewish Society.
5. Letter to Professor Herbert Loewe from Office of Chief Rabbi, 28 November 1931, no. 5692, University of Southampton Library, MS 17S/86/9.
6. Ibid.
7. *Jewish Chronicle*, 31 March 1934, p. 10.
8. Extract from a letter in the Zionist Archives, Jerusalem, A354/19. The letters held in this archive are dated from 1934 to 1945, but many have no dates on them. All further references to letters are from this collection.
9. 23 April 1934, Zionist Archives, A354/19.
10. Hertz's letters to his son from March 1934 through March 1945 are full of references to honours, medals, gifts, and the critical acclaim which he received. He was especially proud of a new leather-bound version of his book and obviously took much pleasure in the reception of it. Zionist Archives, A354/19.
11. *Jewish Chronicle*, 5 June 1938, pp. 11–12.
12. See *Encyclopaedia Judaica*, vol. 8, p. 398.
13. As reported in the *Jewish Chronicle*, 25 July 1941, p. 18.
14. *Khometz* includes food that has flour and/or bread products. It is forbidden to eat such food at Passover. References are from the Zionist Archives, A354/19. However, Hertz did become a strong fighter against Nazism and its manifestations in England.
15. *Jewish Chronicle*, 2 December 1938, p. 17.
16. A branch of Judaism at variance with the mainstream nominally Orthodox practice of England's Jewish community. The Agudath considers Judaism a religion of obedience to the *word* of God, whose laws are absolutely binding and not subject to interpretation.
17. See David Kranzler and Gertrude Hirschler (eds), *Solomon Schonfeld: His Page in History* (New York, 1982), p. 39.

18. Ultra-orthodox Jews believed they would return to their ancient homeland only after the Messiah came.
19. Taped interview with the author, Israel 1996. At the informant's request, her name has been changed in my reporting of her experience. What has been reported is not an isolated incident. It remains the dark and troubling secret of an unknown number of the former child refugees.
20. Quoted in Kranzler and Hirschler, *Schonfeld: His Page in History*, p. 45.

—•◆•—

CHAPTER SEVEN

Five in Cambridge,
One in Norwich

When the shattered family in Leipzig sent their children to England, the only consolation left to the parents was that they had done all they could to ensure the safety of their young. The Leipzig chapter of the Schmulevitz history had ended. There was no longer a family nest in either the city or the country, nor would there be one in the foreseeable future.

A few days after the last of the children arrived in their new country, England was at war with Germany and nobody's survival could be taken for granted. The children lived through the war; over a nine-year period, they grew and reached their maturity in Britain, America and Israel. But they never saw their parents again and are still trying to understand exactly what happened to those relatives left behind.

The exodus of the Schmulevitz children was completed after the three Koppold children left the boat in Southampton, England, on 26 August 1939. Having done what they could for their children, the Leipzig adults hoped to save themselves. Leo and Eva Schmulevitz went off in one direction; Abraham and Trude Grünbaum went off in another; Adolph Koppold was incarcerated in Sachsenhausen very soon after his children left Leipzig; the widowed Yetta Ribetski Piatrkowska and her mother, Rose Schmulevitz, were together until Yetta was expelled from Germany along with all those born in Poland. Yetta returned, and she, her sister Clara and their mother Rose, left Leipzig together on 21 January 1942.[1]

They were all at no. 4 Humbolt Street, Leipzig, confined with other deportees in an apartment building commandeered by the Nazis.[2] The first deportation from the city occurred on 21 January 1942. Clara and her mother are recorded as being among the deportees; their names are entered in the *Deportationbuch* for the years 1942–45. Yetta Piatrkowsky (Vera's mother) is not listed, although she too had been living at the same address.[3] In October 1946 Marta Mitdank, a Leipzig resident and a friend of the Schmulevitzs, sent Vera and Paula her eye-witness account of what happened at 4 Humbolt Street when the first transport from Leipzig was organizing to leave. Mitdank claims that Yetta 'was to stay back',[4] but she went to Riga only because Oma and Clarchen pleaded with her to go.[5] It is not clear that Mitdank is a reliable witness. But she is the only one to have reported the events that preceded the deportation of the last three Schmulevitz women in Leipzig. No one boarding the trains had any notion at all of where they were going or why.

The common wisdom then was that if families or couples separated during attempted flight, each had better mobility and a better chance of survival. There is no indication that any of the Schmulevitz family considered going separate ways. Except, perhaps, Yetta who was alone after Vera left and did much travelling alone, some of it enforced. Because she had been born in Poland, she was declared stateless by the Germans and deported back to that country. She returned to Leipzig and somehow managed to stay close to her mother and her sister Clara.

Yetta ended up in the same apartment and then the same train with them and 702 other people bound for Riga, Auschwitz and Treblinka.[6] When the war was over, Marta Mitdank reported the events that transpired at 4 Humbolt Street prior to the transport. She sent the family a letter composed over a three-day period, starting Tuesday, 15 October 1946 and ending Thursday.[7] Mitdank claims that Clara and Yetta were both with their mother in Riga when Rose Schmulevitz perished there.[8] Exactly where the sisters died is not clear. What is known, finally, is that all the remaining family members in Leipzig were murdered by the Nazis.

It is difficult to corroborate the information in the Mitdank letter. Mitdank asserts that Vera's mother could have avoided the transport but chose to be with her sister and mother because they pleaded with her to join them. It seems highly unlikely that Yetta would have gone on the transport of her own volition because her mother and sister wanted her to join them. But, on the other hand, nobody knew about the death camps at that time. When the people who had been confined in inadequate quarters for several weeks were ordered to board the trains, they had no idea where they were being taken. Even if Mitdank took some creative liberty with the facts, the end result is the same. They all arrived in Riga. Mitdank further claims that she 'received mail from Yetta through soldiers', and learned that 'Yetta worked at the train construction site, our good Clarchen washed windows, and Oma [grandmother] had to sew. Under all circumstances, they were all doing well; and still they were full of hope.' Mitdank reports that Rose Schmulevitz died in Riga. When the Riga ghetto was dissolved, Yetta and Clara were sent to Sudhov where it was reported that they died of typhoid (see Letters below, p. 217).

Marta Mitdank describes the Schmulevitz women as strong, faithful and compassionate (see Letters below, p. 217–21). To Vera and Paula, she echoes what they had been told by their own parents: not to leave the Koppold children, the youngest, most vulnerable and most in need of supervision. She writes: 'Continue to be a crutch for them so that the last won't get lost. I ask that you would do this for your loved ones.'

A letter in the autumn of 1941 from the Red Cross informed Paula Grünbaum that her parents reached Salonika together and were in the ancient Greek city. Jews had been a presence in Salonika since Hellenistic and Roman times; in 1935, 60,000 Jews lived there, in 1945 there were none. It is not certain where the Grünbaums further journey took them or indeed what happened to them. After the war, Paula heard from a Leipzig acquaintance that her parents were seen on a transport 'being sent somewhere'. In response to her repeated enquiries, the Red Cross sent Paula a letter telling her in effect: 'Mrs Balkin, put it to rest already.'[9] They had notified her that both parents were sent to Auschwitz; Paula knows her father was killed on 23 April 1945, 'one of the last ones before peace was declared in Germany'.

The fate of Adolf Koppold is also known. Records in the Sachsische Staatsarchiv, Leipzig, show that he was sent to Sachsenhausen in August 1939 and died there on 5 May 1940. Leo Schmulevitz and his wife Eva tried to escape together, but it is not known where they went or where they perished.

The last of the six children from Leipzig arrived in England on 26 August 1939. On 31 August Hitler ordered the invasion of Poland. On 1 September 1939, the British government ordered the evacuation of all children, nursing mothers and the elderly from London and other sites vulnerable to German rockets.[10] An attack on England was almost certain. On 3 September 1939, Britain and France declared war on Germany.

The young refugee children understood neither 'war' nor 'evacuation', or their implications. Three of the six Leipzig children: two Koppolds (Siegmar and Zilla) and Paula Grünbaum (accompanied by their grand-mother's niece, Dora Binke), were among those evacuated to Cambridge. Harold remained at the farm where he had been placed in the village of Wansford, and the home of the Dorringtons, a war veteran turned postman and his wife. Paula's sister Edith and the Jacobson children (grandchildren of Dora Binke) were evacuated from London to Oakham in Rutland and taken into the home of two elderly single women.

Of the six from Leipzig, only Vera lived in one home for the duration of her stay in England; in contrast, her five cousins experienced multiple moves and a variety of foster-homes. Their oldest cousin Paula, who had been living with her relatives and thus not placed in a foster-home, was able to keep track of the children in spite of their frequent moves.

Multiple-home placements were typical for many children who came to England on *Kindertransports*. Siblings and cousins arriving together often lost track of each other, sometimes for years – sometimes forever. They were separated in the process of being transferred to private homes or hostels and moving from one placement to another. Nor did the committees in charge of the young refugees always know where all the children were. Some youngsters arriving in England paid no attention to the rules and took off by themselves or joined friends to explore the new country. Volunteers for the Refugee Children's Movement and for the CRCC, feeling a strong obligation to the missing parents for the welfare of their children, tried to keep accurate records and to act responsibly towards their charges. But they were no match for those few youngsters who were determined to take control of their own futures. Many of the young *émigrés* desperately searched for ways to help their parents leave Germany or Austria for England. Many were despondent about their inability to get to the right agencies so that they might help their parents. They needed advice and care. But, the first task of the Refugee Children's Movement, before it could deal with the anxieties of the children (and before the children disappeared altogether) was to record the names and pertinent information of the newly arrived young *émigrés*.

Region 4 of the CRCC was exemplary in its scrupulous attention to record-keeping for the 2,000 children who passed through its hands. Indeed, all 12 regional committees did a splendid job of keeping track of the 10,000 child refugees in England. Yet, with the best intentions in the world, the volunteers could not stay on top of every situation and the records were often muddled or misplaced. By the time they were sorted out many youngsters were often somewhere entirely unknown to the people in charge.

Children like Vera who were in one home from the time of their arrival until they left were unusual. Vera's five cousins, who had more erratic histories, were more typical of the children who arrived on *Kindertransports*. Five of the six from Leipzig attended school in England; Paula, who was 15 when she arrived, was too old for mandatory schooling and too young to find a good job. Nevertheless, she worked at whatever jobs she could get, and later managed to get some office training.

Paula had solemnly promised her mother before she left Leipzig that she would always know the whereabouts of her cousins and her sister. That became her mission. Had it not been for her, the children might well have lost track of one another. For some siblings, that was only one of the unfortunate consequences of the *Kindertransport*.

Because the RCM was already organized into 12 regional committees, corresponding to the map of the air raid warning system, the government asked it to take charge of the record-keeping for the evacuated. Overnight, the CRCC had some 800 new files to process.

Dora Binke, Paula, Siegmar and Zilla were evacuated together to Cambridge, and housed in a hostel there. By November 1939 no bombs had fallen and no attacks had been mounted. English parents began to bring their evacuated children home – an exodus that continued throughout the spring. By January 1940 only 55 per cent of unaccompanied children and 12 per cent of mothers remained in their evacuation sites.[11] Many of the remaining children were young refugees who had no parents to claim them and no homes to which they belonged.

In the middle of December 1939 Dora Binke left Paula in charge of Siegmar and Zilla Koppold in the hostel and returned to her home and family in London. Thus she effectively transferred the role of carer for two infant children to an inexperienced 15-year-old not yet fluent in English. Nor did the adult Dora (who should have known better) say anything at all to the committee responsible. Of that time, Paula says, 'I didn't know how to handle a baby. She was teething and crying and I was walking around with her at night. And Siggy started crying. But, we made it. We did.'[12] It never occurred to Paula to notify the CRCC of the change in their living arrangements.

In April 1940 Paula received an unexpected visit from a member of the CRCC. When the visitor learned that Paula was alone with the two infants, she immediately took the children away from her. Paula was heartbroken. Zilla remained in Cambridge. In May 1940 she was placed in the home of Mr and Mrs Stanley. Siegmar was placed in the home of Jack and Peggy Longland, in Welwyn Garden City, about 20 miles away.

With nothing to do and nobody who needed her, Paula returned to the Binke home in London and looked for work. But before she could get a job, she was required to appear for questioning at a tribunal.

While she was not interned, Paula nevertheless felt stigmatized by the words 'enemy alien'. Her foreign birth as well as her lack of experience and skill contributed to her difficulty in finding a job. Nor could she endure London during the period of heavy bombing. She returned to Cambridge, found work in a mattress factory, and rented a room from the Stanleys, with whom Zilla was then living. Paula babysat for Zilla when her hosts went out for the evening. She remembers, 'For the rest of my time, I worked. All I did was go to work. I had no social life.'

The war started in earnest on 7 September 1940. There was a second evacuation of women and children from London and other cities. For about 76 consecutive nights, bombs continued to fall without a break, except for one night when bad weather prevented the night raids.[13] A total of 625

German bombs fell on London. Children who had been evacuated previously and had returned to their homes were once again sent out of London. During this second evacuation the processing of the children went much more smoothly than before. Paula's sister Edith and one of the Jacobson children had remained in Salcombe, Devon, at the country estate of Lady Clementine Waring. For Edith, it was the most luxurious setting and longest placement she had had in England. She remained there for two years, and had some schooling. Lady Clementine invited Edith to stay longer, but Edith, afraid that if she stayed she would be trained to be a maid, chose to leave.

In August 1942 Edith returned with the Jacobson children to their London home. In September 1943 she was evicted. Rose Jacobson took Edith and her suitcase to the RCC and left both there after telling the committee that they must make other arrangements for her. If Edith knows why she was evicted so unceremoniously she does not say so. Subsequently, the 11-year-old was placed in an Orthodox Jewish hostel, which she found oppressive. After ten weeks she sent such a desperate message to her sister Paula (at that time visiting Vera in Norwich) that Paula immediately withdrew her from the hostel. Vera's foster-mother, Bertha Staff, made arrangements with her sister and brother-in-law in London, Florrie and Mickey Hart, for Paula and Edith to move into their home. Paula was with the Harts in March of 1944 when they were bombed. The house was destroyed by a direct hit. Miraculously they all survived, but Florrie and her husband were now searching for a roof over their own heads.

Paula exhausted her meagre funds searching for different accommodation for herself and Edith. The JRC in London was able to help her rent a room with kitchen privileges in Stamford Hill, London, where she and Edith could both stay. Three months later, at the end of June 1944, the sisters visited their cousins in Cambridge and decided to remain there. The CRCC helped them move into the refugee hostel on Parkside, and life began to take on a more orderly shape for them. Paula was then 20 and Edith was 13 and going to school.

At Paula's request, the CRCC agreed that Zilla, then 5, could live with her and Edith in the hostel. Zilla had not been doing well in the home of the spiritualist with whom she lived. The child was frightened for much of the time and appeared to be wasting away. The CRCC, concerned about her condition, had her put under a doctor's care. In his reports, Zilla is described as having large, sad eyes and a pigeon chest. When she joined her cousins at the Parkside hostel, she began to improve almost immediately.

Paula, Edith and Zilla formed a family unit and each had a daily routine. Paula worked, Edith attended a local school, while Zilla was enrolled in an open-air school where she became steadily stronger. The kitchen staff at the hostel looked after Zilla until the older child returned from school and could watch her cousin; they were also available during the day if needed. After the hostel was closed in January 1946, Paula and the two younger children moved to an apartment in Petty Cury (Cambridge). Paula worked at a series of part-time jobs – as a store clerk, an office assistant and as a receptionist in the Ramsey and Pratt Photography Studio – and was able to meet some but not all of their expenses. Her job at Sayles Department Store earned her £2 15s per week, and they were able to manage. The CRCC subsidized Paula and the girls, and helped Paula financially so she could take courses to improve her office skills. Edith and Zilla were both doing well in school. Until they left for America, the three lived together, their lives quietly watched over and guided by the CRCC who now had all six children from Leipzig under their care. And that made all the difference.

The war in Europe was winding down. On 8 May 1945 (VE Day), it was over. Paula and Edith, having established contact with Grünbaum relatives in Michigan, were scheduled to leave for America sometime during the summer. Their passage had already been booked. But there were complications.

In June 1945 Paula turned 21 and fell in love. She announced to the CRCC that she wanted to get married to her fiancé, a 30-year-old electrical engineer. She wanted to remain in England. She sent word to her family in America of her engagement and her intention of staying in England. She suggested to the CRCC that Zilla could go to America in her place. Vera was already in New York and would take care of Zilla.

Greta Burkill learned somehow that her fiancé was already married, and she had to break the news to a distraught Paula. The romance ended, but the deception of the man she loved left her brokenhearted. Burkill, with her usual kindness, managed to secure some money for Paula to go on a two-week holiday with Edith and Zilla, which was both healing and restorative for Paula. When the three returned they were able to finalize plans to go to America.

Paula's dilemma and aborted love affair was not uncommon among young refugee women: many had similar disappointments. They came to England as innocent children and grew into vulnerable women without mothers, aunts or grandmothers to guide them or to be confidantes. Missing their families, the young women had an intense need for love. For some, the need was so strong that it clouded their judgement and made them especially vulnerable.

Nor were these normal times for the young refugee men, whose needs for family were equally intense. They grew into manhood under the shadow of war; their lives were often determined by the country's needs for their service. Difficult times create difficult situations. Young refugee men and women both needed and sought intimate friendships.

When the young seek love they generally find it. Many who had been on the *Kindertransport* made lasting friendships and enduring marriages with other '*Kinder*' or English mates. Most of those who married have celebrated their 50th and 60th wedding anniversaries. But in the years between 1939 and 1945, those who went through puberty and beyond under the shadow of their *Kindertransport* experience, found that life and love, mating and matching, were not simple experiences.

Innocent and inexperienced women craving security and affection were naïve and trusting. They either seduced or were seduced by sincere-sounding young men who promised everything but could give little. Several young women refugees became single mothers and, seeing in a child a family of their own, wanted desperately to keep their babies. They sought domestic jobs which made it possible for them to do so. A few men divorced their wives and married their pregnant girlfriends; others simply disappeared from the women's lives. The dilemma of pregnant young refugee women provided another problem for the English women volunteers staffing the offices of the various refugee committees.

Paula's unhappy romantic interlude was cut short at an early stage with no serious repercussions, thanks to the attentiveness and wisdom of Greta Burkill. Others were not so lucky. In the files of the CRCC there is an entry which reads:

> Eleven new girls arrive in Cambridge with summaries of the difficulties they had encountered. A girl's second pregnancy has the Committee sending her to the Probation Officer and the Movement's lawyer … One girl has been arrested; Mrs Hardisty was making arrangements for her release … Released from prison but destitute. Sent to Highgate Public Assistance Institution where she will remain until the baby is born … One girl is found a domestic position where she can take her illegitimate baby.[14]

Zilla, 8 months old when she arrived in England from Leipzig, remembers little about Cambridge and nothing of her mother and father. By June 1947 she was being adequately cared for by Paula and the women in charge of the hostel where they lived. The two other Koppold children (Zilla's brothers) were in exemplary homes and all were in close proximity to each other. It was the best possible situation for these children under the circumstances.

Harold, a quiet compliant child and the oldest of the three Koppolds, was nearly 7 when he arrived in England. Before joining the Sofier family in Cambridge, he had been in at least two different homes. While he had nothing bad to say about those placements, his cousin Paula was distressed by his situation. She offers as an example that in one of his foster-homes he had to stay outdoors until supper-time when he came home from school; after supper he had to go to bed immediately. Harold does not remember any particular difficulty for him in staying outside after school; he says it gave him an opportunity to play with other children. But, Paula remembers that when she arrived at his foster-home and introduced herself, the foster-mother asked her to wait and then appeared with the boy and his suitcase and told her to take both and leave.

The CRCC placed Harold in another foster-home. Eventually, the Sofiers, a Jewish family in Cambridge, at the urging of their son Norman, asked the committee to allow Harold to live with them. Norman Sofier was two or three years older than Harold. He befriended the boy in 1942 when they both attended Shabbat services at the small synagogue on Thompson's Lane in Cambridge. The young refugee child did not look happy to the older boy, and Norman, reporting his impression to his parents, asked them to invite Harold to live with them. The family lived modestly in Orchard Street, Cambridge, in half of a small cottage without a spare bedroom. Ann Sofier was a clerk in a department store, while her husband was a barber. Ann Sofier promised her son that if they could get the other half of the cottage, they would consider inviting Harold to join the family. When the adjoining cottage apartment became available, Ann was suddenly overwhelmed with the idea of assuming the responsibility for a refugee child. In spite of the promise to her own son, she was afraid to take a boy into her home without knowing what kind of a child he was or whether she would get on with him. Her husband encouraged her to take the child. In fact, according to Norman Sofier,[15] his father felt they had a moral duty to take care of these Jewish children who were deprived of parents.

When Ann Sofier approached Greta Burkill with a request for Harold Koppold to join her family, Burkill, always looking for appropriate homes for children, encouraged her to take a different child who needed to be placed. Harold already had a good home, Burkill asserted, and others were waiting for homes. But Ann was adamant. She obtained the support of Rabbi Kline in Cambridge and the principal of Norman's school, both of whom endorsed her appeal to foster Harold Koppold. Greta Burkill, recognizing that the child would benefit from being in a family that really wanted him, acceded to the request. So Harold joined the Sofiers. Ann Sofier became a surrogate mother to him, and the family became his. The Sofiers also became family to the four other cousins living within a close radius of each other, and to Vera, now in Norwich, about 50 miles away but reasonably accessible by train.

Harold and Norman became close friends, and remain so to the present. In Cambridge they shared everything: trips, excursions, clubs, toys, games. They especially enjoyed playing chess together. 'He was a whiz at chess', Norman reported. 'And he followed me everywhere. But, he was reluctant to talk about his past. And none of us pressured him to do that.'

The Sofier home was close to the hostel where Paula lived with Edith and Zilla, and near the cottage of Elsie and Len Mansfield with whom Siegmar eventually was placed. Thus five of the six children from Leipzig were in close proximity to each other. As Bertha Staff's home was open to Vera's cousins Paula and Edith, so Ann Sofier's home became a second home to all six of the Leipzig children. They celebrated all Jewish holidays together and occasionally Vera joined them. For the children, the atmosphere created was as close as they could get to the family they had left behind.

In her later years Ann Sofier remembered with pleasure and warmth the celebrations that took place in her home when the six from Leipzig gathered together in her small cottage for a holiday. 'They all ended up with us a lot. I ended up having so many', she said. She also reflected on the experience of having taken Harold into her home. With some emotion, she reported: 'As I look back on my life, bringing Harold into our family was one of the most fulfilling experiences I had, outside of raising my own son. Harold enriched our lives in ways I cannot even begin to tell you.'[16]

Ann Sofier knew that the happy circumstance of the Leipzig children surviving so well did not come about by accident. She had no hesitation in sharing her feelings and impressions about Greta Burkill and the CRCC with whom she worked: '[Mrs Burkill] was wonderful ... absolutely marvellous. She loved every colour, every creed, everybody ... [she] had a loud sort of funny voice. She once came to look for me at the store where I worked ... She made me feel self-conscious, she was so loud.' But Ann Sofier fully appreciated the magnitude of her work, even comparing her to Mother Theresa: 'I always admired Greta Burkill. She was always at it, active, always for the sake of the refugees. She adopted two Chinese children ... Like Mother Theresa, she had such a special feeling for all the children. She was a marvellous, remarkable woman. And her husband was very patient, no matter what she did.'[17]

The CRCC periodically visited the homes of the children they placed in order to check their living conditions. According to Ann Sofier, neither Burkill nor the committee felt they needed to visit Harold on a regular basis. 'They ... knew how much we wanted him and they were confident he was doing just fine.' The Sofiers did not accept the customary stipend of 13s 15d given to host families by the RCM, as money was not the reason for inviting Harold to live with them. Ann Sofier says:

We didn't want the money. We didn't want him for the money. We didn't want him to feel any different when he came to live with us. I never gave him anything to wear that was Norman's which he could have. Norman was two years older. But we wanted him to feel he was important enough to get new clothes also. We bought him a new bike. We didn't want anything to do with the money part, we wanted him to feel he was one of us, which he did.[18]

Harold attended the Perse School in Cambridge and also studied Hebrew. The Sofiers helped him celebrate his *Bar Mitzvah* at the small Tompkins Lane synagogue. Mrs Burkill was there to hear him chant his *Haftorah*, and she gave him a gift of £4, which the Sofiers remember as being 'a lot of money in those days'. To the delight of his tutors, Harold continued studying Hebrew after his *Bar Mitzvah*. His teachers refused money from the Sofiers for the lessons. At that time, 'everyone did for each other whatever they could', Ann Sofier said.

Many people who took refugee children into their homes wanted to adopt them but could not do so unless there was proof that their parents were no longer alive. The Sofiers too would have liked to have adopted Harold. Nevertheless, he became an integral member of the family and their emotional investment in him did not go unrewarded. Not only did Norman have a brother, but Ann had another son who loved her. Much later, after he immigrated to Israel, Harold telephoned her every two weeks:

Every other Friday, he calls me up from Israel.[19] I know it's expensive to call from Israel. I told him, 'Look, I write you every month, so don't phone. I'll write you more if you want.' He said, 'No, we like to hear your voice. We just want to hear your voice.' You couldn't say he was much of a talker when he came. He was very reserved. The only one he'd speak to was Norman; I could hear them in the bedroom, talking to each other.[20]

The two other Koppold children and their cousins Paula and Edith were frequent guests at the Sofier home. Edith reports that she confided in Ann Sofier when she visited her, and Ann always made her feel very special – something Edith badly needed. She treasures the memory now. Typically, the cousins gathered at the Sofier home, often on Shabbat, and always to celebrate Jewish holidays and birthdays. Vera also visited about once a month, making the two-hour trip to spend a weekend with her cousins in Cambridge. Siegmar especially remembers the Passover *seders* at the Sofier home with his brother, his sister and his cousins: 'They were the most memorable and beautiful *seders* I have ever attended. They had a tiny room and we were all squeezed in, but to me it was like a palace.'

If all the commotion was a burden for her, Ann Sofier did not remember it as such. Knowing the sacrifice that the parents had made in sending their children away, she marvelled at their strength even while she had trouble understanding how they could have done it: 'Can you imagine it? A mother handed over her three children, one just a wee baby. They were such good, lovely children. You could see they were from a good family, you know. Nice. Nice.'

Harold Koppold grew close to the Sofier family and followed Norman Sofier everywhere he could. They often visited a model kibbutz in Thaxted, a village near Cambridge, and they spent holidays together there. The history and idealism of Israel inspired Harold who continued to live happily in the Sofier home until Norman went to university and then on to national service. Harold then decided to make *aliya* to Israel.[21] Ann Sofier helped him prepare to leave, buying him what she thought were suitable clothes: suits, ties, a dressing-gown, shirts – all formal – to take with him. She did not know that he would be living in a tent.

Harold settled in Israel permanently. He changed his name to Tsvi Shdaimar and lives on a border kibbutz near Gaza. Living on the edge is nothing new to him, he claims. At some point on the kibbutz he began sculpting and painting. His sculptures now grace the kibbutz, many of them reflecting his *Kindertransport* experience. He married, has three sons by his first wife from whom he is divorced, and has now remarried. His sons and grandchildren live in Israel and America.

Siegmar Koppold, 3 years old when he arrived in England and almost 12 when he left, was more fortunate than many who shared in the *Kindertransport* experience. He was in two different foster homes, both of which were exemplary. Siegmar was sent to his first placement in the spring of 1940, after the CRCC took him and his sister Zilla away from the teenage Paula who was doing her best to look after both infants by herself. Siegmar was placed in the Hertfordshire home of John and Peggy Longland who had a son, John, about the same age as Siegmar. John Longland was a headmaster.[22] Siegmar was happily integrated into the family and lived with them until 1942 when Peggy Longland's difficult second pregnancy forced them to ask the CRCC to find another home for him. In 1976 Siegmar, trying to make sense of the various pieces of his life in England, wrote a letter to Jack Longland. Longland replied, saying how sorry he was that they had had to send the little boy back to the committee: 'I think you were reasonably happy in our home, and you and John really got on pretty well together ... In some ways you were almost heartbreakingly self-sufficient, as I suppose you had to be, deprived of real parents whom you were never to see again. In fact, there were astonishingly few tantrums.'[23]

After Siegmar left the family, the Longlands contributed 5s per month to the committee towards his care.[24] Yet more than 30 years on, John Longland was still troubled by their decision to send the boy to another home: 'I still have a bad conscience about you. I think we ought to have kept you in our home and with our family until the end of the war, or at least until you had the opportunity to go to your relatives in America.'[25]

Siegmar's next placement became his home for the rest of the time he was in England. The CRCC placed him with the Mansfields: Len Mansfield, his sister Elsie and their 15-year-old niece Gladys. Elsie Mansfield was a charwoman and her brother Len a butler at one of the colleges. Although the Longland and Mansfield homes were at opposite ends of the social scale, both families provided Siegmar with the warmth and stability necessary for a child's growth and development. For the first time in England, Siegmar had an opportunity to develop a relationship with his brother as the Mansfield's cottage was close to the home of the Sofiers where Siegmar's brother Harold was living. Siegmar lived very happily with the Mansfields for more than six years until he left for America.

Elsie Mansfield had never married (her fiancé had been killed in the First World War). To deal with her loss she fostered children, and was known to the CRCC before they placed Siegmar with her. The Mansfields, especially Elsie, doted on Siegmar and he did very well in their home.

One Cambridge resident who lives on Eden Street, near the former Mansfield home, remembers Siegmar walking with Elsie Mansfield: 'He held on to her hand, and would not let go, no matter how long we stood and chatted. He was a bright child, and there was such apparent love between him and his foster-mother.'

Siegmar lived with the Mansfields on Eden Street for almost seven years. According to his testimony, it was the best and most stable home he had ever had, or ever was to have. As a 5-year-old child, experiencing a second major break in his home life (leaving his parents and then the Longlands), he arrived at the Mansfields looking frail and with major eating problems. Elsie Mansfield pushed him to his school in a pram because she thought the walk would be too tiring for him.[26] (Indeed, the health of both Siegmar and Zilla was the subject of many discussions at meetings of the CRCC. The two were very thin; and Siegmar was somewhat sickly. At one point the committee arranged for consultations with specialists in internal medicine for both children, but both eventually grew into sturdy healthy youngsters.)

Elsie Mansfield adored Siegmar and was wonderful to him. By all accounts, he also adored her. The Mansfield and Sofier homes were close to one another, so while the boys played together the foster-mothers often talked to each other about the brothers they were tending. Siegmar did very well in school, made friends and was an important member of the Mansfield household. He belonged to the Scouts, went on camping trips with them, and also studied Hebrew. The Mansfields made sure that Siegmar went to the synagogue. When he approached the age of *Bar Mitzvah*, Elsie discussed with Ann Sofier what needed to be done. The two women were in the process of planning for the Judaic rite of passage when Siegmar's world literally changed. His *Bar Mitzvah* was celebrated, not in Cambridge as planned, but in Paterson, New Jersey.

Some months earlier, a series of events had been set in motion over which no one in England seemed to have any control, but which significantly affected the lives of Siegmar and the Mansfields. It happened when Vera and her cousins Paula, Edith and Zilla reunited in New York at the home of Vera's uncle and aunt.

Vera had left England for America in March 1947 and settled in the home of relatives in New York City. Soon after arriving, she asked her uncle to help her get her cousins in England over to America. Her uncle, a clothing manufacturer, wanted to help whatever survivors of the European catastrophe he could. Eventually, he was asked to arrange for Paula, Edith and Zilla to come to America. They all left England together on 15 July 1947. After a brief stay in New York, Paula and Edith travelled further to Michigan, where relatives of their deceased father lived. Zilla remained in New York with Vera and was subsequently adopted by another friend or colleague of Vera's uncle, Charlie Schnall.

While Paula was with Vera in New York, the two cousins decided that Siegmar needed to be with the family in the United States so that they could keep tabs on him more easily. That he was doing very well at the Mansfield home, where he and his foster family were totally bonded to each other, was not for them a major consideration. The cousins' focus was on preserving the remnants of their Leipzig Schmulevitz family, and by extension their Jewish heritage. There was also the implicit promise they had made to keep the family together. They also wanted Harold in America, but he had other plans from which he would not be dissuaded.

Vera enlisted the help of her uncle, in whose home she was living, to find an appropriate home for Siegmar. As a consequence, Vera's uncle, armed with a photograph of Siegmar, approached Meyer Silber, a business associate from Paterson, New Jersey, with a plan that he and his wife consider adopting the boy. The plan then took on a life of its own, and neither Siegmar nor the Mansfields had any say in the matter.

Meyer and Gussie Silber, a middle-aged couple, had no children. They looked at Siegmar's picture and decided to investigate his background before committing themselves to adopting him. They commissioned friends travelling in England to visit the boy at his foster-home and to send reports. Arnold Levy, one of those asked to investigate Siegmar, wrote to the Silbers about his visit to the Mansfield home and his impression of Siegmar:

> The boy is cared for most lovingly by the lady and her brother in whose care he is; they are deeply attached to him and he to them ... The sudden break from these loving people and his happy surroundings might upset him ... Material things such as rich food, elegant clothes, expensive toys ... will in no way compensate the child for the loss of the quiet harmonious home ... Though [his foster-parents] are not Jewish, they have seen to it that Siegmar attends religious classes at the synagogue regularly. They are deeply devoted to him.[27]

A week later, the Silbers asked yet another person to visit Siegmar at the Mansfield home, and received another report:

> The boy is a very bright, handsome, intelligent child ... strongly attached to ... Miss Mansfield, and she in turn loves him more than if he were her own child ... She has brought him up ever since he was about 5 years old and he is now 11, and given him the most devoted care and attention that any child could possibly have. Even though her means are limited, he wants for nothing. Even though she is not Jewish, she sees [to it] that he is brought up in his own religion and goes to services regularly. The child lives in great fear of his [being taken away from her].[28]

On the basis of these reports, the Silbers decided that Siegmar was the perfect child for them. They ignored the implied suggestion in both letters that the boy might be better off staying where he was. Reassured that he was of sound body and mind, the Silbers immediately started the adoption process. No one in authority, in either England or America, questioned the decision or the law, although Greta Burkill of the CRCC and the social service workers in Cambridge all felt it was terrible to take the child away from the warm, supportive family with whom he was totally bonded. Neither Siegmar nor the Mansfields wanted to part from each other, but they did not have the means or the sophistication to challenge directives that came to them from America. In addition, his older cousins had testified that he needed to be in a Jewish home. It did not matter that the Christian foster-parents made sure he received religious instruction preparatory for his *Bar Mitzvah* and Siegmar was at the synagogue every

Saturday for services. Eventually, the heartbroken foster-family and foster-child had to accept the fact that he had to go to America.

The simple *Bar Mitzvah* which Elsie Mansfield and Ann Sofier had planned for Siegmar in the small Cambridge synagogue morphed into a gala event held in a temple in New Jersey. The *Bar Mitzvah* gave Meyer Silber an opportunity to introduce his new son to his congregation.

Ann Sofier, who had observed both the boy and Siegmar's life with the Mansfields and the trauma of his leaving the home he cherished, wondered whether the move was in his best interest. She concludes that it was good, but perhaps should have been handled differently:

> The cousins should not have forced him to leave the person he had come to love as a mother. He loved her and she loved that boy passionately … His cousins in New York decided Siegmar must go to America because they were there … They wanted Harold also. But, he is three years older than Siegmar and he paid no attention to their arguments. He decided for himself where he wanted to be; he emigrated to Israel.

The Silbers of Paterson adopted Siegmar. Everything was arranged from America for the boy from Leipzig and Cambridge to leave England and to move into their home.

Siegmar says that his leaving 'was no simple matter'.[29] While he does not talk about his pain, he remembers that his Scout group gave him a farewell party (written up in the *Cambridge News*) and his scouting friends had arranged a last-minute camping trip for their group a week before Siegmar was due to go. Before he left, Elsie Mansfield took Siegmar as a treat to the Red Lion tea room and Len Mansfield brought him home ice cream and some oranges. Siegmar understood these to be 'simple statements of deep attachments'. As an adult, he reasons that the Mansfield's act of kindness and generosity left him with most positive feelings about both England and its people: 'The style with which I was sent off and my experiences from 1939 to 1948 made me a staunch defender of the English. Later in life, I would argue fiercely that the English people were emotional and loving, despite their reputation for detachment and stoicism.'[30]

Siegmar retains only fond memories of his life in Cambridge and at the home of Elsie Mansfield and her brother Len. Before he left for America, the Mansfields gave him books and a few other farewell gifts which he also understood as expressions of genuine kindness and love: 'They chose some Arthur Ransome books and a few volumes on English natural history.' When he arrived at his American middle-class home with few clothes but a 'ton of books', Siegmar remembers the Silbers being somewhat puzzled.[31]

Just before Siegmar's embarkation, Elsie Mansfield took him on what he calls a wonderful day's outing to London. They went to Madame Tussaud's, the British Museum and the Victoria and Albert Museum. She then accompanied him to the boat. Siegmar boarded the *Queen Elizabeth* in Southampton and left England on 22 May 1948, in the company of Bertha and Arthur Staff, Vera's foster-family in Norwich, who were emigrating to Canada. Nine years previously, in August 1939, he had arrived at the same port from which he was now leaving.

The CRCC did not believe that Siegmar's leaving Cambridge and the Mansfields was the wisest move for him, but they did nothing to discourage or stop the plan that had been put in motion. They were well aware of the pain felt by Elsie Mansfield. Greta Burkill wrote a letter to Vera urging her to try to understand both Siegmar's and Elsie Mansfield's feelings on being parted from each other. Burkill wanted Vera to help reassure the Mansfields:

> You must go half-way to help Miss Mansfield to get over this great pain and sorrow and make her feel that Siegmar is going to people who will love him as dearly as she has done, and who will care for him both physically and emotionally in the same way as he has been cared for in Cambridge ... Ask the foster-parents to write to Miss Mansfield personally and tell her [Mansfield] what sort of home they [the Silbers] have got and what sort of life they are going to give little Siegmar.[32]

Vera does not remember whether or not she wrote to Elsie Mansfield. She thinks that if Burkill asked her to write then she probably did so. Siegmar, for his part, did write to Elsie Mansfield and she answered his letters. She also had some correspondence with Meyer and Gussie Silber, Siegmar's new adoptive parents. To Meyer Silber, Elsie wrote that she missed Siegmar very much and wished that she had not grown to love him so much. She said she always wanted only one thing for him: that he should be happy. She asked Meyer Silber never to tell Siegmar that it was his duty to write, but at the same time, she hoped the Silbers would let him do so if he wished. 'He owes me nothing. His love for me while in England has repaid me for everything I ever did for him. But, if he wants to write, then I am sure you will let him.' Elsie Mansfield closed the letter with a wish for Meyer Silber: 'I hope you grow to love Siegmar as much as I do, but do not have such a big hurt to follow.'

Elsie wrote to Siegmar about the small garden they had planted together: 'That small piece of England, that to your Aunt and Uncle will always be "Siegmar's Garden", is looking grand' (20 June 1948). In August Elsie thanked Siegmar for some presents that he sent. She also wrote to him that, on the advice of her brother, she had taken in an 8-year-old girl who

had not been well treated in her foster-home. 'She is not a bit like you ...
She is not clever like you and can only read very small words.'

Like Ann Sofier, Elsie Mansfield, humble charwoman, could qualify for
a humanitarian award as a rescuer of children. Not particularly educated
and not Jewish, nonetheless she cherished a Jewish refugee boy, made sure
he received his religious training in the synagogue, and helped him excel at
school. She loved children and her love saved them. And in saving one
child, it is 'as if [she] saved the world'. In time, a mature Siegmar, a
husband and father with his own children, took his family to England to
visit the woman who mothered him, loved him and never forgot him.

In the aftermath of the Holocaust Siegmar's cousins sincerely and strongly
believed that they had a moral imperative to preserve the remnants of their
Leipzig family and their Jewish heritage. Remembering the plea of their
parents to 'keep the children together', Vera and Paula felt they must take
the young children with them when they decided to emigrate to America.

Whereas in Cambridge the five cousins saw each other as often as they
wished, and the family bond remained strong, in America tensions arose
between the siblings and they became distanced from one another. (There
was no CRCC working in the background to help keep the family together.)
Siegmar attributes the tensions to the attitude of Zilla's foster-parents who
actively discouraged her relatives from visiting. (Siegmar's foster-parents
were happy for his family to visit him.) Paula, who was Zilla's main carer
from her infancy in Cambridge until they came to the United States, could
not visit the child in her adoptive home. This nearly broke Paula's heart.
The foster-parents also discouraged visits from Siegmar, especially after he
wanted to help Zilla manage some assets to which she was entitled. Nor did
they invite Siegmar to Zilla's wedding. But the bond was not broken. When
Siegmar heard that Zilla's husband had died, he took the first plane he
could to be with his sister in North Carolina.

The last wish of Trude Grünbaum was that her daughters, Paula and
Edith, should stay close to each other, 'like two loaves of bread'. In America
they are close neither geographically (one lives in Michigan, the other in
California) nor emotionally. However, both claim that if the other were in
trouble, they would do everything they could to help.

Vera, as an only child, managed to avoid the stresses and strains brought
about by sibling rivalry. She remains on good terms with all her cousins.
And all five claim to feel very close to Tsvi (Harold) in Israel. For his part,
Tsvi gets on with everyone.

Like most of the children who arrived in England on the
Kindertransports, all six from Leipzig grew into responsible adults; they
made stable marriages and established families of their own in their adult

lives. They now have sixteen grandchildren between them. That they were able to achieve such stability in their adult lives is due in no small measure to the work of the CRCC in helping them to preserve their family ties and reinforcing their sense of identity in most difficult times and circumstances.

NOTES

1. See Marta Mitdank letter, 15 October 1946, printed below.
2. On Vera's identity card in the files of the CRCC, her mother's address is 4 Humbolt Street; the same address also appears on correspondence sent to Vera by her mother. It was a gathering place for those to be deported.
3. In the card file of the CRCC, Vera's mother's address in May of 1941 is recorded as 'Leipzig, Humbolt St, no. 4'.
4. Letters from Marta Mitdank were sent to Paula Grünbaum and Vera Ribetski after the war to inform them of what she knew of the fate of their families. Translated copies of the letters were given to the author by Tsvi Shdaimah (Harold Koppold) when the author visited him on his kibbutz, Nir Oz, on the Gaza border, in June 1994. See below.
5. Mitdank reports that an eye-witness knew Yetta and Clara from Riga. When the Riga ghetto was dissolved, Yetta and Clara were sent to Sudhov, where Yetta was a group leader.
6. *Deportationbuch der in den Jahren 1942 bis 1945. Von Leipzig aus gewaltsan verschicken Juden von 21.1.1942 zur Evakuierung Kommender Juden nach Riga, Auschwitz, Treblinka, An m. mit 702 Personen, Sachsische Staatsarchiv, Leipzig.*
7. The letters were written over a two-day period during 15/16 October 1946. No date is given on the letter cited. Presumably it followed the letter before it. See below.
8. See Marta Mitdank, letter, 15 October 1946, see below.
9. Paula Balkin interview with the author, 23 March 1998, transcript in author's private collection.
10. British intelligence had learned that Germany was preparing to attack England.
11. Bob Holman, *The Evacuation* (Oxford, 1995), p. 27.
12. Balkin interview (Spielberg video, November 1966), transcript by the author, p. 7, author's private collection.
13. See Holman, *Evacuation*, p. 32.
14. CRCC, 22 February 1946, Add. MS 7974, Cambridge University Library.
15. Norman Sofier interview with the author, London, 2 September 1997, transcript in author's private collection.
16. Ann Sofier interview with the author, London, 19 April 1994, transcript in author's private collection.
17. Ibid., p. 2.
18. Ibid.
19. It was serendipitous that I visited Ann Sofier for the interview on a Friday. I was with her when Harold (or Tsvi, the name he took in Israel) telephoned.
20. Sofier interview, 1994.
21. The Hebrew word *aliya* literally means to ascend. By extension, one who makes a decision to move to Israel is 'ascending' or going to a higher place.
22. John Longland was knighted in 1970.
23. Letter from John Longland to Siegmar Silber, 4 February 1976, private collection of Siegmar Silber.
24. Papers of the CRCC, Add. MS 7974, Cambridge University Library.
25. Letter from Sir John Longland to Siegmar Silber, 4 February 1976.
26. Sofier interview, 1944. Ann Sofier lived very close to the Mansfields, in Walm Lane, London, and she saw a great deal of both Siegmar and Elsie Mansfield.
27. Copies of the correspondence were given to the author by Siegmar Silber.

28. Copies of these letters were given to the author by Siegmar Silber.
29. Siegmar Silber, 'Leaving in Style: An Unabashed Reminiscence', *I Came Alone: The Stories of the Kindertransports* (Lewes, 1990), p. 312.
30. Ibid., p. 318.
31. Ibid., p. 317.
32. Ibid., p. 319.

CHAPTER EIGHT

Refugees and Jewish Farmers: Old Stereotypes, New Realities

In the mid-1930s German and Austrian Jews, desperate to leave their homes for any destination that offered them a safe harbour, were caught between a worldwide economic depression with global high unemployment and increasingly negative attitudes about Jews, who were blamed for much of humanity's problems. Whilst the conscience of the world was tried – never before had it witnessed the kind of blatant brutality as that inflicted on Jews of all classes: professionals, businessmen and the working class – no country was eager to take on the burden of destitute immigrants needing help. Since 1934 plans were advanced by various countries for the absorption of Jewish refugees and émigrés. Many of the plans came to naught whilst good governments, like good people, stood by and did nothing.

In the midst of the international turmoil *vis-à-vis* the Jews and Jewish refugees, the Jewish world was torn by Zionists who wanted to affirm their right in Palestine (and thus provide a legal and safe haven for the refugees) and the pragmatists who saw the immediate needs of the endangered as taking precedence over anything else. Unlike the rest of Europe, Great Britain remained free of Nazi control or occupation and hence contained an established Jewish community. But like the world at large, it too had internal tensions and a perceived need to be both politically correct and empowered. Often, its decisions were pragmatic rather than humane. In its role as policeman to the Middle East, it limited entry to most of those Jews seeking to remigrate to Palestine and effectively rejected plans for refugee settlement in other places.[1]

Starting in spring 1938, the *Jewish Chronicle* began suggesting to its readers that if Jews were 'prepared to go on the land and remain on the land', then they may be successful in getting necessary exit visas.[2] Thereafter, the *Chronicle* continued reporting on the prospects for farming for new and potential immigrants.[3]

Coincident with the first *Kindertransports* leaving Germany for Great Britain, Whittinghame, an estate near Edinburgh (see Chapter 2) became available for the housing of 200 young Jewish refugees. There they received farm training that would enable them eventually to take up agricultural work in Palestine.[4]

In December 1938, Viennese-born Sidney Pollard, age 13, was on one of the first *Kindertransports* to arrive in Britain. He was sent to Whittinghame, where, it was hoped, a communal life-style would prepare him for a future on a kibbutz in Palestine. He describes his experiences thus:

> Technically it [Whittinghame] was called a 'farm school', but there was no education in the accepted sense. We had English and Hebrew lessons, and classes on any other odd subject the 'teachers' in charge were capable of delivering ... a proportion of us worked 'in house', cleaning, cooking, washing up ... the rest worked in the fields of the proprietor, Lord Treprain, presumably to help pay the rent. 'Outside work' was full-time and allowed no education ... We were highly politicised – not perhaps surprisingly since politics had wrenched our lives out of their courses – and tended to be contemptuous of the philistines who did not think politics the most important thing in their lives. In principle, our political attitude was Zionist, but there was also a strong streak of social-ism, and an equally strong belief, derived from the early kibbutz movement, that there was something highly moral and good for the soul in doing manual work, a ... notion that conditions should be created for everyone to be able to engage in both physical and intellectual labour. Working on the land in Scotland would be good preparation for such a life.[5]

After two years the funds, subscribed by Jewish families in Scotland for the management of Whittinghame, ran out. Pollard was then on his own. The plan had been for the young people to train and then go to Palestine, but the sea routes were closed. Pollard stayed in Britain, working at whatever jobs he could get until a distant relative helped him by paying for correspondence courses and examinations that ultimately propelled him into an academic life.

In March 1939 15-year-old Esther Golan arrived in England on a *Kindertransport* from Berlin. She went directly to Whittinghame with other children aged 13 to 16. Like Pollard, Golan was also caught by the war and could not leave Britain. She retains positive memories of her experience at the mansion and the 'training farm'. According to her testimony, all the children were Jewish. They were served kosher food and looked after by a staff of adults from Frankfurt who spoke the same language as their charges. For Golan, the group became a surrogate family; in fact, her years in Whittinghame were the best she had in Britain. She remained there until after her seventeenth birthday, when she had to leave and support herself. She worked as a domestic and/or a children's helper and felt thoroughly exploited. As soon as she could, she remigrated to Palestine.[6]

Paul Cohn, today a distinguished mathematician and a Fellow of the Royal Society, was also 15 years old when he arrived in Britain in May 1939 on a *Kindertransport*. His cousin, older by one or two years, had preceded him and had been placed on a farm in Dorking. At the cousin's request, the Dorking committee obtained a guarantee from the same farmer, which enabled the young Cohn to leave. He immediately transferred to the farm. The plan was for him to work there until he was 18, at which time he would be shipped to the Dominions, where there was a demand for farmers.

On the farm, Paul Cohn worked long hours – often 70 hours a week. The effect, he says, was that 'work in the open air, and nourishing food, turned [me] from a delicate child into a sturdy youngster' (Newsletter of the Association for Jewish Refugees (vol. 49, no. 2, February 1994, p. 2). But he found the work not particularly challenging, observing, 'For slow learners … it would take about a week to learn poultry farming.'[7] The members of the Dorking refugee committee, chaired by composer Vaughan Williams, helped the young refugee boy by inviting him to their homes and supplying him with books. When he decided to continue his interrupted education, the committee provided him with financial assistance. As Cohn reflects on that period of his life, he says the 'work was boring' but he feels that he was fairly treated and appears not to have regrets: 'I had a very reasonable time on the farm. I was there for about two and a half years; during that time, I was treated well.'[8]

Australia, with its vast under-populated areas, seemed to be a promising destination for Jewish refugees. The Hilfsverein der Juden in Deutschland, a social agency working for the movement of Jews out of Germany, told prospective immigrants in 1937 that Australia was only one-quarter smaller than Europe and had only 7 million people. Thus, it could undoubtedly feed a population many times that size. It had fertile soil for potential farmers.[9] The Australian Jewish Welfare Society formed a company, Mutual Farms Ltd, to control all the agricultural undertakings anticipated by the organization. Plans were made to settle Jewish migrants on farms in the Murrumbidgee area in New South Wales. Somewhat defensively, the society declared a fixed policy against group settlement and proclaimed its intention to assist only those who will not come into competition with Australian workers. Preference would be given to agricultural workers, skilled technicians, domestics and children (*Jewish Chronicle*, 23 December 1938, p. 16).

A rumour of Japanese naval vessels cruising off New Guinea created enough fear in the population for the Australian government, mindful of its weak defensive position in the event of an enemy attack, to consider permitting 50,000 immigrants to settle, but numbers were continually revised downwards. The prime minister told the Labour Party that he would allow 15,000 refugees to enter in the next three years.[10] The *Chronicle* reported consideration of the Fitzroy River area in the far north of Western Australia as the designated site for the settlement of some 40,000 people on 10,000 'small' farms of 100 acres each.

No matter what the numbers, there was reaction to the plan. Michael Terry, a freelance writer and explorer, in ostensibly presenting an argument for allowing Jewish immigrants into Australia,[11] raises objections and repeats well-worn clichés about Jewish farmers. On the one hand, he tries to convince readers of the plan's wisdom, on the other, he incorporates all the stereotypes of Jews: they are interested primarily in money; they have acquisitive habits; their numbers would create havoc in the national economy, depreciate values and make life impossible. He concludes that a horde of new settlers is highly questionable:

> If Australia's full population requirements were to be met suddenly by a vast horde of primary producers descending on to her pastures, her wheatfields, her forests, her orchards (potential or actual) they would inevitably create havoc in the national economy. Increased production flung upon the open markets of the world would depreciate values and make life impossible for established farmers, orchardists, etc. ... Increasing wool, wheat, and other products in excess of buying power of the present population and the new army of settlers is highly question-able in the present state of the world. (*Jewish Chronicle*, 23 December 1938, p. 28)

The writer goes on to acknowledge the 'mental capacity' of the new immigrants would make them 'highly desirable', but only if they could abandon the usual attitude of immigrants in a new, sparsely populated land:

> They must turn their backs on ambition as represented in terms of [money]. They must abandon the 'golden fortune in a new land' spirit. All they must allow themselves to yearn for is security. [If they] can establish a new set of values where three meals a day, a bed, freedom of persecution, tranquility in the future are the highlights – then they will find a new and satisfactory home in Australia.

Terry's vision of the ideal immigrant is one who is satisfied to live a simple life, raises only enough vegetables to feed his family and produces dairy products to fit his needs. It is then that the new immigrant 'can go to bed at night without fear of the dawn'. If these conditions were met, then Australia might take in more than 15,000. But, 'if they [the new immigrants] cannot think ahead without the glitter of material ambition, maybe somewhere else they will find a welcome – but not in the Commonwealth'.

Terry understands that at the 'present, thousands are today yearning for simple security'. For them, he recommends places in underdeveloped Australia where large communities might be established satisfactorily. But he sees a risk; Jews are not agricultural people:

> Whether or not thousands of refugees would farm successfully such land remains to be seen. But, in reality, their success will depend more upon themselves than on the land, its water supplies, its accessibility, its climate. We must be on our guard against the dangerous assumption that because Jewish immigrants to Palestine have surprised the world with their success in tilling its very difficult soil, therefore other Jewish immigrants who also are normally non-agriculturally minded people will be successful in Australia. There is for Jews no historical association, no intrinsic mysterious importance attached to the basin of the Fitzroy River as there is for the Land of Israel. Without this tremendously powerful factor to bolster flagging spirits, and to make suffering a sacrifice and hardship an inspiration, will they rise above the strangeness of occupation, will they at last adapt themselves to new values, a new way of living, and a new country? If they can, and if it is reasonably believed they can – then my sincere hope is that no obstacles will be permitted to hinder ... the settlers who may want to get away from the nightmare of Central Europe.

In common with other plans that had been advanced, this one also carried the warning that a large concentration of Jews may not pass muster. Thus, Terry proposes that the plan 'for mass colonization will be better received by the Australian government if 40% of intending immigrants are non-Jewish, preferably British. Because naturally no country wishes to foster different communities within its social structure.'

As to the question of whether Jews can rise above the strangeness of a new occupation and adapt themselves to new values, a new way of living, and a new country, the writer is confident they can. He urges: 'No obstacle should hinder any organization with *financial backing* [emphasis added] which may want to prepare such a place and the settlers who may want to get away from the nightmare of Central Europe.' As to the people who unwisely fear that a 'community of Jewish farmers ... might upset the whole of Australia', Terry concedes the perniciousness of the stereotype.

He concludes: 'It has been used to side-track attention from this undeveloped portion of Western Australia.'

Like many other schemes for saving or rescuing Jews, Australia did not come to fruition. By the end of 1938, 3,300 central European immigrants were reported for Australia, and a total of 7,000 Nazi victims (of all kinds) arrived between 1935 and 1940. Secure in its global distance from the 'cosmopolitan culture that created it and sustained it, [Australia] failed in 1938 to follow the motherland in yielding to liberal impulses ... the November *kristallnacht* had no repercussions "down under"'.[12]

Nevertheless, the *Jewish Chronicle* did all a newspaper could to provide support for Jewish farm settlement in Australia and elsewhere. To refute the lie that Jews cannot or will not farm, the *Chronicle* reprinted a survey of Jewish farmers in Galicia, Poland, commissioned by the YIVO Institute for Jewish Research in Vilna in 1936. The most reliable account of Jewish farmers available at that time, the survey results clearly contradict widespread insinuations that Jews refuse to dirty their hands in farm work, a stereotype that has been inimical to them.[13]

[A] census of Jewish farm-holdings in Poland [shows] 124,389 Jews, or 4% of the Jewish population of Poland, are engaged in agriculture. More than half of the Jewish agricultural population is concentrated in Galicia, chiefly eastern Galicia, where about a tenth of the entire Jewish population are deriving their livelihood from the land. In the whole of Poland there are 22,164 Jewish farms, more than half of which are in Galicia, over 5,000 in the eastern provinces of Poland, and about 4,000 in the central provinces.[14]

In the same issue of the *Chronicle* a third story appears indicating happy relations between Jewish and Christian farm boys in England. Fourteen young Austrian, German and Czechoslovakian refugees, all receiving agricultural training at a farm at Hambledon near Henley, were guests of the High Wycombe Young Farmers' Club at their annual dance. According to local reports, the *Chronicle* writes, the refugee boys seemed to have become rapidly acclimatized, for they are said to have joined in heartily with the fun of the dance,

swaggering as blithely as any cockney in the Lambeth Walk and Palais Glide. These homeless youngsters ... are being made to feel thoroughly welcome by the farming community of Buckinghamshire. After they have finished their training, the refugees are to take up farming in the Colonies. The training scheme is under the aegis of the YMCA working in conjunction with the Society of Friends and a Jewish society, and it is hoped that one hundred refugees will be given instruction in the course of a year.

With the manpower of many countries being diverted for military purposes, there was an acute need for inexpensive farm labour to maintain food production. Yet, the rhetoric to deny entry to Jewish refugees seeking such work continued to draw upon old stereotypes. In 1939 Jewish farmers were discussed in Britain's Parliament during a debate to allow refugees to enter the country on agricultural work permits. Apparently, some MPs were sceptical of the plan, whereby 'refugees admitted to the country pending emigration will be allowed to assist in harvesting operations during the summer and autumn months' in those locations where there is a legitimate shortage of agricultural workers *(Jewish Chronicle*, 14 July 1939, p. 14).

A Member of Parliament, Mr Hanna, found the idea offensive and he asked why old England did not follow the example of New England (America) and fill up the 'countryside with really desirable immigrants'?[15] He had an ally in Lady Astor, who resorts to an old cliché: 'Is it not true', she asks, 'that there has been great difficulty in getting Jewish immigrants to go on the land, because the race is not particularly given to agriculture?'

Samuel Hoare, MP, vigorously defended the plan and cited the example of the abandoned and run-down army camp at Richborough. A group of 95 Jewish refugees had been sent to the camp to clean out the rubble, take away the rocks, dig out stumps, and prepare the ground for planting. Within a month the camp had been totally transformed.

But Lady Astor persisted: 'I have been informed that they do not find it easy to get those young men to go upon the land.'

Another MP, Mr D.M. Foote (Liberal), suggested that there was too much emphasis on the Jews. He asks: 'Is it not a fact that there are many refugees not of Jewish origin and should they not be considered also?'

In the same issue of the *Chronicle* there is a story from another part of the world: Slovaks were depriving Jews of their land.[16] Where a tolerant government in the Austro–Hungarian Empire had permitted Jews to own land, the Slovaks in 1939 confiscated Jewish farms and introduced ration cards for the dairy products the farms had formerly provided. The journalist exposes the lie in the assertions that Jews are not farmers:

One of the usual charges made by anti–Semitic demagogues against Jews is that they do not engage in agriculture, conveniently ignoring hundreds of thousands of Jews engaged in agriculture in Palestine, Poland, Argentina, the USSR, Canada and the USA.

By September 1939 Jewish refugees in Britain were reported as helping British agriculture, working at a training farm in Tingrith, near Harlington, Bedfordshire, and establishing good relations with their neighbours. Ninety-three refugees, working under expert guidance, were getting a thorough grounding in all aspects of agricultural work.

> Here refugees are not being dealt with on a charitable, blind-alley basis; they are being taught how to fend for themselves, armed with a knowledge of how to produce the main cereal and market crops and of dairy-farming and poultry-raising. (*Jewish Chronicle*, 1 September 1939, p. 20)

The trainees' first job was 'to revive the neglected fields and restore the run-down buildings [which] they did with energy and imagination'. The 18-month training period was in expectation that 'the refugees will then be able to fill posts in Palestine or overseas'.

In Ireland, 100 Jewish refugees turned a farm at Mill Isle from a derelict estate into a highly prosperous one. They supplied their own food needs and put on the market 45,000 heads of cabbage, 30 tons of potatoes, 16 tons of corn, as well as poultry and eggs (*Jewish Chronicle*, 21 February 1941, p. 22). In January 1944 vacancies existed at Poulton House Farm School in Scotland.[17]

In 1939 the total number of refugees permitted at any one time to be trained on individual farms in England and Wales was limited to 1,000, with an additional 500 allowed training in agricultural institutes. At the time of the *Chronicle* report (8 September), 1,194 permits for visas were applied for and issued but only 960 of the applicants arrived in the UK. One can only guess at the reasons why 234 did not.

A month earlier the *Chronicle* had reported (11 August) that Jewish organizations in Germany were frequently experiencing the greatest difficulty in tracing children for whom permits of emigration had already been obtained, because of their continual wandering from place to place. Whole families were turned out of their flats at a moment's notice and compelled to wander the streets, staying for a night or two with more fortunate friends. It was rarely possible for them to leave Germany in the allotted time. When the permit expired, the children became outlaws and were automatically liable for arrest.

As events in Europe grew more sinister and the need for Jews to leave their homes on the Continent became more pressing, the *Chronicle* continued reporting agricultural opportunities all over the world. For at least a century, small groups of Jews had established farm communities in Argentina, Canada, Palestine and America.

The Hilfsverein der deutschen Juden was founded in 1901 in Berlin as an aid organization to eastern Jews. The initial mission was to help Jews from the east return to their countries of origin.[18] After 1933 the Hilfsverein took on the responsibility of helping émigrés from Germany to go to all countries except Palestine, where they were not permitted to enter, and eastern Europe, from where they could not leave. It obtained immigration permits, found transportation and provided a wide range of financial assistance: travel money, expenses for visas, overseas passage, transportation of household goods, and so forth. It helped more German Jews leave Germany than any other agency. The Hilfsverein and the Jewish Colonization Association (ICA), which was set up by Baron Maurice de Hirsch, settled 'several thousand immigrants' as farmers in the Avigdor colony in Argentina.[19]

At the end of the nineteenth century the ICA established agricultural colonies in Argentina for beleaguered Jews. Of the 79,000 Jews arriving in Argentina between 1918 and 1933, a considerable number entered without valid immigration visas. By 1925 over 20,000 Jews were farming or engaged in agricultural work there. The Hilfsverein der deutschen Juden estimated 4,500 German Jewish immigrants were among the nearly twelve thousand Jewish immigrants who had landed in Argentina between 1933 and 1936.[20]

Other places in South America also hosted Jewish farmers. The Hilfsverein ran its own agricultural training farm in Choele Choele, in the territory of Rio Negro. In Uruguay, with a Jewish population of 30,000, Jews established a farm colony in Tres Arboles, and opened an agricultural school. Bolivia granted a permit of residence to those who entered with an agricultural visa, but for a year only, and this, provided they were effectively engaged in agriculture (*Jewish Chronicle*, 20 October 1939, p. 20).

In trying to plan for refugees, President Roosevelt was instrumental in convening a conference at Evian in July 1938. The conference may have marked a crucial turning point in Germany's attitude towards the Jews, since at this time it became clear that no country was prepared to assume responsibility for Jewish refugees. That being the case, the Germans may have reasoned, no country would care how Germany took care of its unwanted population. Of all the countries represented at the Evian conference, only the Dominican Republic offered to take in refugees.

The United Kingdom advanced a plan for Northern Rhodesia to admit 50,000 refugees during a five-year period. The European members of the Northern Rhodesia Legislative Council opposed the admission of any Jewish refugees, offering as explanation the prohibitive costs involved.[21] Rhodesia agreed to admit a maximum of 150 refugees to be trained for farming, and would start with 25 selected Jews already trained in agriculture (*Jewish Chronicle*, 2 December 1939, p. 17).

Out of sixteen plans advanced for new agricultural settlements, only one, the Sosua Project in the Dominican Republic, materialized. From its initial offer in 1938 to accept between 50,000 and 100,000 refugees, its estimate was continuously revised. In 1940 it reported a potential for 28,000; in 1941 it had an absorptive capacity for 5,000. Eventually 500 refugees settled there.[22]

Only Palestine was eager to settle Jews and support them on the land. But Britain, caught up in its role as policeman of the Middle East, did not permit unlimited immigration to the country. Perhaps to compensate for its obdurate position in the case of Palestine, Britain opened its doors to more refugees than did any other country, proportionate to its size. It is estimated that fully one-quarter of all European Jews who survived the Holocaust, survived in Great Britain.

NOTES

1. See Herbert A. Strauss, 'Jewish Emigration from Germany: Nazi Policies and Jewish Response, (II)', *Yearbook, 1981*, Leo Baeck Institute (London, Jerusalem, New York), pp. 343–409.
2. *Jewish Chronicle*, 25 March 1938, p. 42.
3. Ibid., 5 August 1938, p. 16.
4. Ibid., 2 December 1938, p. 17.
5. P. Alter (ed.), *Out of the Third Reich: Refugee Historians in Post-War Britain* (London, 1998), 'Sidney Pollard, in Search of a Social Purpose', pp. 198–9.
6. Transcript of interview with Esther Golan, 9 June 1995, Jerusalem, author's private collection.
7. Transcript of interview with Paul Cohn, 20 April 1994, London, author's private collection.
8. Interview with Paul Cohn.
9. Strauss, 'Jewish Emigration from Germany', p. 388.
10. *Jewish Chronicle*, 23 December 1938, p. 16.
11. Michael Terry, 'Australia and Jewish Immigration: Changing Opinion in the Southern Continent' and 'The Question of Mass Colonisation: Settler's Psychology All Important', *Jewish Chronicle*, 23 December 1938, pp. 28, 33.
12. Strauss, 'Jewish Emigration from Germany', p. 389.
13. See Gertrude Dubrovsky, *The Land Was Theirs* (Tuscaloosa, 1992), pp. 1–25.
14. *Jewish Chronicle*, 30 December 1938, p. 26.
15. What must be understood is that Jews were not permitted to own land anywhere in the Pale, a large geographical area where 95 per cent of the Jewish population in eastern Europe lived. Without land they could not farm. Nevertheless, the stereotype was repeatedly used against Jews. Eventually, they themselves internalized it; modern Jews will often laugh at the notion of Jewish farmers. The exception, of course, is in Israel, where the idea of reclaiming a country from the ground up is a source of pride. However, Jewish farm communities in the United States, for example, predate the first collective farm or kibbutz in Israel. See Dubrovsky, *The Land Was Theirs*.
16. There is an unintended irony in the remarks of MP Hanna. In the great age of exploration and discovery, England released prisoners and sent them as settlers to the New World.
17. 'Slovak Jews Must Not be Farmers: No Pleasing the Anti-Semites', *Jewish Chronicle*, 14 July 1939, p. 20.
18. Minutes of the Joint Committee for Religious Education and Welfare of Jewish Refugee Children, 5 January 1944, p. 2, University of Southampton, MS 7S/139/1.
19. At the end of the nineteenth century unrelenting pogroms in parts of Poland and Russia produced a wave of westward-bound immigration. In the USA the German-Jewish Board of Delegates, worried about how the new immigrants would affect their own precarious position as new Americans, tried to convince government officials to place more restrictions on immigration as a

way of limiting the numbers of eastern European Jews arriving. See Dubrovsky, *The Land Was Theirs*, note 20, p. 236. The Hilfsverein der deutschen Juden, founded about the same time, was also interested in helping new immigrants return to their countries of origin.

20. See Strauss, 'Jewish Emigration from Germany', p. 371.
201. Ibid., pp. 396–7.
22. Ibid., 'Appendix: Planned Agricultural Settlements, or Settlements with Limited Success', p. 409.
23. See Segal, *Other People's Houses* (New York, 1964).

Letters from Leipzig

CHAPTER NINE

Letters from Leipzig

Much of the real stuff of history comes from events in the lives of ordinary people who generally have very little control over those events. Some 'take arms against a sea of troubles' in an effort to end them; some try to remove themselves from harm's way; some succumb quietly to the inevitable. And some try hard to record their perilous journeys so that others may know.

The letters from Leipzig provide a valuable historic record of extraordinary events affecting ordinary people who had to meet the horrendous challenges of a world gone mad. Innocent families were forced to break up. Parents sent their infant children to strangers in a foreign country, while they desperately searched for some means of survival themselves. Everyone's life depended on luck and the kindness of others. Theirs are not stories written by novelists, yet their struggles are at one and the same time heroic and mundane.

The events in the lives of the six children who arrived in England from Leipzig, and in the lives of their parents, are recorded by them in the letters they wrote as they tried to maintain contact with each other from a distance. The letters – full of longing, pain and love – are from the hands and hearts of desperate people in the midst of an historic struggle. They provide an intimate look at the Schmulevitz family dynamics as they tried to cope with an impossible and insane situation. Their hope for survival rested on the ability of their children from Leipzig negotiating a safe haven in England for their parents. The parents did not survive, but letters they wrote did. Paula Grünbaum Balkin, one of the six from Leipzig, preserved all the letters she received from her family and others while living in England. She has achieved her adult lifetime ambition of publishing her family's story as it is revealed in the treasured notes and letters they wrote to her.[1]

In 1946, a Marta, aka Mariane Mitdank (a Christian woman from Leipzig) began a correspondence with Paula, although the salutation in the first letter included Vera and Edith. None of the six from Leipzig had ever met Marta Mitdank and both Paula and Vera assert that they never had heard of her before she initiated the correspondence. While Mitdank claims to know the family very well, she misidentifies Paula's father, calling him Otto instead of his name, Abraham. According to Mitdank, her motivation for writing was to inform them that she had been a friend of the Schmulevitz family and had tried to help them. She felt an obligation to report to them on the last days of the family in Leipzig. Eventually, Mitdank describes her own difficult situation and her own needs. As she had helped their family, she was now looking for help for herself and her family. Although neither Paula nor Vera had ever met or heard of Mitdank, both responded to her need by sending her packages of food and clothing from America.

Whatever her real motivation was, Mitdank reported on the chaotic situation in Leipzig before, during, and immediately after the war. She obviously was a witness to some horrific scenes in Leipzig and describes them with what appears to be authentic detail.

Her retrospective account starts in 1942. All six Schmulevitz grandchildren were safe in England. But the parents and relatives they left in Leipzig were in peril of their lives. Vera's mother, born in Poland, had been sent back there and had returned to Leipzig; Abraham and Truda Grünbaum had fled, seeking a safe harbour in Hungary, and ended, presumably, in a concentration camp. The children's uncle and aunt, Leo and Eva, were killed in a bombing raid in Kolamea, Hungary; and Abraham Koppold had been arrested and died in Sachsenhausen. Left in Leipzig were Clara Koppold, her sister Yetta Ribetsky, and her mother, Rose Asman Schmulevitz.

At the beginning of January 1942, Clara Koppold and her mother were forced to leave their home and were directed to no. 4 Humbold Strasse, Leipzig. Yetta Ribetski, the oldest Schmulevitz daughter, visited her relatives there. On 21 January 1942, Clara and her mother were among 702 persons put on a transport to 'Riga, Auschwitz, Treblinka'.[2] Somehow Yetta caught up with them; the three were together at their final destination in Riga.[3]

Some of this particular history comes from two letters, dated 15 and 16 October 1946, written to Paula and Vera by Marta Mitdank.[4] Mitdank might have helped the Schmulevitz family send and receive mail to and from their children in England.[5] She claims to have visited Clara Koppold and her mother during their enforced confinement with other Jews from Leipzig at no. 4 Humbold Strasse. She apparently kept track of the Schmulevitz family's movement, whether for altruistic or selfish motives is hard to say. Evidently, she saw some advantage in being involved with the family. After the six from Leipzig emigrated to America, Mitdank wrote to Paula to ask for help. In support of her petition, she reminds them of the help she offered their family. Mitdank obliquely implies that either she or others in her family were Jewish or had Jewish relations. At one point, she says: 'As Jews, we were marked and often visited by the Gestapo. We were always lucky, though we were often called to police headquarters.' At another point, she implies that she and her husband went to 'Jewish streets, and not to be conspicuous, we also wore a [yellow] Jewish star.' While explicitly stating that she is not Jewish, she cryptically suggests a Semitic past. She continued to write to Paula and Vera after they had emigrated to America, and hinted that they might be able to help her also get to America. Her letters in translation follow.

Leipzig, 4 December 1938
[actually 1937 is written, but Vera left in December 1938]
[Following three notes were probably sent in one envelope.]

My dear Vera,
I read your letter today, and rejoice that you arrived well. I hope that you will get used to London very soon. How was your trip and was it boring? Are you living in a house with another person or alone? How are the girls?
You should be happy that you're already away. Our whole group wants to go to Erez, only Ruth and I want to go to America. I don't have anything else to tell you.
With happiest greeting,
From your friend, Bella.

Dear Vera,
I was very happy when I heard from Bella that you arrived safely. You can really consider yourself lucky. That is from my heart; I don't begrudge it. That's all for today.
Your Elsie

Dear Vera,
I was very happy that everything is well with you. Hopefully, you are getting used to life there. Write to us soon about how you are doing. By us, Uncle Leo is proud of your report. Exert yourself that the unimportant mermaids [?] will leave. About that, Uncle Leo eagerly wants to read.
We send you regards lovingly,
Aunt & Uncle, Eva and Leo

Leipzig, 9 December 1938
My dear Vera!
I received your lovely letter. I am quite delighted with it because I could tell

from it that you are doing well. According to your letter, you sent it out on December 6, and I got it on December 8 in the evening. I want to try to fulfil your wish as soon as I can. Warm regards and kisses from your mommy and grandma and everyone else.

Many regards from your Aunt Clara and Uncle Adolf, Harold and Siegmar.

Leipzig, 11 December 1938

My dear Vera,

Today I received your letter, and I was quite astonished to have you write me that I should describe everything to you exactly. I did do that in the letter I wrote on Sunday. Do you still have it? If so, read it through one more time. To turn things around a bit: I would like to ask you to give me a somewhat more exact report. I am already happy with what you write, but so much more can be reported, such as, for example, whether you are well cared for at Miss [Staff's] and where you're sleeping and how the food is. I would also very much like to know how school is and whether you are making a good impression in the household, because you must not forget, my dear child, that you are away from home, which means that you must make a good impression. Did you receive your mail from the [?], because Aunt True and Clara sent a package to you there. Aunt Clara also sent a beautiful birthday card, which will certainly give you pleasure. If you don't have it, make sure to get it. I will send you a knitting book so that you can pick out your pullover for yourself. You just have to give me the page and [?], and then I'll send you the pattern. How about the organization of your things? Is everything put away nicely, including your socks? What kind of socks are you wearing these days? It is surely cold over there and you have enough dresses. Are you wearing your wool skirt? You see, dear Vera, I want to know a great deal more than what you write. Uncle Leo has been back in the community since December 8, and they now live in the 11. It is not clear at this point when Paula and Edith will be travelling. Aunt Clara has had the affidavit since Wednesday, and we cannot say at this point when they will be travelling. I worked at your uncle's house the whole week, because when I get subsidies, and will immediately be brought into compulsory work, which begins at [?] o'clock in the morning. Should I register for it? Grandma's dining room set is sold and already taken out of the room. I am sleeping on the chaise longue so that it doesn't look quite so bad in the room. Grandma and I are in pretty good health, which I hope is the case with you as well. I also wanted to tell you that on Monday I got a clipping from an English newspaper from Mase with you sitting in a coat having coffee and cake right in the front, and on the right side you have a card. Two other girls were sitting next to you. Grandma was so delighted with your note to her.

She was already thinking that since you hadn't addressed anything to her personally, you had forgotten her completely. Please write her every time, a couple of extra lines. I am enclosing your document with your birthday. I have not yet been able to get hold of a Jewish calendar. I will also send you our picture and I hope you like it. With your next letter, include a note for Mrs Schönbradt. I will send you a ruled piece of paper also, so that you will write better, and please make it look nicer next time. For today I have written enough and want to close with the most heartfelt regards and kisses from your mommy.

Your grandma also sends you many regards and kisses. She longs for you so much and would love to help you with your sweater. Uncle Leo, Aunt Eva, Aunt Trude, and Uncle Abram as well as Paula and Edith, Aunt Clara, and Uncle Adolf and Harold and Siegmar in addition to the Schönbradt family all send their greetings and wish you all the best. Good night.

[along margin of first page:]

Please give the Staff family my regards. I would like to write them a few lines; will they [Xerox is cut]

Leipzig, 12 December 1938

My dear child!
I am sending this card along with a sewing book with patterns. When you find something you like, you need to trace it and cut it out. I hope you find something to your liking. I have also included the book Goldkäppchen, which you can explain to the little girl. Yesterday I sent you a picture. Please make a note on it, which I forgot to do. The picture is from 30 November 1938. I'm at Aunt Clara's. Siegmar is sleeping and Harold is playing outside. Your aunt and uncle are in the shop; they are taking inventory. Have you already taken care of your mail, which [?] and have you already written to [?]? I can't tell you yet when Paula and Edith will travel.

Many regards and kisses from your mommy, grandma, and all the others. Many cordial greetings to the Staff family.

Berlin, 16 December 1938

My dear child,
As you can see from the card, I am in Berlin. I was called [?] a man by means of Ribet. Please write to them for help for your grandma and mommy. You have the address. When I get home, I will answer your letter. I hope you are doing very well. In the meantime, warm regards and kisses from your mommy.

[in a different handwriting]

*My dear child, I hope you like London. [?] a happy future and perhaps
[?]*
Best wishes, Josef [?]

Leipzig, 2 [22?] December 1938

My dear Vera,
*When I came home on Sunday evening, I found your lovely card and letter
waiting for me. I was quite delighted about it. It was very nice in Berlin. Did
you receive our picture in the meantime? On Monday I sent you the pattern
you wanted and your wool socks. I hope you have them by now. It was also
quite cold here and we have quite a bit of snowfall and no coal, which is also
hard to get in this weather.*
   *I sold your bicycle for 15 marks and right away got myself a pair of shoes
with that money. Uncle Adolf's store is still closed and he will board it up,
I can't tell you how, so I worked with him. I am sending you the address of
Uncle Sam and I ask you please to write him a very sensible letter about me
and your grandma so that he calls for both me and grandma as soon as possible so that we can get out and come to take you with us, which is certainly
your wish as well. I am enclosing a Jewish calendar as well.*

Mr Sam Ribet
New York
Style art [?] 79 5 Ave.
USA

*Are you dressing up nice and warm? I would also like to hear whether you
have organized your things yet. You can already do somewhat more work
than just washing the dishes. It would certainly not be a mistake if you were
to do it. When you write, please write more clearly. Surely you have enough
time. And don't make so many mistakes. Aunt Eva and Uncle Leo are
temporarily living in the 11; they will definitely move to the Grünbaums.
We also unfortunately have two back rooms free and are weighing the idea
of subletting. Your grandma cries every time she sees a letter from you. She
misses you terribly. Our schools are still closed. Paula and Edith often go to
the nursery school. For today I'll close this letter because I don't know what
else to write you. Many, many regards and kisses from your mommy and
grandma. Everyone sends their regards. Is the watch still working? Are you
wearing the silver necklace and the coral necklace?*

The Schönbradt family also sends regards.

Leipzig, 30 December 1938

My dear Vera,

This time I had to wait a pretty long time to get a letter from you. I was already getting worried about you. I completely lost my peace of mind. Actually I was quite happy about your letter, but my joy would have been ever greater if you had been clever enough to send me at least a little picture of yourself for Chanukah. It was such a small thing for you and a joy for me. You'll soon have more income per week than I do, but please don't fritter away anything, because you know how times are, and we have learned how to keep hold of our money. What kind of silver shoes did you get? I ask you to be nice and obedient so that people also are nice to you, and don't forget that I like to see that you're neat. Are you wearing the wool coat and are you using the socks? Do you wear long ones now? How big is the neckline in your party dress? Please pay attention to errors when you're writing, otherwise my daughter will embarrass me, and you don't want to do that. Dear Vera, I am sending you the address of Uncle Sam [Ribets?], New York, USA [?] 5th Ave. He is the oldest brother of your papa and wants to help me to get away from here. I also wrote to him about grandma. You should write to him in the same spirit as you felt before your left. I hope you understand me. I cannot express this more clearly. Can you communicate with Lotte better now? Doesn't Lotte have a father? Please give the whole family my regards. Dear Vera, please write soon and you get warm regards and kisses from your mommy, who would love to see you. Grandma and all of your aunts and uncles as well as your cousins send their regards. What colour is your party dress? In London, are green and pink popular? What does your hairdo look like?

Many regards and kisses.

Leipzig, 10 January 1939, 9.30 in the evening

My dear Vera,

Now that it is so quiet around here, since grandma is upstairs, I want to answer your letter. The Rotensteins are upstairs as well, and I sent your regards to them. They send their regards to you too. In the last letter, I had only forgotten to mention that I received the stamps, but they are once again already used. Dear child, I also received the English letter from the Staffs, which made me extremely happy because I am starting to get some hope for a better life if things work out. Dear Vera, in the letter I had asked the Staffs to help me get a job. Would I need a security for that? Isn't it possible for these people to get me a work somewhere? I have heard something about a Wolpern [Woburn] House that gets people work. Mrs Hurwitz read the letter out loud to me and then wrote a reply to it. Who is Miss Keller? Can't you speak to her and tell her that your mommy would be willing to do any *kind of work? What kind of school are you attending, and please make sure that you can pick something up while you are listening. Pay careful attention when you cook not to make things look sloppy when it's your turn to cook. I was terribly happy about your package sent as a free sample, or did this come from the Staffs? The reason I don't know is that a letter [?] and name of them was in it. If this is the case, please don't forget to thank them for me; otherwise, I thank you with all my heart for this. Today I went to get my forms stamped; I hope that I will get support. Aunt Clara also told me that she is writing you a letter. I also get quite a bit of mail from the Schreiers. They always ask about you. If you can, please write them a card some time. One child or another of theirs is always sick. The address is: J. Schreier, Krakow, Poland, Dietta 74 le Nattel. They will certainly be delighted. I have not heard from Helmut in a long time and don't know what's going on with him. I have also written to America and am waiting for mail from there as well. How are all of your things? Have you organized everything? Can't you be a little more hardworking with your pullover? As far as your not feeling like doing it, what do you mean by that – you have to make yourself like work, and then everything works out. You absolutely cannot imagine how much Paula would like to leave. There is no school here yet. Goldscher is not here yet either. He is still on vacation and no one knows when he will be returning. Zelasek was also here, and no one can do anything for him. Uncle Leo now has a great deal of work to do in the [Jewish] community because the subsidies are paid out from upstairs. Grandma, however, comes at the old place; isn't that great? Your letter was censored because it was too long, apparently. You must use a larger envelope, or are you out of them? Otherwise I can't really think of anything else to write. Warmest regards from your mommy and grandma, who would love to see you. Please give Miss Staff our regards and give her the reply. Mrs Hurwitz does all of that for me, isn't that nice of her? Stay healthy and write soon.*

[along the side margin] *Everyone sends their regards; I'm going to the train now.*

Leipzig, 15 January 1939
Sunday, 3 o'clock in the afternoon

My dear child,
This morning I received your letter with great joy. I hope you enjoyed yourself at the party. How happy and proud I would be to have seen my child in her first party dress, how she wore her hair and whether she has everything else in perfect order. But I must be satisfied with being happy to know that she is with such cordial people, who take care of her like her own

mother. The book Elisabeth is from Aunt Clara. I will give her thanks from you. I found the stamp in the letter. The Schreiers' address is: Dietla 74 [?]. I think that you gave the English supplement to Miss Staff. Nothing is mentioned in the letter. Has any action been taken? You cannot imagine how much grandma and I are counting on your help. On Wednesday, Jan. 18, I will be getting the first support payment. I don't know how much it will be. [?] I have the address of this uncle, if you write them a very sharp letter, perhaps they will help him to get out. The address: Mr L. [Evelyn?], London, Clapton 65, Moresby 1 [rest of address is illegible]

(reverse side of card)

My dear Vera,
I have no news as yet from America. Every day I count on mail. Can you communicate with Lotte yet? Have you begun work on your pullover? If not, do start it soon, otherwise the winter will be over and you have the knitting wool. In the next letter I would like you to include a few lines from Schaubradts. They would be very happy. Grandma, Uncle Leo, Aunt Eva, Uncle Abram and Aunt Trude, Paula, Edith, Aunt Clara and Uncle Adolf and [?] and I send you many thousand regards and kisses.

> *Leipzig, 6 February 1939*
> *Evening at 10 o'clock*

My dear Vera,
This morning Grandma brought me your eagerly awaited letter. She could hardly wait until I opened it, because I have been for 8 days at Aunt Clara's. First, your picture fell into my hands. The joy, you simply can't imagine, but the women understood. Finally, Aunt Clara said she excited herself too much. Then we came to your dear letter, which we, of course, had not forgotten. With wonder, after the picture she [Grandma?] looked somewhat [bad? Ill?]. Is this [?] the situation?

My dear Vera, you can't think how happy I am for you, that your wishes came true, and that you find distraction in this joy. Don't worry about us, because we do [not?] want it to change. [Do not be impatient. It's not that we don't want it to change.] We have to wait for help, that hopefully will come soon. Our God still lives, and about that, dear Vera, please, I ask you, pull yourself together and leave our fate to the future. Keep your strength up, and I must ask you to look after your health. Don't drink any water when you are overheated.

You know that I always worry about your health, and that you are my one and only, and I have had no [other] joy from my life. I have also been happy about your steps forward in school, and I hope that I hear good news from you. I believe that you were happy about the blouse, you always liked it. I also think that your sweater will be done this year.

Dear Vera, we are healthy as always, only that this week I am nervous [excitable] because the three kids were difficult. Siegmar is today very much out of sorts, and still does not want to sleep. He complains of pain (Weh-Weh) that isn't there and he wants to be with mommy, where Pippi is.

Have you heard anymore about our stuff? I am very worried about how things are dragging on [langen]. There is no hope at hand. The only saviour [?] and help may come from London. Otherwise, I don't know what will be. Have you heard anything? It looks like it will not be easy to overcome.

Say, Vera, how do you like yourself in the long dress and the shoes with the red shoelaces? You would look like a little lady. And the beautiful ring should replace the watch. I think you look thinner, but perhaps it is the picture which makes you look like that. Today, Grandma cried more than she laughed over your letter and picture, but you are not aware of it.

Dear Vera, I still have to make it to the mailbox on Konigsplatz. I will end now with heartfelt regards and kisses. Your mother, who sleeps with you tonight. Also, from your Grandma I send you a thousand greetings and kisses, and the same from all the others: also Frau Schönbrod who sends regards to you and the same from Frau Menz.

Leipzig, 11 February 1939
7 o'clock in the evening

My dear child,
I received your lovely letter. Did you also see yourself in the film? Everything is the same as ever with me. Have you written to Helmut and the Schreiers yet? On the [?] you drew a beautiful flower pot, which Harold tore out right away and put it on the night table of Aunt Clara, who, thank God, is in good health. I really hope that in the matter of [Mr Gold?] some help comes along, because I cannot do anything further on my own now. I feel terribly sorry for him. My dear child, I still have hope that I will be travelling; have you heard anything? Mrs Schönbradt, Paula, Aunt Trude, and Edith are visiting at Aunt Clara's right now. Aunt Clara is already up and about to some extent; although she is weak, she is out of bed, thank God. I hope that you have already received something from me and Grandma, which will certainly make you happy.
With warm regards and kisses from
Your Mommy

[Reverse side of card]

Regards and kisses from Grandma.

My dear Vera! Now I know that you have received my package and I will send you another one on Monday. You only need to write Mommy to let her know whether you have received it, but do answer Paula soon. Many regards from me and all other [?]. [Lora?] Grünbaum. Wait! Now I know who Zilla got her nose from. Next time [?] your Clara, Uncle Adolf, Harold, [?] and Zilla send their regards.
[?]

Leipzig, 17 February 1939; Friday afternoon

My dear Vera!
I received your lovely letter and was happy that you got the blouse and the nightshirt. I was starting to get worried whether they would arrive. The nightshirt is from grandma, as you had already correctly guessed. Aunt Trude told me that she sent you a pair of socks. I did not send that package and I didn't see any socks or else I would have known more details about it. I will not ask her, as you can imagine. This letter will arrive one day later. I can't do anything about that because Paula brought it to your aunt on Thursday evening. Today I have enclosed a letter in English for Miss Staff in which I tell her about myself and provide her with Langen's address. I will write Helmut's address for you again: Pzustak [?], Lodz Legielusiana [?] Ul. 25 u 41, c/o [?] Assmann.

The address of the Schreiers is: Schreier le Nattel, Krakow, Dietla 74. Write soon.

I spoke to Bella's mother. She told me that you wrote to Bella. I was quite happy that you wrote the girl already. As for the English letter from Mrs Staff, I had gotten up my hopes, first that maybe some help will come for Langen and for me some prospect of getting out of here. Dear Vera, Paula gave me what she wrote so I could read it. I would like to ask you on her behalf: if you can help this girl, please do so. It makes no difference where she goes, just that she gets out of here because they have no understanding. So I am asking you to help this child on my behalf. Harold was delighted with your vase and said: 'well, she can keep sending me things like that.' Siegmar and the doll [Zilla] are doing quite well. When you see that, it gives you so much pleasure. Grandma was here this afternoon and I had to read your letter to her again. [?] a letter to you is already on the way. She is already counting the days until the answer comes. Otherwise everything here is more or less fine. The rooms are rented and grandma at least doesn't have to worry about that. Please write me a bit more in the next letter, about the way you live and how you spend your days. Hugs and kisses, many thousands of them from your mommy, and grandma tells me to give you the same from her.

[Different handwriting]

Dear Vera!
I am hereby confirming once again that the doll [Zilla] has a wide nose like
you. Of course she could still change. What else are you doing? You never
write me details about yourself, and I was quite surprised about your
handwriting. It doesn't look like the handwriting of a child any more, but it
does have to become more even. I have nothing new to report about us. We
are living from one day to the next and in great uncertainty.

Many regards and kisses, Your Aunt Clara, Uncle Adolf, Harold,
Siegmar and Zilla.

Harold was really delighted with your letter.

Leipzig, 25 February 1939, 9 in the evening
My dear Vera!
This morning I received your lovely letter. It just got somewhat delayed; I
would have expected it sooner. You know how I anxiously wait for mail, and
you are the same way. Paula received your letter, and you surely have her
reply by now. In my last letter I had put in an English enclosure for Miss
Staff. Has something been done about it? In the matter of Langen: he is still
there. Dear Vera, I got the address of Helmut's sister Dora in London from
Helmut. I tried writing a card and to my delight I received an answer from
her. I had asked her to look around for a job for me, which she has certainly
done. She sent a form for me to fill out from the [Jewish?] community. I
have to sign it and send it back together with 3 photos. She added that I
should be able to be there in about 8 weeks if things work out well. Tomorrow
I'm going to send her everything and I think I did the right thing. On the
form, I listed Miss Staff as a reference. You will also be receiving a little
picture of me, of course – will that make you happy? I hope that everything
proceeds as rapidly as possible because I was at the authorities today because
I was asked to come. They noted down who is still there among those slated
to be deported, and I think that in the near future something like this can
happen again. For this reason I'm in a hurry. There is still no notice
concerning grandma, she probably won't be considered. I will also write you
the address of Dora, Helmut's sister, Mr J. Binke, London Nr. 15, 19
Vartry (?) Road, Stamford Hill.

Dora is also asking for your address, which I will send her – is that OK?
Because she wrote that she would want to visit you. You do, of course, know
how it was, and right up to your departure you experienced everything along
with us, so I would advise you to write about all of it to her, including every-
thing about Uncle Leo and your Aunt, because I want Aunt Eva as well as
Leo to be able to come along as quickly as possible, because your uncle is also

going to lose his job. Uncle Abram has been doing compulsory work since Monday, so there is less complaining, right? I've spent the second night in a row at grandmas because I would finally like to get a good night's rest. The doll [Zilla] often cries during the night and when you've been working the whole day, you'd like to rest up at night. Harold was quite delighted with your vase; when something comes from you, he turns red with pleasure. I have mail from America, full of complaints, but how can I help out there? They also mentioned you and Miss Staff, which upset me, because the letter was written in Yiddish and Mrs Schönbradt read it. It was in real Yiddish, and is not appropriate for our difficult times. Now, dear Vera, the sandman is coming to me, so I'll close this letter. Lots of warm regards and kisses from your mommy and grandma. Everyone else sends their regards. Mrs Schönbradt, Mrs Menz, and all of our good friends send their regards. Good night!

Leipzig, 1 March 1939

My dear Vera,
Today I got your lovely letter and I am very sorry that you can no longer receive these little things. I'm hoping for good luck so that I will be able to see you soon. Today and tomorrow I am being tested in housekeeping and cooking and then the certificate is issued in order to get me a job, so I'll keep this letter brief, because I'm quite tired. Grandma sent you the nightshirts. I hope you did not need to pay any additional charges. You haven't mentioned anything about your spring coat; have you gotten it? Uncle Abram's brother and sisters are also coming to the fair on Thursday. I am now at Aunt Clara's house and am going to put your card right into the mailbox so that you will get news promptly. Otherwise I wouldn't know what else is new to report, so here are many warm regards and kisses from me and grandma.
    Your mommy

Dear Vera!
I also don't want to miss the opportunity send you my best regards. Little Zilla makes a commotion at night and sleeps during the day. Many regards from all of us.
    Your Aunt Clara

Leipzig, 9 March 1939

My dear Vera,
Finally I have mail from you. Every day I have been waiting for the mailman, but only in vain. I passed my exam with flying colours. On Thursday I sent off my application, report card, and cover letter and am anxiously awaiting the answer. Uncle Abram's brother and his wife are here

from Poland. I have mail from Dora. She wrote that she is expecting my papers, but they were already gone. She also asked for your address and she thought that I didn't want her to visit you because I had forgotten to send her your address. You must certainly have an answer to your letter by now. They also wrote me in German. Have you heard anything concerning the matter of [Mr Gold?]. Doesn't he have any help yet? I was happy to hear that you have your coat and I want you to wear it in good health; I would like to put aside this worry at the very least. Please write me soon, somewhat more about what you are doing. You certainly have more to write. Describe the area where you're living and the walks you take or how you are communicating with others. With all of this waiting around for you to write, grandma forgot to drink her coffee this morning. Paula is sleeping with me this week because of the house guests. Edith's birthday is on Sunday. On Sunday, Harold travelled alone [?] to grandma with the [?]; how do you like that? Zilla is doing fine. We couldn't travel yet because of the weather. Would you like to go bicycling and roller-skating? Answer this question and don't forget. Otherwise everything is as always. The warmest regards and kisses from your mommy, grandma, all of your aunts and uncles, cousins as well as our friends.

Leipzig, 12 March 1939; 6 p.m.

My dear Vera!

Today I was absolutely delighted to get your detailed answer. I went to Edith right away to congratulate her. Then she showed me your card with indescribable joy. She received a nice card from Paula, but she said to Paula: Vera's card pleases me the most. Grünbaum's visitors have already left. We also have April weather here, but we can't change the weather and will have to wait until it's nicer. I was quite annoyed that you lost a year. You probably have a big gap; couldn't it be [?]? What's going on with your knees? Are you in pain again? How is your comprehension these days; are you getting better at understanding Lotte? And the boys and the family itself? Should I send you gloves to go with your coat, as well as for Lotte? I would like to give you something nice. I hope that I can accomplish what I set out to do, but you must have some patience. It's always the same old story and no one has made any progress. I spoke to Bella's mommy. Ruth should be travelling on March 13 to Poland [?] and Bella herself has also come down with a cold. Lippmanns' address in Volkowsilaus [Vilnius?], Lithuania is Turgavite 262. Have you also written to Helmut and Schreier? Why the bad penmanship; were you in a big hurry? Today I did the laundry for the first time since October and I am very exhausted and I am writing you nonetheless right away so that you won't be concerned. I am going to close my letter, and send regards and kisses until there is good news soon.

Your mommy, and grandma also sends you the same regards. The Herwalds, Grünbaums, [?], Goldkrauses and [Lessdowskis?].

14 March 1939

Dear Vera!
We were grateful to receive your last letter. But unfortunately I did [not?] get around to answering it right away and in the evenings I am very tired. To make up for it, I am sending you two little pictures of our kids, which will certainly cheer you up. It is so lucky for us that your mommy comes to see me every afternoon and helps me out with all kinds of things; otherwise I don't know how I would manage. When she goes to London, which I very much hope, I will really miss her. Your mommy gives me all of your letters to read. I am so happy that you are enjoying school and that you have made a lot of progress in English; keep up with it. As far as the climate goes, dear Vera, take special care not to catch a cold. Don't make your mommy worried about that, and all the rest of us too. You wrote me about an English special-ity, 'fish and chips'. Is that something you buy ready-made or do you have to prepare it yourself? According to my dictionary, it is fish and roasted potatoes. Is that correct? Your writing has improved remarkably. I now want to close because Zilla has been making life very difficult for me this afternoon, making it impossible for me to continue writing a letter. Stay healthy and accept our warmest regards and kisses from your Aunt Clara, Uncle Adolf, Harold, Siegmar, and Zilla. The Koppold family.

[Handwriting now changes]

My dear Vera,
Since I am at Aunt Clara's house and there is still space on the paper, I also want to write you a few lines because you will see that I am always think-ing of you. I can report to you that last night Paula was at the departure of the train for the trip to Palestine, Ruth as well, and also Horst Rotenstein. Now all of the Rotenstein children are gone. This week the bride got married in London and the dressmaker also went to London. Yesterday, Uncle Abram got a letter from his brother Chaim in Canada that gave him great cause for hope. God willing, he and his family may really make it there. That would be great, wouldn't it? Siegmar and Harold are eating their dinner and are making quite a racket. I'm going to put them to bed in a minute. Then it will be quiet right away and that's a nice feeling. It is time to stop writing now, regards and kisses from your mommy, who is longing for you. And I must report that the same goes for grandma, who also sends you her warmest regards and kisses.

[Author's note: the right margin of this letter is cut off, and the left margin has several blots, so that restoration of the full text without the original is not possible.]

Leipzig, 19 March 1939; 5 o'clock p.m.

My dear Vera!
Yesterday I received your lovely letter. I was not very happy to learn from it that your knees are causing you pain again. Are you in great pain? Do try to keep them warm; you know that warmth has always helped. It has already been 14 days since I sent the papers to [?] and still there has been no word. I don't know what to think. I already have my certificate of a clean record, and it will already run out on the first of [?] if I don't have a permit by then. It will run out and take a while until I get it. I had thought that you had already taken care of the mail, but what for a long time [?]. The fact that you are going to the theatre [?]. I hope you are understanding something and are learning something in the process. What has happened with Paula's case? She does need a claim, or, to put it better, a guarantee. It does have to happen soon, because Paula will turn 15 soon and then she will need a permit. However, she will only get that if she has a position. So, please take care of this; it is urgent. I have nothing further to report to you from here, only my general wish, which you know about. Otherwise, nothing is new, my dear Vera, other than that I expect good news from you soon. Regards and kisses from your mommy and grandma, all of your aunts and uncles as well as your cousins.

Leipzig, 25 March 1939

My dear Vera!
Last Friday I received your lovely letter [?], which made me very happy to hear that you have visitors from London. You must have been pleased by that, weren't you? Did they bring you something? You cannot imagine how proud of this niece Uncle Leo was when he read that you are helping him out. Do you always have to walk a long distance, since you're feeling pain in your knees, or is it the climate that you need to get used to? Have you tried to treat the pain with heat? My dear child, I beg of you not to take so much to heart that you have no leather. It's not the worst thing. Many people would be happy to be able to hold the leather the way you can. We do have to realize that God wants things to be this way, otherwise He would have made things turn out differently for us. So we need to console ourselves with hope for a better future. Have you gotten mail from anyone? Harold is planning to come to the school on Gustav Adolf Street on April 12. That's a long way, isn't it? Zilla is a charming child and is thriving. Today is the first nice day in a long time, and Harold has been with us since early in the

day. He is playing with the children in the yard. He loves to come alone, and when he has finished walking, we call up Aunt Clara. Siegmar always cries terribly when his big brother goes. He can already say many different words. Mrs Schönbradt came upstairs today and asked about you; the next time you write, add a few lines for her, if you have the patience to do so. Please write me more details about your things and about your life, as well as more specifics about the other people there. At the moment, I can't write anything very specific about myself, since my days are spent in ways that are already familiar to you. Warm regards and kisses from your mommy and grandma and [Magda?], we are just about to go out. Uncle Leo, and Aunt Eva, the Grünbaum family, and the Koppolds as well as all of your friends send their best.

Leipzig, 1 April 1939

My dear Vera,

I received your lovely letter on Friday afternoon. The postage stamp is marked from Norwich on March 30, so the delay is not on this end. Today, Saturday, I got a letter from Dora, in which she urgently asks for the certificate of birth and the doctor's form. I got examined by the doctor today and am sending the papers along immediately. Maybe it won't be too much longer now and I can see you soon, and how beautiful you look with your hairdo. Lange was released on March 20, under the condition that he emigrate, and he will travel in mid-April to Shanghai with the chief executives of his town, who were together with him. Your teacher [?] also went there. I wonder whether he will also become a teacher there? I saw Bella and she told me that she wrote you twice already, but did not get any news. I gave her your exact address. Surely by now you have mail from her. The fact that you are using the money from Dora for practical purposes made me happy. I can imagine you in your new coat and shoes as a little lady already. My fantasy tells me that you have grown somewhat slimmer. Dear Vera, please don't get so concerned about us. We will celebrate the Passover holidays as best we can. We have gotten limited quantities of matzzos from the Jewish community. As soon as I can, I will send you a garter belt and a pair of slippers. Everyone was delighted to read your letter, and I think that everyone will be writing to you. The Schönbradts' son Fritz has already been gone for 6 weeks and his mother has not heard anything from him yet. She is quite worried. I hope that she will soon hear good news.

For now I send my warmest regards and kisses from your mommy and grandma. [?] a very healthy Passover. Everyone sends their best wishes.

Leipzig, 4 April 1939, 9 in the evening

My dear Vera,

I received your letter of January 2. It was a bit on the short side, but I was happy that you answered me so quickly. Since you were so absolutely delighted about the book from your uncle, why didn't you add a few extra lines? He has already been saying that he has earned it. As you already know, they are now living at the Grünbaums', so if you can, write to them specially. The calendar is from Aunt Eva. Here it is very muddy these days, but it is no longer cold. There was also quite a bit of snow here. I also wrote to New York, to our uncle and to the grandparents. I hope to have good news because my situation is quite desperate. I am not getting any support, not even from the [Jewish] community, and no subsidies. In this letter I am enclosing a letter from the Staff family. I had Mrs Hurwitz write it in English. In this letter, I also ask them to help me if they can. I said in the letter that they might be able to lodge me as a domestic or some kind of household employee somewhere. But of course I can't leave grandma alone; she would have to come along. Dear Vera, since you already know the contents of the English letter, I think that you will also figure out how to get your mommy and grandma out of here as quickly as possible. The schools for you are still closed. We began the new year in complete desperation. I was at the train station when [the Simons?] travelled away. I spend a lot of time with Aunt Clara. Your uncle is also always there because the shop is closed and all the other shops are closed as well. Harold and Siegmar are two wonderful boys. You should see how Siegmar can [?]. It is really terrific to see this. Soon they will probably have to have the [?]. You wrote your letter in a beautiful handwriting, but the errors, Vera! You tell me that you never write letters using capital letters, but please try to concentrate on your writing more. You know, of course, when a letter from you comes everyone wants to see it and then I get ashamed when I find those mistakes you make. Edith is going to the nursery school, from 8 in the morning to the afternoon, and the children learn only English there. Well, when I am together with my Vera, she will teach me English, won't she? At our house, the rooms of the Italians were unoccupied. Yesterday, when the rent had to be paid, someone came and rented. You can imagine grandma – how happy she was. I went right to the landlady and paid the rest. Well, now I have written you enough for today and you can't complain. Dear Vera, many warm regards and kisses, and stay healthy –

Your mommy

Many regards and kisses from your grandma, who cries every time we get a letter from you.

Your aunts and uncles and cousins also send their regards.

Leipzig, 7 April 1939
Friday afternoon

My dear Vera!
I received your lovely letter and was happy to hear that you are well. Grandma got your birthday card and was extremely happy about it. You can imagine that she didn't spare any of the women from admiring it. She longs to see you so terribly. Otherwise nothing around here has changed as yet. For the moment, everything is the same as always. I am awaiting notice any day now, because I don't know how I can carry on. You need a great deal of patience to wait. I haven't had any news from America in quite a long time. I also wrote to Uncle [Schimen?] in December and to this day have not received any answer. Were you able to write a Yiddish letter anyway? Don't forget to describe your vacation to me. As to your telling me that you have not gotten thinner, I was pleased, because I don't want you to become thin. You should always remain nice and chubby for me. Don't be surprised that they are going to the place where your teacher went. There is no other way there and those who left have to leave. I have mail from [Lauteff?]. He wrote me that he also had mail from you. He was very happy about it. Helmut wrote me the same thing. That is everything for today.

Warm regards and kisses from me and grandma, Your mommy

Leipzig, 17 April 1939

My dear Vera!
Today I received your lovely letter and I can report to you that all of us are well at the moment. Your uncle was quite delighted with your letter. I was even more delighted with my daughter, and you can believe me how proud I was of my girl, and I hope that we will continue to have pleasure from you. Your grandma also shed a few tears while reading your letter aloud, because she too longs to see you, as I have already told you. But dear Vera, we have to pull ourselves together, because you hope, as we also do, that things will change. Aunt Clara told me that she wrote you a card. I imagine you have it already. I can tell you that the children are terrific. Siegmar has short hair and looks great, and he babbles about all kinds of things already. Mrs Schönbradt was here earlier today just when your letter came, and she sends her regards. Hans is in Sweden and we have heard nothing from Fritz for 6 weeks, which makes her very unhappy. The school is only for general students; everything is together on Gustav Adolf Street. Uncle Adolf brings Harold to school. I get to Aunt Clara's house less often these days, because I am organizing everything for myself. I am learning some of the English. [Note: this last sentence is written in English!] Straight away [?] about the mother spoken girl [note again: text is in English here!] Paula is now

taking care of a little girl and again has a little pocket money. Now, dear Vera, I also sent you a garter belt and two blouses, as well as some books. I hope that everything arrives without your having to pay additional costs. For today, I send you my warm regards and kisses from your mommy. Grandma also sends her best wishes and kisses. From the Schönbradts, [?] as well as all your other acquaintances, best wishes. Your relatives will write to you themselves.

Vilko ... [Vilnius? Lithuania], 19 April 1939

Dear Vera!
Received your card, which made me tremendously happy that you are well. I have heard from your mama that she is preparing to travel to you too. It will be good when she comes. Otherwise things are well with you. I am quite astonished by your good and factual writing, and ask you please to write more often. Have you heard anything from Paula? As the Grünbaums wrote, she is also supposed to have gone to England. I have no news to report about myself. Be healthy and [?] [Illegible signature]

[*Note:* This is a poor Xerox throughout, which cuts off the right margin. I have speculated on the meanings of some words, and indicated other gaps with brackets.]

Leipzig, 24 April 1939, 10 p.m.

My dear Vera!
I received your lovely letter today and was quite delighted to learn that you are well, thank God. I can say the same for us. Thank God we are all right in terms of our health. You will be surprised to hear that I am writing to you so late. I am sitting on Aunt Trude's chaise longue and I have your letter on my lap, because the men are playing cards, as usual, and I am passing the time [?] and am thinking of my child. This afternoon I was in town with Paula for a while, and then we made a stop at Aunt Clara's. Yesterday the weather wasn't good enough to go out. Your aunt was especially happy because Uncle Adolf had flown out and your aunt was alone with the children. Harold is doing quite well in school. I got a school picture from Aunt Clara. Dear Vera, I am sending you the picture and I hope that it gives you pleasure and when I come to my child, I will also be able to look at our dear Harold on the picture. Mrs Schönbradt was here this morning. She was able to show us a picture of the house. He is now in Sweden and works in a (gardening) nursery. He is doing well. Unfortunately there is no news from Fritz yet. She left me with many regards for you. Paula has a new job in an Irish [the word could also be read as: Aryan] cleaning company as an errand girl and doing easy sewing jobs. Every evening her

*muscles ache, because you don't get paid for nothing. Pretty soon she will be
earning 9 [?] per week; isn't that nice?*

*Dear Vera, I was so sorry that Miss Staff had to incur so many extra
expenses and that she has, unfortunately, not been thanked properly thus far.
Unfortunately, I can't do anything about that, because I saw Dora 23 years
ago and don't know how things are there. But the way of the world is that
ingratitude is the universal reward. I also don't know what to think about
the fact that Dora got my document and birth certificate 3 weeks ago
already and there is still no answer. You cannot imagine how worried that
makes us. It wasn't so bad, but my passport ran out in February and will not
be renewed until I can produce an emigration document. Otherwise I will be
declared stateless, and I would like to avoid that. Now you know the reason
for my concern. How are things coming along with you? Are you getting
along in the inhuman heat? How does your skirt look? Do you have more
mail from America? I have nothing from either Uncle Shimen or from the
parents. I imagine you can communicate with Lottie quite well. How are
things with the boys, whom you haven't mentioned in your letters at all, and
Mr and Mrs Staff? Are you still happy there?*

*Now, dear Vera, I want to close this letter with the warmest regards and
kisses from me and grandma. Many regards to the Staff family. Your
mommy and grandma. Everyone sends their regards and kisses.*

Leipzig, 29 April 1939; 8 p.m.

My dear Vera!

*Today I received your lovely letter. Also, a card came from your grandpar-
ents and a letter from Helmut, who also sent us a little picture. Helmut
already wishes he could be away from that place and he thinks that he will
be able to come back to Leipzig for a short time. Also, he believes that he will
travel to London. There is no good news concerning your dear grandparents,
because the father is, unfortunately, sick. Your dear cousins Paula and
Edith were terribly happy to get your message and they will write to you
specially. Harold was also quite proud that his Vera wrote him a letter. Herr
Wiesner, who gave me lessons, had to read the letter from Harold right
away, and he said that 'it was from my Vera'. I feel that you have nothing
to fear in your case. I'm begging of you to keep warm for now and dispense
with some of your gymnastics, and if it doesn't get better, then you had better
find a doctor. I do hope, however, that it gets better by itself. I don't have
much news to write about me and grandma. Thank God we are healthy. The
Schreiers also got mail this week, he sent a little picture of the 3 boys. They
also look well, thank God, and little Karl is recuperating in [?]. Uncle
Abram's brother was in Krakow and visited them. They were very happy
and he was able to send best wishes from us. After all, we long for every*

person that we have come to love. The incident with the boy in Hamburg is very regrettable. I hope that by the time you get my card he is better. Dear Vera, I am asking you to be cautious and make sure that you don't catch a cold in the bad weather, because then Miss Staff will certainly be [?]. That's enough for today. I send my warmest regards and kisses from your mommy and grandma. Everyone sends regards and kisses. Mrs Schönbradt sends her best.

[Upside down, top of first page of letter]

Regards also from Mrs [Heilung?]

Leipzig, 12 May 1939

My dear Vera,

I was overjoyed to get your lovely letter this morning. When I read it to grandma, including the part you wrote to her, she ran to the bathroom and had a good cry, just the way little Vera would do it, isn't that true? Aunt Trude gave me two books, which I will be sending you soon for Aunt Trude. But since I gave your shoes to Bella, I have been weighing this in my mind and bought you a pair that I found on the way to Aunt Clara and I had them on the whole afternoon at your aunt's house, so I will most likely be able to send them to you tomorrow. Did you receive those peppermint sucking candies last week, which you love so much? I sent you a few to give you my regards. Harold already goes to school all by himself and went to the movies alone this week, organized by the Kulturbund (cultural league), he sat next to Bella and told about how he had seen London. He didn't mention you. He already has a very firm grasp of school; today at 3 o'clock I had him take care of the little ones, and he was downstairs [?]; he's already a good babysitter. Otherwise I really don't have much to report, only that Mrs Schreier will come to Leipzig next week to take care of her affairs here. I can also tell you that Lea and her mommy are in Latvia. We can really be happy about that, because they really have suffered. I got a card from London from the ship. It is on the Hamburg Africa Line; where is London [?] we don't know. Paula may come on a [?] in order to reach her goal that much sooner. Please don't be angry with her for not writing so quickly. She is always in the shop until quite late, and when she comes home, she is quite worn out, as you can imagine.

Our Mother's Day has been postponed until May 21st. Your [?] came at the right time [?]. Regards and kisses from grandma and mommy and from HAROLD.

[Postscript on the first page, top upside down]: *Regards from Aunt [Clara?] as well as the youngsters.*

Leipzig, 24 May 1939

My dear Vera!

I received your lovely letter. I was not pleased to learn about all the irregularity in your things. Write down the dates so that you can figure it out. At the right time, it should arrive 4 days earlier. I hope you did not have to pay any duty on the dress that we already sent off to you. Is this customs duty something new? I would have liked to learn more about your sports festival, as well as details about your instruction in school and how your school is on the whole and your activities throughout the day and the things you eat and so on and so forth. When I am with you, I will certainly not need to ask you these things, because I think that my own view of the situation will suffice; you can believe me on that. But for now, I have to be content with the written version. Today is [Shavout] and right now grandma is making a cheesecake for us and Aunt Clara. She is talking about you, saying that this is meant to be your cake. The weather is beautiful and right after our meal, grandma and I will go to the [Gauselalein?] family to take them on a walk. Otherwise they get out so little. Your aunt always waits for my help; you can well imagine that I am happy to oblige. I sent you the book and I also read it. I liked it very much. You have certainly received a letter from Aunt Trude, and you will also get mail from Aunt Clara. She has not forgotten you; it will just be one with a surprise. I have let Bella know and she said that she is expecting mail from you. Here people are celebrating Whitsun holidays; there too? Are your things in order? How are your socks? That's all I can think of to write today.

Warmest regards and kisses from your grandma and mommy.

Leipzig, 31 May 1939

My dear Vera,

As you can see from the lines I wrote at Aunt Clara's, we have to leave by June 20. I have already made a petition to the committee and asked for an extension, since I also have had bad luck with my papers, which got lost. I also wrote to Dora, as well as to the committee, in which I have asked for help for grandma. In Dora's letter I also enclosed copies of our identity cards, and I hope that I get good news. You can also impress on Dora how dear grandma is to us. The address J. Binke, London, N.15 Partry Rd, 19. Dear Vera, I have already organized everything and I hope that I can send off our things. However, since I don't know where to send them, the thought occurred to me to send them to you, where they would be safest. I also hope that Miss Staff will allow this, since she also has a heart. You could also write to [?] in your hand. Maybe we will get a few dollars. Then we would have some money right from the start when our things arrive. Otherwise we are healthy, dear child, and I ask you please not to take everything so to heart. I am doing everything possible so that all will go well. I also sent you two books that I got and I hope you like them. Uncle Leo has already taken care of something else, which I will also have to send you.

Many warm regards and kisses from your mommy and grandma.

Leipzig, 2 June 1939

My dear Vera,
Today I received your lovely letter. It gave me a great deal of pleasure. Nothing has changed here for now; I sent an appeal to the committee and requested an extension. I have also organized everything to send off and I am impatiently awaiting some positive word. I have also made application for grandma to the Committee Jewish Aid, Bloomsbury House, Bloomsbury Street, London, and we are hoping that God the Almighty will stand by us in our time of need to let us go there. Maybe you can write to Dora again; she already knows what steps I have taken. It is, after all, possible that she can do something. I gave your letter to your girlfriend. She was delighted with it. They suffered the same fate as we did; the circumstances have become crazy. Aunt Clara was quite happy with the lines you wrote her. She said: 'at least one person from whom we hear things that are tolerable.' Around here, everyone is going around with very hard heads. Everyone is saying: 'What are you doing?' We can't complain about our health, and it is getting quite warm outside. It is already Shabbas, and I am hungry, so for now, regards and kisses from your mommy and grandma.

Leipzig, 8 June 1939; 8 o'clock in the evening

My dear child,
Receiving your lovely letter today was my only pleasure. Yesterday I received a letter from Dora, in which she wrote that I should send her the papers from grandma right away, since she was at the Committee and the papers were required there. It would be a very great pleasure for us if we were to get a favourable response from them. Whether it would help to extend our stay is not yet clear. I have already submitted all of the things required, and await word from the foreign exchange office, then I will give it to the shipping agent. Helmut's sons will travel to London on June 12. As far as the others go, I can write you that they have not yet received anything in writing, but in the matter of extending their passports they were told when the time is up. Otherwise, grandma is remaining quite brave. She has no other choice; she really enjoyed your words to her. Last week I sent you several books and Uncle Leo's address. Did you get them? You also did not write about Paula's birthday cake. Please don't always forget to write about that! We are having beautiful weather right now; it does not match our mood. It is also quite warm. As you have seen from my letter, we are not the

only ones and we must cope with this, because there are many thousands of people. So, dear Vera, be strong and if we trust in God, help will come in the next time of difficulty. For today, I will close with best wishes and kisses from grandma and mommy.

Leipzig, 12 June 1939

My dear child,
This morning I received your lovely letter. We were just going to the train to accompany Helmut's boys, who travelled to London today. They're happier, aren't they? God willing, grandma and I would also get this kind of notice, but as it seems, we still have a difficult task ahead of us until we get what we desire. But it doesn't really matter; we are people who must take everything in our stride. Yesterday I also had a letter from Dora, in which she says that everything is going along. Dear Vera, I saw from your letter that you are losing your courage and your hope. You must not do this, dear Vera, because if we were to lose our hope, we would no longer have any strength to fight. Keep in mind that life is indeed a fight and an individual cannot structure it according to his own wishes. Mase told me that he had written to you. I also have mail from Schreier. He also writes that people need to be brave and grit their teeth. Then things work out and you deal with everything more easily. As of yet we have no word. We hope that we get a respite from the gallows. Charming little Siegmar is at our house this after-noon, I brought everything to grandma so that she would not be so despondent. It should be a passport. The Grünbaums are hoping for Palestine and the Koppolds, for help from America for a transit camp. Also, Trude is counting on going to Lodz with her [or: your?] aunt. The Schönbradts to Warsaw. We will thus be scattered throughout the world. In the same mailing I am sending you 3 books that I got from your uncle today. Have you been having trouble at the Staffs? My reason for asking is your bad mood. Today I don't know of anything new to report.
The warmest regards and kisses from your grandma and your mommy.
[Upside down, top of letter]
For our little doll we are having YOUR earrings made, right?
All of your loved ones send their regards and kisses.

Leipzig, 18 June 1939

My dear Vera!
I have received your lovely letter and I can let you know that our extension is valid until July 15. I hope to have taken care of everything by then and to have gotten a positive word from London. None of us has been deported and we will not risk that. For grandma the prospects are good. Dora wrote, and Helmut's boys have been in London since Wednesday, Trude's children

already have notice that a guarantee will be issued and that they soon will have everything they need to travel in. Rolf wrote us a card from Bremen. He promised me to write you as well. So, as you can see, you will soon see people from Leipzig there too and you will also somehow be able to make yourself understood. Aunt Clara and her family are here this afternoon, since they will not have us for very long, after all. Please do write me somewhat more about yourself, including how you spend your days. Have you begun a new piece of needlework? Just be sure not to go swimming once the weather has cooled down or when you are very overheated, since you're a bit sensitive. How is your relationship with Lotte and the boy now, and with the Staff family as a whole? Please always give them my best, even if I neglect to mention that sometimes.

Did you get something new again? Or do you need something? I would love to fulfil your wishes if I can. We're having bad weather here this week. [Mase?] didn't write a card, but he meant the greetings he added on. Lippmann as well as Schreier have both tried to help somehow. They both want things to work out. That's enough for today – lots of regards and kisses from your mommy and grandma, everyone who loves you sends their regards and kisses, Mommy.

Leipzig, 22 June 1939

My dear Vera,
I received your lovely letter today with great happiness. Before I tell you several other things, I don't want to delay letting you know about something wonderful. Our Paula got her notification today that she will be on the transport that leaves on Tuesday, June 27. Now you can look forward to seeing your Paula. I hope I will be able to write the same news about us soon, but my child has faith in God and her wish may soon be fulfilled. The Grünbaums have the prospect of getting a certificate soon. I can't write you anything new about [?], nor do I have anything to report about Uncle Leo or Aunt Eva. Everything's the same as ever in their cases. How did your sports festival go? Let me see you on a little picture. After all, for a short while to come I have to be content with that. How happy I would be if it were already otherwise. The Schönbradts have residence until August 31. He is already in Poland. Anna and her mother will certainly travel to Poland without any difficulty. Your aunt will finally see her son. I have not had mail from America for a long time. Mail has arrived from Schreier. He is going to great lengths for us and he tried to help us with advice. It is quite clear how sympathetic he is to our situation. Grandma and I are in good health. The others are well too, which is our only solace. Everyone got your lovely letters and they were all delighted. You will soon get news from all of them. I hope, my dear Vera, that I will be able to write you something good

in the next letter, because I am very much hoping that there will be news concerning our travel. For today, I really don't know anything else to write, and send the most heartfelt regards and kisses from your mommy, who loves you, and from your grandma, who loves you too.

Leipzig, 6 July 1939

My dear Vera!

Today, after some delay, your letter arrived. I was already getting worried, since there was no mail from you on the fifth for Aunt Clara's birthday. Paula also sent mail. She writes that she already sent you her things and that she already wrote to you. Edith travelled on Tuesday, July 4; at the time she received my card she was already in the country. Regina was also [?]. She promised me that she would write to you. Nothing much has changed around here. Paula wrote that I should send various papers again, and we are waiting once again for help, because our deadline will have run out by July 15. I have already written to you: if you get something, you should look at the return address. The card for Mr Eisner was in the book that he sent you, as a memento. I also have mail from Schreier, as well as from the Lippmanns. I have gotten nothing from America in a long time. Other than that, I can't tell you any news about us nor can I write anything to cheer you up. At Aunt Clara's birthday yesterday the mood was somewhat sombre, but that's the way these times are here. Everybody asked about your party, but it's over. Your grandma is as well as can be expected these days, and everyone is walking around with a sullen expression, as you can well imagine. Uncle Leo gave me two more books for you. You must have a real library by now, right? Next week I will certainly send you our things [?] and I hope that everything will arrive in one piece. Once it is there, your wish will be fulfilled. That's all for today, dear Vera. The warmest of regards and kisses from mommy, also from grandma. All of your loved ones send you regards.

Leipzig, 10 July 1939

My dear Vera!

I am answering your lovely card immediately. I received it today. I imagine that you have already received the regards I sent via Paula and that everything is working out well for you. On Friday, the shipping agent is picking up our things. Let's hope that we have received something more promising from London by that time. I can't tell you at the moment what we will do if we should need an extension. But I will leave no stone unturned, as you can well imagine. [?] Wolf is travelling today and we hope that everything will work out well for that girl. I am absolutely certain that you have already seen Paula and Edith in one way or another, which would make me very happy. Mr and Mrs Eisner were really delighted about the card you sent them. As far as we are concerned, I can report to you that we are feeling well. Have you heard from Helmut's boys yet? Please don't always neglect your writing so much; the last time you wrote more nicely than this time. I hope you will not need to worry about us all that much, because we must hope for a speedy reunion, which is what is keeping us going. I see very few girls from your class. I think most of them are already gone, which I hope is the case. In the hope that we hear good news from you, your mommy and grandma send you regards and kisses.

Leipzig, 14 July 1939

My dear Vera!
I received your lovely letter today and I was quite delighted to learn that you have already gotten your things and that you like everything. Paula was annoyed, as she wrote me, because she already had everything ready for you and then accidentally left it lying around. Did Edith write to you? Today our things were picked up by the shipping agent and they are going to London. There are also lovely things for you in this shipment. You will be really delighted with them. Dear Vera, today, I am continuing this letter today, July 15, because I wanted to tell you something additional. I can write you now that our stay has tacitly been extended until July 31, 1939, and I am hoping that by that time a better result will have emerged for us. A guarantee of 50 has already been issued for grandma and we have great hope that the permit will arrive very soon. Soon you, dear Vera, will have someone with you once again. I am happy that you are well. What else can I say about us? I can't write you more at the moment, because Siegmar wants to [?]. For today, the warmest of regards and kisses from your mommy and grandma, who love you. Many regards from everyone.

Lodz, 19 July 1939

My beloved child!
I think there is mail from you at home today, at grandma's house. As you can see, dear Vera, I am no longer in Leipzig. I got grandma's stay extended. As you already know, staying longer really makes no sense for me, since I certainly cannot come until I am free, so I decided, with a heavy heart, to come here, and my dear ones must remain behind. May God protect them. However, I want to, and must, achieve my goal in order to get free, so that I can soon be together with you once again. Therefore, dear Vera, you shouldn't consider my interruption as a [?] tour for me, because I also want to visit your aunt in Warsaw. Our things are at the shipper's and when grandma has her permit, everything will be sent off. I have not had mail from Paula yet, and the good news from Aunt Trude, which is that I cannot

come until she has the divorce in her hands. [Note: since this doesn't appear to make sense (was Aunt Trude filing for divorce?), it is possible that the word Schneidung (divorce) was intended to be Entscheidung (decision).] I will now close, because I am very tired, after having travelled for the entire night. Uncle Abram's brother is taking very good care of me.

Warmest regards and kisses from your mommy, who loves you with all her heart.

Lodz, 24 July 1939

My dear child,
After waiting anxiously for word from you, I received your lovely letter today. I am finding my way around here quite well, the circumstances are not especially good. You see a great deal of suffering. But both of us keep hoping [?] a brief period of separation. Several people have already taken up my cause and I hope to watch everything develop quickly. [Lumpriedt?] is here. Helmut came to me on Friday and is going to great efforts on my behalf. He is making sure that I don't get lonely. Abram's brother Jankel as well as his daughter Pelte are also very kind and thoughtful. The others are in the [?] fresh. I looked up the [?] family yesterday. They are in Lodz and send their warmest regards, as do the Nudelträgers. Today I received my first letter from grandma and I had been quite worried about her, but my fears were unfounded. Our dear grandma got a letter from [?] which said that her case was being processed. I had only been able to get an extension for her, which I didn't write you about because I didn't want to worry you, but since I'm there and I'm healthy, it's better for my dear child, since people get old on their own without additional anxieties. Enough for today. Warmest regards and kisses from your mother, who never forgets you. Mr Grünbaum and his daughter send their regards.

[Postscript from Helmut]

Dear Vera,
[?] I am also happy about you. I hope it doesn't take long until you have your mommy there; many kind regards, Helmut.

[return address says Leipzig] [postmark says 29 July 1939]
My dear Paula!
Now I must write again, because I cannot wait any longer. What is wrong? Don't you have any interest in or sympathy for our children or us? I have written to the Binke family as well as to you several times already and we have no answer or pictures as yet. What's to happen now? The money from America may have arrived in the meantime. Please, once again, hurry up,

because we have gotten our stay extended for the last time, to the 30th of August. I will always send you a double card, so that I get word right away. If you write to your parents, we have to wait too long until we know something, because it's so far away. As far as grandma goes, why should she have to wait so long? Her things have been with the shippers for two weeks and every day costs storage money, and the apartment is already rented out. As long as grandma does not have a permit, she doesn't have permission to send her things. Many of our acquaintances who began at the same time and even later already have their permits. Grandma is also, like me, quite desperate. I will close now, so that I don't make your heart so heavy. I am asking you once again for speedy news, since I can't be calm until I hear something. Regards and kisses from your Aunt Clara, Uncle Adolf, and the children. Many warm regards to the Binke family. Special regards from grandma for Dora and her family, as well as to you, Paula and Edith. She would love to see you soon.

[This letter is from Clara and Adolf Koppold.]

Lodz, 31 July 1939

My dear child!

Today, after a long delay, I received your lovely letter, which I had awaited with great impatience. I was especially pleased about the lovely lines you wrote to the Grünbaums, since this demonstrated to me that you already know the proper thing to do. Also, I noticed once again that my daughter is already a big girl, which means that I'm already getting old. Dear Vera, you want to know what kinds of things I have along, you can imagine, as much as I can wear; that was the best for me because I unfortunately had to give up my little suitcase. Helmut has just brought me the news that the Engels have also already arrived. You are right that half of Leipzig is here. I don't need a lawyer yet; the gentleman from the committee is so kind and gives me great cause for hope. If I need a lawyer, I will get one. You shouldn't worry about me. Unfortunately I haven't gotten any mail from grandma yet. I don't know how far along she is. Nonetheless, I have taken care of every-thing when I was still there. Grandma's, your and my things are all at the shipper's. When you are at Paula's, dear Vera, she will certainly tell you what is in store on the trip to London, because when grandma travels, a lot is involved. I'll travel to your aunt in Warsaw when the right time comes and I can tell myself, now you can relax for a few days. She doesn't know yet that I'm in P[oland]. I had a nice letter from Paula on Tuesday. She as well as Edith are counting the days until your arrival. I would have been happy to have counted twice as many days if I knew that we would see each other soon! I hope that when you are in London, you remember that I would like to see my dear girls. Even the tiniest picture won't make me angry. I am happy for you about your new dress and wish my girl a really nice voyage, beautiful weather. And all the best to Ms Staff as well and a speedy recovery; where is Lotte staying? Since I promised Helmut some space, I will close with many regards and kisses, Your mommy. Mr Grünbaum and children send their warm regards; his wife is in the [?]. Mr and Mrs Nudelträger send their regards. Since Helmut has not come yet, I won't wait any longer and make you worry; I know how that is. I am also not getting any mail from Leipzig.

P.S. Helmut came late, which is why the card will be arriving one day later.

Bad Bentheim, 22 August 1939

My dear Vera!
Today I brought my three children here [?]. You can imagine how hard it is for me. At the same time, I am sending you the best of regards and kisses. Your Aunt Clara

On Wednesday at approximately 2 o'clock they will arrive in London.

22 August 1939

My dear Paula,
Up to here I brought the children and now I have to return alone in the night. Take good care of Zilla, Siegmar and Harold. They have three suitcases and luggage receipt, travel permit and one pram with contents, a bag, etc. Take good care.
   Many kisses.
   Your Aunt Clarchen

Lodz, 27 August 1939

My dear Vera!
I received your lovely letter and found your many kisses quite amusing. It would have been better to have them in reality, but, God willing, it may happen soon. I hope there will be no [?] before that. Everyone here is back from their summer apartments already, including Uncle Abram's mother, children, and sister. Now I have enough company, but as you can imagine, I'm not really in the mood. Today I have not even left the house yet. I don't feel like getting dressed. I had mail from Aunt Clara from Bentheim on Thursday. Our poor aunt; I can imagine how broke her poor heart was, but we are all in a [?] that can do anything. I can tell you that my head simply can't think any more because I hear absolutely nothing specific from them. They just write me a card in grandma's name. They arrive as double cards,

which I then answer right away. My lawyer has already informed me that the divorce date is set for September 23, but he, through his attorney, was able to provide an advantage that he signed the request along with this state that both parties are in agreement. So he can no longer undertake any retreat, because I have not seen him since August 8. Therefore, he is very [?] at me, and for this reason he has already [?]. I got a nice card from Schreier, which made me very happy. It was written very sweetly. I have not answered it yet. Do you have any word yet from Paula as to how far along my case is? I hope that it can't take much longer now. I have a document from the committee, saying that I was [?] by Miss Staff. Paula also did get the Jewish [?] from me. I hope that I soon get some positive news. Since I want to leave some space for Aunt [?], who is Paula's youngest aunt. So I will close, and I send you, dear Vera, many regards and kisses from your mommy. Everyone you know sends you cordial regards, but I have no space left to name them all.

[The remainder of the text is in Yiddish (or Hebrew).]

Leipzig, 9 November 1939

My dear child,
Finally, I am able to write you a few words [like this, or in this way] and I hope you'll do the same as soon as possible, because I am waiting for a message from you as if it would be like my daily bread. You are probably wondering why you are getting this letter from me, so I will tell you directly. I moved and since the 1st of November I am staying at tante Clara's and Grandma is there as well. I hope I'll be able to stay there. Have you heard from the others: Paula, Edith, Harold, Siegmar and Pippi? How is it going with you, my dear Vera? I believe you have much to tell me, because we didn't hear anything from you for a long time. I hope that you will not let me wait too long, and you will write me about you and the others. Kisses and hugs from your Mother. Grandmother, Uncle Leo, Aunt Eva, Aunt Trude and Uncle Grünbaum also send regards and kisses.

[January 1940]

My dear Vera,
Your dear lines I received with great joy. For we three who remained behind, the only joy is to receive mail from you children and from our other loved ones. Through this separation, we have nothing else.
*   My dear Vera, I am actually very proud of you, that my second niece, at about fourteen years of age, has become very mature and you are already in Backfisch [?] and a young lady and I consider myself now like an old aunt. What kind of career do you actually want to study? It is very important in life to have some skill with which you can earn money.*

Dear Vera, have you actually seen my children? Are they healthy? You have no idea how much I worry about everything. You have no idea what kind of worries I have about everything. My little sweet Pippa will be one year old on January 30th, and I could not come here to hold my child to my heart.

My dear Vera, I will now close. I congratulate you again, and we sent congratulations to the Gold Cross quite a while ago. Be well and remain a good person. Greet your mother often with happy mail. She has such a great longing for you. Write back soon.

Heartfelt greetings and kisses. Your Aunt Clara.

P.S.: Dear Vera! I almost forgot to send Frau Staff heartfelt regards and wishes and many thanks for everything she does for my Vera in addition. Please do it in my name. Your Mother

Budapest, 5 [January?] 1940

[Here the left margin of the Xerox is cut off and parts of the Xerox are too light to read, so again I have extrapolated and/or peppered the letter with question marks.]

My dear Paula!

After a long wait, we have received your lovely letter. You, my big girl, can imagine how I longed for a letter from you and please wait and make sure that my little one writes, even only a few lines. You needn't worry too much about us [?] write to Aunt [?] that she should get in touch with Uncle Mayer as soon as possible, because we can no longer count on support, so see what you can do. [?] otherwise everything is absolutely fine. [?] Stay healthy and regards and kisses from your mommy. Regards and kisses to Vera [?]. Best of regards to the Binke family.

Dear Paula and Edith!

I was so delighted to get your letter, and don't be concerned, but I need to ask Edith to write. In the last letter I gave you all the details and am asking you please to take care of everything so that we will be able to come to you. Regards and kisses to you and Vera and [?].

Leipzig, 15 January 1940

My beloved child,

Finally, I have received once more a sign [letter] from you, my dear child. My joy was indescribable. From you writing, I understand that you, thank God, are healthy and doing well. I was so happy that you had such a good birthday and that you had dear Paula as a guest. Hopefully, you enjoyed the few days. Dear Vera, how wonderful it would have been if I could have celebrated your 15th birthday with you and could have my dear Vera as a young lady in front of me.

Where Helmut and his wife find themselves, I cannot say. He would have left from there also and is far as I understand it. From our other dear [friends] you must have surely learned, they are in Hungary. Have you seen any of our dear friends. Paula wrote us about our Pippa. She should be an example for the world because of the way she takes care of the children.

For today, dear Vera, be [surrounded] by regards and kisses from your Mother, who so eagerly waits to see you. Dear Vera, with great joy I read your dear letters and I hope and pray to God that it will come to pass that will see [my] beloved grandchildren.

So far, I am healthy, and I hope the same for all my dear ones. Besides you, my dear child, and also my Paula, Edith, Siegmar, Harold and my Pippa, Zilla, heartfelt regards and kisses from your oma [grandma] and the others who think about you. Please give my regards to the dear wanderers [Priukes – and Augehorige] from me, those whom I had most willingly welcomed.

Budapest, 18 March 1940

[No addressee listed here, but the letter is for Paula.]

I have made you wait for an answer for 3 days. Papa really wanted to write to you, but his eye is not better yet and I don't want to make you wait any more, because I know more than anyone how that is. My dear girl, be sensible, fate has been relatively kind to us up to now. Don't complain; everything will improve again, and if anything at all is on your mind, I understand you better than anyone. I don't want to be just your mother, but also your friend and your confidante. I am quite astonished that you [?]; they are, after all, also on the copies sent along with them. I had also sent you the address of Dr [?]. Here we have been given every reason for hope that we will be able to get to you soon. Many things are being promised to us, but unfortunately very few of them are kept. Thank God, I have very positive letters from home. I have not gotten mail from Helmut for a long time, which is a good sign that he is on the way to [?]. Have you sent off the [pound?] that you once wrote about? I know that my big girl doesn't have much time, but if you can manage it, you certainly have to look up Mrs [Baader?], who lives near you, because the [children?] are in great distress, and also little [Mogen?] [?] Did my Edith get her birthday cards? I was so delighted with your letter and with what Vera wrote, please do it again soon, Harold as well. Is he well? Many regards and kisses from [?] Papa,

Uncle Leo and Aunt Eva [?] Dora, as well as [?] and the family. I hope you are all healthy. And you know how we are from Trude. It would be so wonderful to be able to repay your good deeds in London soon, as soon as we have news from [?] we will send it on to you. All of you should stay in good health, and regards and kisses, Trude [?]

[Postage stamp indicates that this was sent from Hungary.]

23 April 1940 [or 1942?]

My dear Paula and Edith!
Oh, how impatiently we are awaiting mail from you. You dear children, I hope you are not too afraid. Just have faith in God and everything will get better once again. And don't be nervous. It is now [?] everything is fate and determination. Above all, be brave and [?] especially Paula and Vera, you take everything so [tragically?]. Pull yourselves together and think about the fact that in Paula [?] the children [?] so that you can all stay together, because with God's help we will see each other again, so we will have no need to search elsewhere. May God grant us a reunion very soon. So be sensible. How are things? Have you received the pictures? And has my big girl sent pictures again, because as of today nothing has arrived. A whole week ago I sent a very detailed letter, which also included the address of Lombeck, which has to be taken care of. So once again for my Paula: Lombeck, c/o H. [Leser?] 8 H [Lorence?] [Mansions?], [Vivian?] Avenue London Central [1?] W.4. I think my Paula can read this. Please take care of this quickly, because we don't know what the next days will bring. You needn't worry about us. As far as we go, everything is just fine. Thank God we have good news from grandma, Aunt Yetta, Aunt Clara, and Uncle Adolf. Today mail came from Poland too.

[On the reverse side]

My dear Paula and Edith,
The warmest regards and kisses from your papa; many regards and good wishes to the Binke family. Everything is fine there. [?] it is high time for him to leave, so for today he adds his regards. Please write back very soon, because you dears can imagine how we are waiting for your reply. Keep in mind that even if you don't receive an answer right away, write anyway. Many regards and kisses, Your mommy and Aunt. Many regards and good wishes to the Binke family. Warm regards to all, Aunt Eva and Uncle Leo.

[Top of letter is cut off, but addressee is Paula; no date]
[Letter is sent from Budapest]

By the time you get this card, nothing will have changed here with us. You are our only concern, whatever may happen. My big girl should always be sure to stay with the children, because that is a great relief to all of us when the mail gets delayed. Always write at least once a week. Do you also get mail from Vera on a regular basis? Write about everything and don't be so worried. We have to bear our fate with courage and hope for a better future. Keep in mind: be brave and strong. Thank God we got good mail from home. Lipman sent us a package again and wrote us a very cordial letter. He gets the [?] from grandma, and gets mail regularly from Poland and helps as best he can. I would have been greatly delighted to see the other pictures. All of you should stay well and strong, many regards and kisses from your mommy and aunt, papa and uncle, and many regards and all good wishes to the Binke family.

[In another handwriting]

My dear Paula and Edith!
We are fine so far, and you know everything else from mommy. With best regards to Uncle Leo.

[No place or date noted – sent by Aunt Trude and Uncle Abraham, Uncle Leo and Aunt Eva]

Dear Vera!
Uncle Leo is asking you to send an exact travel itinerary, and how you made out with your things and with customs. And please do write a nice thank you letter sometime to Mrs [?]. Please don't forget. Aunt Trude

Monday, the 1st of [?] [Margin is cut off in Xerox]
Dear Vera!
Finally I am getting around to writing to you, since I am too lazy to work today. I really do not know what I should be writing you because for me, one day passes just like any other and is filled up with work right into the evening; then I am quite tired. So, don't be upset with me if I don't answer you right away. I hope to improve, because three children make for a lot of work. To make up for it, your other aunts will write you more because they have more time.

My report about the children: Well, I'll start with the oldest. He is going to school and thinks he is very important. He tries very hard to write his ABCs, and I will try to get him to write something for you soon. Harold wants to send his thanks for your letter and wants to keep it together with the other one and even bring it along to America. Siegmar is still too lazy to talk. He is very wild and clever. Runs around quite a bit. If you ask him who goes to school, he raises his index finger and says it (me!), who is in bed (me!). He is always pushing something with his finger and laughs a lot and is terrific. Our little doll Zilla renamed herself Avi. Av (who is developing nicely) has gotten fat. When she is hungry, she screams as though she's been stabbed. Your uncle says that she can wake up the dead. Then, when she is full, she gets a mischievous grin and laughs. It looks as though she will wind up with black hair. Everyone says that she looks like me. I have a very beautiful white deep baby carriage. The front has a seat for Siegmar. We bought it used because a new one would be too expensive. You once asked me whether I would be sending Harold to our relatives. We are not going to do that because he is still too young, and some day I hope that we will be getting away from here. This morning I was at the American consulate. He said that we can leave in the very near future and I was quite happy. Unfortunately, it wasn't real; it was just a dream. I woke up and was so disappointed. Dear Vera, it has already been half a year that we have been sitting around and waiting until we can travel. Who knows how long we still have to wait? We are always delighted to get a letter from you and you write that things are going well for you. Don't be so concerned, because it doesn't help to worry. And we also think that any day your mother will finally get the right notice to travel. So I'll close for now. Stay healthy and we send you our regards and kisses, Your Aunt Clara, Uncle Adolf, Harold, Siegmar and Zilla. Grandma has just arrived and also sends you her regards and kisses. Please give our regards to the Staff family.

[No date or place indicated]

My dear Vera! [followed by one word in Hebrew: I think it reads: Shalom] I was so delighted with your letter, which you addressed to all of us. Do you know for sure at this point whether all of you will be going to private families or living in a group home? Did the English people give you a good reception? Please tell me what kinds of things are most important there, because there is a possibility that I will be coming to England on December 23rd, and I of course only want to bring along practical items, so that I won't be taking along useless things. Uncle Leo is now working on the matter of the children's emigration to England. That's why Uncle Leo has arranged for Horst Rotenstein to travel to England also on December 8, since he has just come from the preparation camp and is not supposed to remain here any longer. On Friday I visited the Rotensteins. Lore had written another airmail letter home. She wrote that everyone should send their regards to you and to me. She would have written us a letter, but she didn't have the money for postage and will be writing us the next time. How is everything else with you, dear Vera? How does it feel to be a newborn English girl?

Have you found a girl to be friends with yet? Do you all get along with one another, and have you all gotten used to life over there? I can already imagine myself as a governess in England.

So, warmest regards and kisses from your Paula. Your whole group sends regards; special greetings from [name is illegible] [additional text along the side margin – illegible]

[Still the same Xerox, and still undated, but new handwriting]

My dear Vera!
Although I did not read your letter, your mommy was bursting with happiness when I got here, and told me what her daughter had written. We all hope that you will soon be getting together with Paula and Edith. You're certainly not upset at that prospect, are you? What other good things are you doing? Please don't be lazy about writing, because you can well imagine that we are all longing for a detailed letter from you, especially details of where you are, what you do all day, what you get to eat, and how you are sleeping. We're petty nosy, aren't we? But I think you will understand why. How is your English going? Have you already started your lessons? How is the weather? Is it very foggy, or is it not as bad as they say? As soon as you get this letter, please think about answering it right away, but please make it nice and pretty, because your uncle wants to show it off, right? You are becoming quite a little prodigy against your will, but you don't need to get upset, because we all want to be proud of you and we all believe that you will not let us down, because when you want to do something you don't disappoint us. So give it some thought. Give your mommy and all of us so much pleasure and above all, stay healthy. I think I have written enough. Regards and kisses from your Aunt Trude and Uncle Abraham.

By the way, as of yesterday, we are members of the SPCA (Animal Protection League). When the weather is bad, we can't go out. Isn't that nice?

[Undated]
In the evening around 22 o'clock – in bed

Dear Vera,
First, we thank you for your mazeltov. Hopefully, the little girl brought us good luck. I had imagined the birth of the child to be much worse, because I went through very much in the months before. Sunday to Monday night, I had pains. Then I woke your uncle and he [went] to get [someone to call] your mother and, at the same time, the midwife from the [place?] and at around 5.15 in the early morning the little one came. You can imagine the joy that it is a girl. It only weights 5 plus pounds and is 46 centimetres long.

Otherwise, she is very cute, has long black hair, dark slit eyes, a wide nose, and a very tiny mouth. My little daughter, as well as I (she came one month too early) find ourselves [upon examination] healthy. It is not a [miracle, wonder?] because of the care of your mother, that our loved ones are well.

There is not much more to write except to say that by us nothing much has changed and we wait from day to day for an exit pass but, unfortunately, till now, in vain.

Your picture pleases me a great deal; you look like a little lady. When I have enough money, I will have a picture done by Leyboth.

Siegmar still does not sleep. He needs a slap for his stubbornness. Harold is sleeping. Uncle Adolph is at the Grünbaums playing cards. Your mother and I are writing. And so that is the end for today.

Best regards and kisses. Your Aunt Clara, Uncle Adolph, Harold and Siegmar and also from your little Zilla.

Please, Vera, do not forget to give heartfelt regards to Mrs Staff, and to Lottie, from me. And give her my warm thanks for her dear picture which brought us so much joy.

Your devoted mother

[Undated]

Dear Vera,
We all hope you're fine. Please write back to us soon. A thousand greetings and kisses. Your Aunt Clarchen.

What are our beloved children doing? Say hello to our Paula and Edith. We are looking forward to seeing you. Your Aunt.

Grandma sends all her grandchildren greetings and from me all the best regards.

[Undated]

My dear big niece Paula,
As it is time to write, I do not want to miss writing to you. How are you? Do you have a lot of work with my children? Where are you staying? Is it not possible to give me a more detailed report? Why is Harold not with his brother and sister? I like to be able to understand everything clearer. The worry about everything is hard to take.

How are you personally and your little sister? Write to me real soon about my sweet children. How far is Harold in school? And Siegmar in talking also, my little doll. Are my children well, as they are so frail. Please write soon; the next time I will write more. Can't write any more now; too much grief! Stay well and kisses, your Aunt Clarchen. Best regards to family Binke and the whole family.

My dear big son Harold,
How are you, how are you managing in school? Are you able to write, and
how are our sweet Siegmar and Zilla? Papa has gone away; hope he will be
home soon. Do you think about your Mutti and Papa sometime? Think
about how you left sugar on the balcony. By Aunt and Uncle Lipman the
stork came a few days ago and left a little girl. Such pleasure, isn't it lovely.
I am closing now, be brave and stay well. Also our Siegmar and Zilla.
    Lots of kisses, your Mutti.

                                                                    [Undated]
My dear Paula,
Many thanks for the report about my children. It was a diversion for me in
my present condition. I am glad they are doing well. Also you, Edith and
Helmut's children. It is too bad that Uncle Adolf is not able to read you and
Harold's letters. Today I am not able to write too much as my nerves are
shattered, but Aunt Jette insists that I write a few lines as she is in the mood
to write.
    Dear Paula, please always write to me a very detailed letter, as this is the
only thing that I have left from my life. Have you heard already from
Lipman? There I wrote to every one of my children. When I get an answer,
I will write again to all of them. I was very happy to get a few lines from
Harold. I will close now, stay well, best regards and kisses, your Aunt Clara,
also to Edith, Vera, Jossi and Karl. Regards and kisses to Harold, Siegmar
and Zilla. Especial warm regards to the family Binke. My dear grandchil-
dren, received your letter with a lot of pleasure. May God help us that our
wishes will be fulfilled and I will be together with all of my children and
grandchildren. Also I thank you my dear Paula for the comforting words, it
was good for me. Well, I will close. Stay well, all of you.
    Regards and kisses from Oma. Special regards to Dora, Husband, her
children. From Your Aunt.

The letters from Leipzig that follow were sent to Paula Grünbaum and
Vera Ribetski by Marta Mitdank, who claimed to be a friend of the family.
Neither Paula nor Vera had heard anything about her from their parents.
She informed them of what she knew of the fate of the Schmulevitz family
remaining in Leipzig after the children had left. Evidently, Marta or
Marijane (they are the same person) helped the Schmulevitz family by
sending and receiving packages and mail to and from the children in
England. The copy I have used to transcribe the letters was given to me by
Tsvi Shdaimah – formerly Harold Koppold – when I visited him on the
Niz Oz kibbutz on the Gaza–Israel border in June 1994. The original letters

were written in German and translated in America into English. I do not
know at this point who the translator was. In a few places, I have added in
square brackets what I think may have been the original intention of the
writer. Otherwise, they are unedited. Evidently, a reply was received from
both Vera and Paula, and another letter was written by Marijane dated
simply 'Thurs. 3 p.m. afternoon'.

From the evidence I conclude the letters were written over a two-day
period, from 15 to 16 October 1946. The letters are addressed primarily to
Vera and Paula, the oldest two children, who were sent to England. I have
been able to corroborate one piece of information contained in the letters:
Clara Koppold and her mother, Rose Asman (Schmulevitz) are listed in a
deportation book in the Bundes Archives in Berlin as living with many
other people in an apartment on Humbold Strasse, Leipzig, from where
they were put on a transport on 21 January 1942 to 'Riga, Auschwitz,
Treblinka'. They were among 702 persons deported that day. Vera's
mother, Yette, is mentioned by the letter writer as living in the apartment
on Humbold Strasse with them. She is not listed among those in the deportation book.

It is not clear to me whether Marijane or the other members of her
family were Jewish or had Jewish relations. At one point she says: 'As Jews,
we were marked and often visited by the Gestapo. We were always lucky
though we were often called to police headquarters.' At another point she
implies that she and her husband went to Jewish streets, and 'not to be
conspicuous, we also wore a [yellow] Jewish star'. Near the end of the letter,
she writes: 'You should know that I was for yours as well as other good
friends never a "Martha", since I still retained the name "Yuliane". I
became a "Marijane". Everyone knows me and of me when you mention
the name here in old circles. Should we continue to leave it at this? I am
your Marijane.' My guess is that she was married to a Christian man, and
was herself in jeopardy much of the time. At one point it appears she was
arrested and sent to a work camp in Poland. [She claims to have been much
involved with the Schmulevitz family.]

Marta Mitdank
(10) Leipzig 05, Riebeck Str. 22.11.1
Russ. Zone. Deutschland
Tues. 15 October 1946, 2 p.m.

My dear girls,
This morning I received, with much joy, your two letters from Oct. 9. I
thank you with my whole heart for your lines. Because mail can only be sent

in weight of 20 grams at a time, I'll begin my answer with letter number one and will continue in more letters. I am typing my response so both Vera and Paula might understand; since you both are interested in the fate of your loved ones.

I thank you wholeheartedly, for the trust you have put in me. To find you was the last promise I gave your beloved at the time of departure, a promise that I saw as my Holy task, and hoped to fulfil it. To write you is one of the hardest tasks I have ever put myself through; especially knowing this all these years was horrible to me, since we weren't just people who knew each other, but people fate brought together – the Family Schmulevitz and us. You may be disappointed when I tell you that we aren't a Jewish family; but that doesn't matter because ever since we were little we were always around and part of the Jewish 'clique' so really no one should be able to tell a difference. My father owned the booths that were erected for the Leipziger cafeteria; there, your grandmother Schmulevitz was one of the customers. You really couldn't know that since that was before your time. While I was in school, I had two close friends, Dora Ganger and Toni Kern. We grew up together and I met many other Jewish people. My husband at the Felsenstein (mountain stone) Company, Rauchwaren(cigarettes, tobacco, etc.) in Brühl. We continued meeting many Jewish people and to this day are still in contact with Felsensteins who are now living in England. Many Jewish friends were welcomed at our house; one family you know – the Feliners. We kept Jewish holidays and Sabbath just like you; and ate matzo at the right times. Our children, still small at that time, knew more Jewish Uncles and Aunts than Christian ones. We were steady customers at Uncle Adolf's store in the Turner Street and when the boycott began we stayed with him. The year 1938 you remember and exactly on 9 November 1938 we were in the store and became witnesses: a man entered the store demanding his suit, finished or not. He was a very demanding man who couldn't be turned away. We later learned that this man knew what was to take place this night. On this evening I met Yette, as she tried to calm the man. What happened during this night [kristallnacht] you know.

Since that performance there was no more peace for the Jewish society. The next morning we were befriended with the Koppold family. You know, the whole situation took on a threatening character and we helped Uncle Adolf as best we could to hide his belongings. We later sold these things so his family could live. Soon after, you left for England. Why didn't I know you? In that time of chaos, it was important to help as many families as possible so my husband and I parted and went to different camps. Then we brought various (non-Jewish) helpless people across the border. Before that, I was in Austria and Hungary to try and import various goods. But in November 1938, we had to make our move.

I think November '38 is when I visited Uncle Adolf and Aunt Clarchen, Emilienstrasse, and met the rest of the relatives and friends as well as the two small boys Harold and Siegmar. Siegmar, with curly hair, is as sweet as a doll, and Harold is a little older. Uncle Adolf and Aunt Clara's meeting was in such a style that both Jews and Christian could mix and find whoever they wanted or needed. The conversation never dealt with the sorrowful situation all were in, and no one knew what the future would hold, but no one knew anything good. Any mention of sorrow was always towards the children that were out of the country. Being separated was painful. Your mail brought much happiness and everyone visiting was a part of that, including me.

January '39 I was able to go to Paris and make some overseas contacts. I used our belongings and took what I could and worked there. When I returned, I found a newborn baby, 30 January 1939. Lawfully, we had to pick a name and 'Zilla' was the nicest name we found. In the Spring – March/April – the en-gross messe was held. Our friends came. I introduced our 'Molly' to Uncle Adolf.

[It seems as if Marijane were hiding Zilla (Molly). Perhaps they laid the groundwork for a future plan of hiding a child.]

Uncle Adolf was able to send some valuables to America. I knew that these valuables arrived because I received a response from America at the Koppolds' address. The code was 'Uncle arrived at 4.00.' Koppolds, believing they had a basis for leaving the country, were very happy. Uncle Adolf was a citizen of Poland, so leaving was put off since this brought about difficulties. Hope was left for summer. When summer finally rolled around, other reasons to postpone came. Sometimes, homes were searched. If that was the case, we would have Uncle Adolf and other Jewish friends at our house for guests. It wasn't easy because (as Jews), we were marked and often visited by the Gestapo. We were always lucky, though we were often called to police headquarters. Afraid? No. We weren't afraid because we were doing what we as humans should do.

War clouds came closer together and our good Yetta was sent to Poland. We decided to bring the Koppold children in safety. I can remember when Aunt Clara would do the shopping and Uncle Adolf would sew the children's clothes. When all was finished, Aunt Eva helped sew names into their clothes. We all were at Koppolds. It was then that Aunt Clara began her painful journey up to the Holland border. She had to leave her dear little children. We were all so sad, but the thought of bringing the children in security gave us new courage. For the Koppolds – the hope of leaving here diminished.

Exactly on 25 October 1939, Yetta, who came from Poland, stood at my door. I was so happy, I could hardly believe it. She was able to get permis-

sion to come for a visit. On top of all that, she had no exact date written out as to when she was to return. We were at war and had food stamps, so Yetta had to report her whereabouts to the police. Everything went fine. In the meantime, Uncle Adolf was arrested. One day he received a card stating he must report to the police station (court-house). He never returned. Because this happened to other families this matter was looked into.

In the work establishment building on Riebeck Street (not far from us) is where they were being held. I hope you'll save me from giving a description of their treatment there. Grandma and Yetta had to give up the apartment on Lohrstreet and lived on Emilienstreet. And there too, according to law, all apartments had to be given up. The whole family (Clara sold her furniture to a butcher family that still lives there today) moved into the rooms on Humbolt Str. 4. It was a large floor in a corner house which they shared with two other renters and with Mrs Issachsohn, whom I'll tell you about later. They had 3 rooms. It was enough and they did decorate them nicely. There was a nice small kitchen, but more important of all, a door of wallpaper in the hallway that led into a small alcove where one could hide when guards came. The door was hidden by a chiffrobe. I must tell you, it got harder for everyone since these houses were known as Jewish houses. You couldn't find any more excuses for living there for the isolation area continued to grow larger.

In December, they brought Uncle Adolf to the camp in Sachsenhausen. We saw him here in Leipzig when Clarchen would bring him sewing materials. But with the overtaking this also became impossible. You can imagine what an effect it had on Clarchen, who was always being hurt (she was always so sensitive). The thoughts of the children, and the husband, the happiness of a sign of life from Adolf, to be in contact with him, being able to send him things – things he never received at all – these were all comforting moments and small rays of hope.

Grandma Schmulevitz began sewing. I was a customer. The kitchen remained the meeting place (Jews were allowed to go out from 6.00 a.m. to 8.00 p.m.) The women were brought to cheap work areas, Yetta worked with smoking necessities (cigars, cigarettes, etc.); Clara in a print shop, where she injured her hand. Mail was always under control. Work picked up in the Humbolt Street because there was always someone who needed workers. Since Yetta and Clarchen were known as 'good help' and were associated with Christian families many of their situations were eased. They were able to help those in need on both sides. My dear Yetta, for example, took over my Jewish correspondence while I took over her Christian one. Therefore, I was able to help my friends in foreign countries, before the war began, with the 'Pound packages' that you are familiar with. They almost all got there. And so we all were entwined with each other, even more than sisters. We celebrated all holidays and took part in all family occasions. Letters continued to flow. It was hard to live, but we survived, and the worries over the relatives were settled. So far, this is the life of Grandma, Yetta and Clarchen. Now begins another section.

In the year 1939, I looked for relationships in Budapest. One didn't need a visit to Hungary if you were German and you could take plenty of money with you. With good friends, I took advantage of this possibility and went there. We had the intention of transferring this money over to France in case of any danger. A sum of money was still with Doctor Klein in Budapest, at my disposal. I put it at the disposal of 'Trude and Otto'. (That's how we called them.) Grünbaums crossed the border to Hungary illegally before the war, and arrived safely after many hindrances. The mail system was pathetic, and Grünbaums got in touch with you. Grünbaums intended to go to Palestine. Soon after, Leo and Eva followed their path. They met there [Hungary?] and both families sent for their belongings. It was packed in the Humboldstr – and they did receive it. We believed them to be well taken care of for the time being. The threat of war forced them to move on and all traces of them were lost when war broke out.

During the war, I found out, after Yetta and everyone had left here, that Uncle Leo and Eva lost their lives during a bomb attack in Kolomea. It was told in Jewish circles, but nothing further could be found out. And since no news has come to this day, the story must have its truth. But that it happened in such a way will never be known. In any case, it can be believed. In the year 1942/43 many circles (friends, families, etc.) parted since most close friends weren't around anymore and no one heard anything anymore from them. We who stayed together were so sorry. The rage and murdering on the daily agenda was pathetic with all that happened. But now, I must include another friend of your loved ones who was also friendly with Grünbaums. He was a soldier at this time near Saloniki. A transport passing through the mountains was delayed by a bridge bombing; we saw that a group of people were being herded on foot by SS troops. He heard well and notice that it was Jews that passed at a distance. As always, when something like this happened, he [the soldier friend] paid attention and is positive that he saw Trude in the group. To do something, or to show himself was hopeless, but he reported it immediately and stayed with his story. Otto was not among them, Trude was alone. That was the last we heard from Grünbaums. No one has answered as of yet, and it is assumable that they were deported. Where to? A question mark. What happened to them? Unknown. That's all that I can report from Leo & Eva, Trude & Otto – mostly things I've heard. Now I'd like to return to the Humboldstr in the year 1940.

1940

The year began with even greater limits for the Jewish society. Yetta &
Otto worked and Oma sewed at home. In May 1940, our dear ones received
a telegram from the camp in Sachsenhausen saying that Uncle Adolf had
died of bad circulation. The pain was indescribable. The fear that the news
would come one day was always there since the ones captured were all dying
one by one.

The death announcements came to the courthouse and were made known
to the relatives there. After a while a wood box with the ashes of the dead
one arrived at the same place. Then the funeral was held for all. It was terrible to have to think that those ashes were Uncle Adolf. I really can't describe
the mental agony that went on then. Clarchen saw nothing to hold her up,
and it was difficult to get her over the tragic situation, since no one believed
Uncle Adolf's death to be a natural one. The reasons were all so obvious.
Telegrams came from all camps and then the ashes followed. We carried the
pain deep inside us. We couldn't show our feelings, especially in front of
Clarchen. We covered our feelings up with lies and tried convincing Clara
that the death could have been a natural one.

And second, who anyway was interested in the death of a Jew? Just us,
who daily fought against this inhumanity. The daily anxieties and exagger-
ations caused 99% to become blind. They were compelled to believe the
human criminals; that the past couldn't be made good [remade] anymore.

In the meantime, through mail, I found out that the Red Cross was
involved, and as you know, everything had to be told in twenty-five word
letters. I know with how much love, hope and wishfulness these 25 words were
written on paper. I was always there when messages were sent. Always the one
thing … 'the kids live, they are healthy, they are fine'. And with all that, a
spark of hope, of seeing one another again. Everyone always hoped for a
miracle. One saw the war as a crazy affair. 'Dear God. Is there no one who'll
end this?' No, there was no one. Every day, the war machine rolled on,
deceived; cheated continually more. That's how the year 1940 went and
ended.

1941 began. Everyone grabbed for goods and belongings. Gold, silver –
anything worth something was taken from the Jewish folk. Furs, wool,
cloths, musical instruments, radios, gramophones, electric appliances (all
sorts), house pets, even the bird in his cage. Work could only be found in the
worst places, with very little pay. The streets, beautifully planted with trees,
were made legally impassable. Jews were banned from parks, benches, street-
cars, trains. This left poor people imprisoned. Enduring all, we were meeting,
the same as before. And then, in the fall, the wearing of the Jewish star was
implemented so that people everywhere could be easily identified. All situations became more complicated. The Jews avoided many of their Christian

helpers out of fear. It was forbidden by highest law, with extreme consequences, to even speak with someone Jewish. Even during working hours, everyone worked separately and spoke only with their supervisors. The star, a yellow piece of cloth; the Star of David outlined and in the middle, printed 'Jude'. It had to be sewn on so that it couldn't be switched. Various streets were only Jewish populated and it wasn't easy walking through these streets because anyone else really had no business there. So, not to be conspicuous, we also wore a Jewish star, and if anyone Jewish came to our house, they would always leave with a purse or briefcase with which to hide the star. In all our miseries, we always found great opportunities.

In 1941, we heard from officials that our Yetta was leaving for Poland. This was investigated. Aunt Yetta was brought before court and was able to prove with her visa that she legally entered German territory, and that there had been no return date stamped on it at the time of issue. A 'mild' judge sentenced her to 4 weeks in jail. She tried changing the sentence to a money fine. It was allowed, and she paid 150 DM fine. She complied happily and we were glad that she had gotten off easy. We expected a higher sentence, especially in those hard times. Besides other episodes, this was another stone we stumbled over. With always caring and fearful hearts, the year ended and 1942 began.

1942

1 January 1942, the day I'll never forget arrived. On Sunday morning a messenger arrived and asked me to come to the Humboldstrasse. I didn't expect anything good. It was cold, very cold. I still remember small details. I found the whole apartment building floor like a bee-swarm, everyone excited, mixed-up, confused. Transport. That world [word] drove me crazy. I continually heard – Transport. Today all had to be packed for the Transport scheduled for Monday. It was the first one to [from?] Leipzig. Clarchen and Oma were part of it all. Aunt Yetta was to stay back. My dear girls, save me from explaining; I really can't describe it to you even though I still retain it all in my memory. – No, I can't! My heart aches – each word is much too impersonal to even tell what I experienced. It was so horrible that the actual fact of it was impossible to grasp. Coming! Going! Searching! Asking! Saying good-bye! Until evening arrived. Everyone that knew Yetta and Clarchen and Oma was there – and since other families were involved in this – and everyone ended up sharing one room and the floor was crowded – I still don't know to this day how to describe that day or which category to put it in. I was there until evening – advised [them] on this and that. Helmut Schroeder later joined me, who was also a good friend, and a Miss Wagner, also a close acquaintance. I believe it was 11 p.m. when we left the apartment. How, I don't quite remember. I only know that the three of us parted not saying a word to each other. It was the only way we could express the last wishes of Oma, Yetta & Clarchen. Constant kissing, handshakes, hugs & tears. It was too much for one day. We still discussed all possibilities.

They were no longer thinking of themselves, only of their children – this brought on a good-bye from everyone. With little desires, leaving their furniture behind standing where it was, these poor people were robbed of their last possessions: their home, the roof over their heads. They were the first taken from us in that way, but not the last. That year, 1942, was considered the wave of Transports. One of the most faithful friends of the house was Bernhard Issachsohn. His mother lived with your loved ones. He had a Christian wife and therefore was spared for a while. He lived with his family in the basement of the same house. It was impossible for us to return to the apartment on that following Monday for the house was surrounded with defenders of the Reich and the Gestapo. The last opportunities for helping anyone were only permitted for Jewish people. However, we always received an account of what was happening. They were transported to the Uferstreet school and from there were brought to Riga for two days. Bernhard pleaded with me to search for you. I got very close to Bernhard who also now was my personal 'care child'.

In the beginning we heard nothing of the transport. Not until mail was smuggled, but that was pitifully little. We only knew for sure that they arrived in Riga. In the Fall, Schroeder became a soldier and was stationed in Norway. His desire was to go to Riga. He accomplished his will. I received mail from Yetta through soldiers. Schroeder wrote me carefully, and then he came for a visit and told me, 'Yes!' He had met everyone. He even was in the Ghetto where they all were staying and visited with them for days at their jobs. Our good Yetta worked at the train construction site, our good Clarchen washed windows, and Oma had to sew. Under all circumstances, they were all doing well; and still they were full of hope. Schroeder, a courageous, risk-taking fellow, discussed with them that the next time he came he would bring papers and take them to Sweden with him. They agreed, but the next time was far off.

For us here there was now more concern for those that were still living here. The torture and embarrassment and harassment continued here too! In the Fall, on 1 October 1942 – exactly – I was forced to work in Poland for four months. I had to leave my family, also my almost 90-year-old, invalid father-in-law. I left, heart-broken. Our son was in Woronesch/Russia, fighting. My father-in-law died 26 October, three weeks after I left. I never saw him again. Except for mail, I was separated from everyone and everything.

In January '43, I returned, but was sick. In March, I started working again and in May I was to be sent to a repair workshop on the Front in Athens. I fought as hard as I could and stayed here because of my sickness. My courage was unbroken and the old acquaintances came in sight again in January. Schroeder came for a visit and on his way he went through Riga. He came upon completely different situations. Everything was run more strictly. It was hard finding meeting places. He found them anyway. Oma was very sick. Yetta and Clarchen were still working. The intention of taking the two girls with him was possible, but both of them did not want to separate themselves from their mother, for one simple reason. If one Jew escaped, ten others within the Ghetto were hanged. They couldn't and weren't going to risk their mother's life. The escape plan was dropped. Both girls remained full of hope and were healthy. They sent greetings home – which really wasn't home anymore, and greetings to the kids. That was all.

In August, I had a major operation, but I recovered, grievingly. From August 1943, the air raid alarms increased. On 3 December, in the morning, shortly before 4 a.m., we experienced the first 'terror attack' that ended terribly. All of Leipzig was in flames and almost 50% of the city was destroyed. For days and nights Leipzig was a sea of flames. We thought the world was going under. In April or May of '43 there was a second transport from here to Poland; and in September one went to Theresienstadt. With that, a nice clean-up of Jewish people was accomplished.

Outcasts among the fold were left behind; with them, Bernhard and those who were sick. These transports became more secretive towards the public. Our Yetta went to Riga only because Oma and Clarchen pleaded with her to go. [Did she have the option? The letter is inconsistent here. G.D.] *After the attack in December, Schroeder again visited. He could not return to his home; he lived in the Packhofstr; and his family had fled. On his return trip he went to Riga again, but with no luck. He found no connections. From there on, we also were left without any news.*

In 1944 we went through continuous attacks. All around us, everything was being destroyed. A gracious God protected our house. Though things were destroyed our house remained standing. Still, I watched and helped my friends that were here, for they too weren't saved from the attacks.

After every attack, we looked for each other and found each other. The situation became completely comfortless, and still the war didn't end. We were without light, water, gas, or decent living materials. Doors and windows were broken. Everyone was desperate for a roof over their head – and for everything they owned – for laying on the streets was bitter. So started the year 1945.

The last transport was 13 February to Theresienstadt. Our last friends were on the transport. Among them, Bernhard with his 10-year-old son. The vision that this war would only last for a few more weeks brought some comfort, but not a definite one. We knew that no long proceedings were held for the Jewish. But to give up all hope? No, that meant giving up yourself. February 27 was the biggest bomb attack. Noon, at exactly 2.40, the first bombs were dropped, in a terrible manner. They fell in front of us, behind us, beside us, everywhere; and we didn't expect to see daylight ever again. It was horrible.

My husband was drafted into the army a few days before. And my son in September 1944, wounded, found himself on his way from south Germany due to an overfilled hospital. Not healed, and one day later, he arrived here. Oh yes, our house still stood, but we were badly ruined. Our son had to leave 8 days later, still not healed, to a division used in case of emergency. My husband stayed in Leipzig, to my relief. From then on we had not one minute of peace. Continual alarms. Dresden, Chemnitz, Plauen, everything was bombed. Though they just flew over us that time, no one knew if we were to be exempt. The invasions started across the German borders. It all went very fast and we waited everyday for the end.

April 18, 1945, Leipzig was taken over by the Americans, on the 20th, it was yielded to them. With that, the fight was finished for us. My husband was taken captive. I was left alone. The reactions to the stressful situation that had been overcome became evident. People were exhausted and still nervous – needless to say. Our son was taken captive in Russia but was set free because he was wounded. There was no trace of my husband. I searched everywhere. I didn't find him among the dead and there was no organization for the wounded or captured.

End of May our boy returned, looking like a labourer, but he lived. In June, my husband returned from Kreuznach in a much worse condition. His body was completely decimated, worse than a labourer. The only clothes he had were rags – but he lived. We fixed our house a little and began rehabilitating and helping those back up that were in worse shape than us. In September, my husband began working again at his business; and soon thereafter our son began working also. End of June, Bernhard returned with his son and our joy was great. Most of the last deported lived through Theresienstadt. He stayed as before, a true friend of the families, but also the only one.

In June, we became Russians – according to zoning laws. Things became easier and mail communication started up again. That's what I had been waiting for. That meant starting my search. I had much success and am endlessly happy. I did, however, receive some sad news. My mail to Vera came back and I continued my search. You know I found our Paula and with this I had accomplished one mission. Many others still waited for an answer. Enquiries from England, America, France, Switzerland and Palestine came. My dear girls, few could save themselves, many were sacri-

fices of this crazy Regime. Now I always waited for who came back and who knew what, and that's when I learned of a Mrs Besser who was also in Riga. To find the woman is my next task.

She said (but I must hear it for myself because I give little credence to stories), that she knew Yetta and Clarchen from Riga. The Riga ghetto has been dissolved and the prisoners were sent to Sudhov. (If it is written as such I am not sure.) Aunt Yetta was supposedly group leader and well know. It is in this camp where Yetta and Clarchen were supposed to have died of typhoid. Hearing this, I almost lost all courage to believe. I still wait for news, for information, but it has been such a long time, and to write would have been the first thing they would have done. Should one believe Mrs Besser, or her story? No, I must know where this woman lives; she was only here for a visit as I was told. I must see her and speak with her so I might become familiar with what I have heard. This, my dearest girls, is the worst I could inform you of. I wrote everything according to the truth, the way I know it – but I still hope. I beg you will hope with me and I plead with you to enquire from where you are since mail doesn't go from here to Riga. There must be a place where information can be obtained, something like a public courthouse would know, where the camp Sudhov is and most likely may still have reports and files on its prisoners. It seems to be the only way. No, I don't want to quit yet, until positive evidence is found that our dear ones are among the dead, unless time or the future would let us anticipate such.

My dear girls, I write you these lines and my tears stream endlessly for my dear, dear girlfriends whom fate so cruelly allowed to be sacrificed. One should despair over oneself and humanity, that these cruelties could actually be carried out. Where was the reasoning? A part of my heart went with the family. Deeply hurt, I stayed back. Lively [as if alive] they are with us daily, not one day passes where we aren't reminded of them. Mrs Wagner, who also was a true friend of your family, has been living with us in our home since May 1946. Miss Wagner, who always was our 'Hans' because her name was Hanni [Khana], has become a dear friend of mine since we met in the kitchen of your loved ones. She and her mother lost their home in bomb attacks three times. And guess what? It was possible for us to give her mother and her brother and her an apartment in our home.

We still live in the past because our 'Hans' also lost someone dear to her in Theresienstadt. She had a business with Mr Hagens. This was our Uncle 'Max'. And as the situations became more complicated they had to give up their business relationship. Uncle 'Max' could not stay in the apartment anymore, so he went into an old folks' home in Gustav-Adolf Str. The meeting point for Uncle Max and Hans was the Humboldtstr, where he also was lovingly taken care of by your loved ones. He also was sent to Theresienstadt and probably also died there. We had communication there, through a Mrs Hahn, with Jdl [Yudel?] Kohn, and one day she wrote that Uncle Max went to Laura. We knew, though, that Laura had already said good-bye to this world. That's how Hans was tied to us all – she shared our fate. Since the future for us isn't complete, we only speak of the past. Hans and I become sad as we live through the frightful, horrible, time. That I could get in contact with you made her happy, for she also yearned to learn about you, as I did. You'll find a few lines from her also – of our Yetta, Clarchen, Oma, and the children.

Do you remember how they were? What they looked like? What pictures do you have of them? Clarchen, our dear Clarchen, really fitted her name. Fragile and small like a flower out of a different world. Good and loving, understanding of everyone, always helping with a soft still hand. Wise thinking, smart handling, carried pain until she could no longer, she carried herself through this world of viciousness. Prideful until she was broken, hateful to anyone mean to her, all without compromise. Sundays became painful to her. When it rained from Heaven, that's when she felt her world most of all. Sadness is what almost ruined her health. She was always the soft one in fights, always giving, always making someone happy. Dreaming, that's how I often found her, always tastefully dressed, and always with the simplest. We often spent quiet hours philosophizing; in candlelight, she seemed peaceful. Her heart beating softly, she tried picking apart the word 'Why' – always trying to bring an answer together. Giving up the children, the death of her husband – this took everything from her. Softly she whispered the names: Harold, Siegmar, Zilla, and my Adi. Gentle and small, the deep black hair, parted in the middle, huge dark eyes – this is how she remains in my memory. 'My children, my husband.' […]

Yette, or Yetta, carried the sorrow deep with her – energetic, helpful, even laughing when her heart was at the breaking point. Never blameful, ready for anything, without thought, always impulsive, full of life. Goodness, love, balanced in every way, readiness; this was all hers. Full of temperament, her circle closed itself to completeness. Sun, Rain, Snow, or Storm, she always remained Yetta. Always giving advice, never letting down [seeming depressed] always helpful, always friendly, even in her deepest sorrow – making others happy. This was keeping her alive. She thought of herself last. First came Oma and Clarchen. And then a few others. Making something out of nothing – only she could do that. A band, a bow, a flower – her hands never empty of doing something. Harmonious, true, completely giving up herself, never a traitor to a friend. She shone through all shadows, and all sorrows were stilled by her. Always optimistic in situations, always finding more energy, who only cried for and by herself, worrying about her children and for all poor souls. Yetta, the fresh stream for all who needed a place to turn; always friendly, laughing even when pain and sorrow hurt her. Blond, light-eyes, youthful, a little idle [idol or doll?], a curl here and there, a necklace, a flower – chic and charming, never able to be brought to her knees, always on top even if it hurt her – but never to show anyone, not letting anyone see how difficult everything got for her; that was our Yetta. Proud of her girl, full of plans, happy when mail arrived from England. From a distance, you could hear her cheering – 'Vera wrote, my big daughter.' […]

Between both girls, Oma stood. She always took care of daily chores. She had daughters, grown-up daughters, independently fighting for life. But she was the mother, she reigned over her small regiment the way she learned to as she grew up. Strict and systematic in belief, she accomplished as much as was sometimes possible. At times, the daughters kept things from her out of necessity, especially because of her health. She carried the worries deep within her, not always able to understand what was happening, working, cooking, taking care of all business. Like magic, old became new, and taste-fully made, too. Nothing was too much for her. A button here, a stitch there, a bow here; something new from house to house – pitiful and also happy things – these were all her additions. Always ready to help. My mother and Oma, in the right words, always full of worries and love for their children. An hour alone with her always ended with her reminiscing of her childhood years, her marriage, she never wanted to understand that there was a world full of sneakiness, nastiness, dirt and viciousness. So lived a one-of-a-kind woman in the midst of viciousness and cruelty. A mother and a grandmother. That's how I see them in front of me – unforgettable. Each in their own place; one they kept until that painful good-bye arrived. Heroines, who fought and took everything for their belief and life – still and courageous in their fight for life, in their fight for their children – in the midst of hate and envy. Cursed at, marked, brought to their knees, undressed of any human characteristics, tortured, murdered, emotionally destroyed, all for only a principle. Game for everyone who wanted to cool their mats – that's how far a man was brought down. And that was supposed to be a Victory? No, my dear girls, what your loved ones experienced is enough. You should be proud to have such fathers and mothers who understood it was better to sink than to be parted from their families and homes. Thinking of the torture they went through you should fight for life with all your might, to witness and fight for that what was to be destroyed, Judaism. Cry, yes cry, but show in your tears courage and hope. Let your loved ones be amongst you and live with you, because they were good and whoever is good has won Heaven. Wind and clouds always brought their greetings and wishes; and their thoughts built bridges on which you were never forgotten and aren't to this day. It would be good to raise the Koppold children in the way the parents wanted. They dreamed of them growing into hard-working people who are to continue where the parents left off – with the will and decision to finish what has been started.

To you, my dear girls, I speak of hope. Be and remain strong and brave and live in the way of your loved ones. I knew that one day I would write you and that I'd find you, but I wanted that this could have been a different chapter. And now I have brought you so much sorrow. My heart wants to break because of it. How can I help you? Patiently, the paper; automatically the fingers; but the heart sad. Won't you promise me to be brave and strong? I beg you for that, remember your loved ones, who would be unhappy if they knew they had caused you so much sorrow against their will. Be proud of them, very proud, and build them an altar in your hearts, an altar of quiet heroism. On this day, I end my report. (It is the 16th of October '45)

In order to try to find out if Riga was the End, I will search for Mrs Besser. Would you please write to Riga as I suggested before? Try it, maybe you'll find something out. Oh, how happy I would have been had I been able to write you happy news. I always had such hope. My girls, what was I to your loved ones? In all hardiness, such a tiny flicker of hope, a short guide along the way. I'm 47 years old today. I had a good harmonious marriage, without worries, well situated, always visited by guests; we had friends with whom we shared happiness and sorrow. Yes, life was OK.

As the year 1933 came, I knew I had a mission to accomplish. But I didn't know that fate would play your loved ones into my hands. In them, I realized the most valuable thing a person could carry with them. Being human to one another – and that filled me with such satisfaction. That we had to part from each other is still unbelievable to me. Within me and in my heart, they still live as if they never had gone away. In you, I find the continuity of my loved ones, and to you I also want to be a good friend, as I am to my good Yetta, Clarchen, and Oma, with true inner thankfulness.

You should know that I was for yours as well as other good friends never a 'Martha', since I still retained the name 'Yuliane'. I became a 'Marijane' [Mariane]. Everyone knows me and of me when you mention the name here in old circles. Should we continue to leave it at this? I am your Marijane and you are my dear, dear, girls. And if I may ask you, if I am a friend, then please, without 'Sie' [formal you]. Isn't it amazing how friendships can be made through such a distance from home, which never was a homeland to you. And with such faithfulness towards your loved ones. We'll leave it at that. I am always and forever,

Your old thankful friend,
Marijane.

Thursday, 3 p.m. afternoon

My dear Vera, my new friend!

I received your letter at the same time as Paula's – and to take dear Paula's advice, I beg you, in relationship of our new friendship to use that small word 'du' [informal you]. My dear girl, I think it will be your desire to continue what your dear ones began and I am glad to have found the same understanding kind of people in you. I thank you for the sweet lines and for your trust. It is a hard task to let this mail reach your hands, but I hope you'll be a real tough girl. I only wish that my report to you could have been the best and only good. In answer to your plea to also want to find out the worst, I wrote this terrible letter. Can I curb your sorrow? My dear Vera, probably not. You are 21 and understanding, but even this doesn't help against that inner pain. It is so hard for me, and I am with you in my thoughts. We can't reverse anything, can't cancel all that's happened. We were all helpless during this horrible time. Otherwise, we would have done everything we could. May God keep you safe, dear Vera. We'll always be your good friends.

I wrote everything, as wished, on a typewriter – many mistakes, many corrections, my thoughts always running ahead of me and my fingers unable to keep up. I had to write everything out of my heart and then came the day I had long awaited. To find you was my duty, because from you I still had the 'Norwich' connection. It was bad luck that I didn't find you the first time, but it happened anyway. It makes me so happy that you are still with the good Staff family, and so filled with joy to know that the earth still inhabits people with good hearts. The biggest joy for your loved ones was to know that you were well taken care of, knowing that you found each other. Of course, they didn't want to leave you alone; there was a plan to reunite in America. Now it is happening; you are going there. A long distance will be between us, but every way can be bridged. Sorry that it isn't possible to get to know you anymore, unless I came to America to visit you – or perhaps you'd find the way here. You would always find a home with us. Let's wait and see what the future brings us – life can still be long – as long as we stay healthy. I also wrote Paula and am delighted to hear that you both have been doing so well. I am also very happy to know that the Koppold children are in such good hands. I wish you, with all my heart, that you'll stay in contact. I know the grandparents in New York from stories and by their names only. Your dear mother herself believed to find refuge there. Now, grandfather is dead? Oh, how painful. It would have made them very happy to be able to see you.

You wrote once that you wanted to become a beautician (learn hairstyling)? You were 14 then, and now I hear you are working in an office. How did you survive the hard times? Norwich was also bombed, wasn't it. We thought of you often and hoped that you were healthy. Do you still have the coral necklace from Oma? Oh, she was so happy to be able to send it to you. She spoke of it – that it was to keep you in good health. I hope it has been going well with you. Of course, I understand your lovely letter, when I read it I always see Vera's mail to home – all small details were always mentioned – a new dress, a new coat, and every line began 'My dear mother'. Oh, how happy we always were to hear good news. All our love and worry was always for the children.

Dearest Vera, one plea I have. Would you please send me a picture of you? I would love to know how the grown Vera looks. I only remember her with her mother when she was small. Dearest Vera, since you are so big now, and Paula also, I beg you with all my heart that you would carry your sorrow together. No, the Koppold children are too young to know how cruel the world could be. Don't leave the Koppold children. Continue to be a crutch for them so that the last won't get lost. I ask that you would do this for your loved ones. As soon as I can, I'll send a picture of us. I'll send one to Paula at least, so you'll know how we look. We are not doing so good, the war has retarded our health and still we are hopeful that different times may come where we'll be able to live [rise up] again. Right now we are satisfied that it's peaceful and that we still have our home. If I can help you in any way, I'll be willing anytime – (so don't forget your addresses). Considering the situations, we are doing well, so far. That's why we don't ask for much and are satisfied with even the smallest. It's a little difficult sometimes, but a person can get used to anything. We have been living off the past, but that's over now. Provisions are minimum, often barely enough. Living among the other people isn't nice. Someone always thinks that the other one has more. The still closed zones also create more difficulties. Still we think that with time, things will get better. We've gone through so much, and yet it has to continue like this. The war only brought misery, grief and sorrow to humanity.

Dearest Vera,

I hope this letter reaches you in good health. I'll complete everything in three letters since only 20 grams are allowed at a time. I truly believe that you'll go to Paula, and I know it will be your saddest day. May God give you strength and courage that you may be able to take everything you know courageously – always with your loved ones in mind. I hope to get an answer from you real soon; and I will be thinking of you.

Wishing you well, I want to be your friend in memory of your loved ones. I send you greetings and remain faithfully, your old friend.

Marijane

Letter from Zvi Shdaimah (Harald Koppold) to Gertrude Dubrovsky,
Clare Hall
Postmarked 27 July 2001, Israel (Kibbutz Nir Oz, D.N. Negev 85122)
Dear Gertrude,

Thank you for sending us the work you did about the Kindertransport and us six children from Leipzig. I knew that an e-mail is enough to say that, but I have remarks of my own to make. I know that now that the work is done, whatever I say is meaningless. However, I feel that I need to say more about myself. Maybe it will interest you.

The first thing that comes to mind is the little part about Vera departing from her parents and saying 'nobody cried'. I, too, remember our father and mother taking us to the railway station, saying goodbye to my father and then waving to him from the train. Our mother got on the train with us and came to the last German station before going into Holland and to the sea-port. I remember her leaving us. It was all quite easy. I think I did see tears in my mother's eyes. There was no crying and I did not feel that I could or should. I was still only 6 years old and did not understand what was happening. No family or parents. I am saying all this because I feel that together with this, I have altogether lost my sense of feeling and absolutely any ability to express feelings. All my life has been like that. No sorrow or crying, at going to funerals, etc. My lack of expression is also a great lack in my everyday life. I am not a psychologist but I feel that everything I have said is a result of the past. There is a lot more to say on that subject. I shall only add now that I cannot express love or closeness to anyone, however good the relationship.

Another matter that I feel I should mention is that the story about us three little ones says that we came to London, a few days later we were sent to Cambridge. About myself – I know nothing about what happened to the others – I was put into a school nearby. We were sent to a little village near Peterborough. We were in the local school and people from the village came to take home one of the children. After a while, I was the only child left. I suppose it is difficult to take care of a child that one can't talk to. However, after a while, a family was found. (I don't know how or who.) I was in that village and [with] the family three years. In those three years I had no contact with any one of the family. Nor did I know anything about Cambridge. I must add that until now, I always thought that going there was incidental, via organizations and committees. About the family and the village, after a while I was quite comfortable there. I don't remember any difficulty with the language. It came naturally, like any child. I can't understand how, at the age of 7, I began speaking a new language without any effort or difficulty. Also in those three years, I did not hear or speak a word of German. Altogether, I forgot the language. Some years later, when

I went to the Perse School in Cambridge, I could choose to study another language. I chose to learn German. I thought that maybe there was still something of the language stuck in my mind. Also, there was still a possibility that some one of the family was still alive and I would want to hear what he had to say. On that subject, I can only add that my attempt to learn German again altogether failed. Also, no one of the family survived, as you know.

My time in the village was quite alright, also the three years I went to school there. Now, I must add that I did not learn to read and write then. That matter caused me much anguish for quite some time. Later, when I began to go to school in Cambridge, the teacher took care of that, and found one of the staff to teach me. It was quite easy, it was only a matter of days until I could read. I could read and I read quite a lot. It was never really fluent and without difficulty. I always read rather slowly until this day.

Another matter about the life in the village. I used to go to chapel regularly on Sundays. That was part of the life. After quite some time someone came to tell me about being Jewish and I should not go to chapel. Who or how this person came to me, I had no idea. I think he was a rabbi and he also talked to the family I was with. I ceased to go to church; there was no question about that. Some years later I got into religion seriously, even before I was with a Jewish family.

My time in the village came to an end when the evacuated children were taken back to their families. I guess the family I was with did not feel that they had to keep someone's child. Then Paula came to take me to the house of the Binkes. I had no part in this; in fact, I was taken by surprise and tried to resist. Again losing my home, I even cried, which was very rare for me.

I was with the Binkes again some days and then I was taken to Cambridge. At first I was taken by a young lady who wanted to take care of a child. After some days, she decided that it was a mistake because she had to leave where she was living and find a place to live near to where her husband was doing his army service. Then I went to live with another family and was with them some months. In those days, I was interviewed by a lady of the Refugee Committee who came to the conclusion that this family was not good for me and they should find another place for me. I am hardly aware of any complaints I had. I do remember that once I said, 'they are dirty'. I have no idea why I said that, I suppose that was a feeling. One other thing that very much bothered me. I told her about a dream I had. I knew that she had a special interest in dreams. (She was a spiritualist.) I told her that my mother was calling out to me from the back window of our apartment while I was playing in the back yard. At one time, that was quite common. She said, 'Your mother is calling to you from out yonder.' I immediately understood what 'out yonder' means. I always thought that what she said was nonsense and impossible. However, the thought about that was often on my mind and bothered me a lot, in spite of what I said before.

I was moved to the Sofier family with the help of the Refugee Committee. They found that I needed to be taken by a Jewish family. At the same time, their son Norman – their only son [child] – used to see me every Saturday at the Synagogue. He told his mother about me and also that he is alone at home all the time. Then the Refugee Committee was looking for a home for me. How the contact was made, I have no idea. However, I came to a new home, which remained my home for about six years. It was perfect. They took good care of me. They saw to it that I go to a good school (the Perse School), a high school. The school I went to previously sent a recommendation: 'eminently suitable for further education'. My everyday schooling went well enough, but I was never a real success in examinations.

My life with the Sofiers was very good, including schooling and a big Bar Mitzvah. *Six years I was with them. No complaints, nor any complaints about other families that I was with. The fact remains that after I left home, I never really felt at home again wherever I was. I remember being asked, 'call me Mummy'. Or 'call me Aunty', and I could not bring myself to do that. I guess that is because of the age I left home. I really don't know. I haven't heard of that with anyone else. I can add now that feeling is with me all the time, wherever I am. The feeling of not really feeling at home.*

There was much said about religion. At that time, I knew nothing about orthodox religion, etc. Also, after I was a short time in Cambridge, someone came to talk to me about being Jewish. I think a rabbi. At the time, it was very serious. I was coming back to where I belonged. I went to the Synagogue regularly every Saturday. I also took with me my little brother, as I was told to do. The people he was with felt that they should agree. They were very good with him and agreeable to the matter of religion, although I don't believe they had any part in doing anything in that matter. As we are told, in the story about the six from Leipzig, his family was eager about his development in religion.

As for myself, I continued some years. When I came to the Sofier family, I was already in that routine and, of course, continued. After my Bar Mitzvah, *I was quite serious on the matter of religion and some time later, together with Zionism. Then, I also got into the routine of going to see the farm in Thaxted on my school holidays. That was a training farm for those who intended to go to a kibbutz in Israel. It belonged to a religious movement (B'nai Akiva). It became my ideal that I must go to Israel. When I was about 14 years old, I decided I must go. I was told that I must have the permission of the Jewish Refugee Children's Committee. I remember going to their office and after a short talk was told definitely that I am with a good family and am going to a good school and it is for my own good that I should continue for at least two years more. I understood, but was very sad and disappointed and even cried.*

I stayed and was at school for another two years; [I] also continued my connection with Thaxted and was looking forward to kibbutz life in Israel. Then, the matter of our going to America began. I knew vaguely that one day we shall all get together again in the USA. At that time, I felt that it was hopeless. My brother and sister were taken in by families and all was well, and then they were adopted. I, myself, could not even consider being with another family. However, all went well with them and now, of course, they all have their own families. I myself led my own life and finished my schooling and came to this country, etc. That, of course, is the beginning of another long story. I shall not go into that long story.

*I suppose I should say something about the beginning. I finally came to this country in August 1949, exactly ten years after I came to England. I came to a place called **Kfar Hanoar Hodati**, a religious place for teaching the young the language and farming. I was there two years. After that, I did my army service, most of that in a kibbutz. In that period, I also left religion and came back to reality. (I think so.) I did my army service, after the elementary training, at first in a religious kibbutz and then in another kibbutz without religion. Then my everyday life and my family life also continues in a kibbutz, etc., etc.*

That is as much as I have to say about myself in this story. I have said more than is necessary. I am sorry about that. After I began, I was drawn into talking about various details. About our everyday life and the connection between us all.

I see it somehow differently than it was told. It was always calm and pleasant, not special events or festivals. Also, my cousin's relationship to Mrs Sofier was pleasant and nice. No special occasions. I can also add that our relationship is continuous, all these years and in spite of the vast distance between us. I suppose that is because of our past that we had together. I think I have said enough. Best wishes to you.

Zvi Shdaimah

NOTES

1. Paula Regina (Grünbaum) Balkin, *Strong Family Ties: A Story in Letters* (published privately, 2002). Many of the letters from which the material in this chapter was drawn were shared with me by Paula Grünbaum Balkin, Vera Ribetski Nussenbaum, Tsvi Shaimah and Siegmar Silber.
2. Deportation Buch, Bundes Archive, Berlin (no pages numbers).
3. Clara, her mother, and other deportees from Leipzig are now memorialized in a Deportation Buch, Bundes Archive, Berlin. Yetta is not included among the people listed for deportation on the transport that carried Clara and her mother east.

4. Translated copies were given to me by Harald Koppold (now Tsvi Shdaimah) when I visited him and his wife on their kibbutz, Nir Oz, close to the Gaza border. I make no attempt to explain Mitdank's motivation in this lengthy correspondence. Neither Paula nor Vera knew her and, in fact, Mitdank claims that the family were new friends.
5. I can make no judgements as to the veracity of the history Mitdank reports.

Pictures from Leipzig

1. Vera Ribetski, four years old, *c.* 1929.

2. Vera Ribetski, first day of school in Leipzig, *c.* 1931.

3. Vera Ribetski, Leipzig, 1934.

4. Vera's foster family, Bertha and Arthur Staff, with Lottie, in Norwich *c.* 1945.

5. Vera and Seymour Nussenbaum, New Jersey, 1995.

6. Yetta Ribetski (at the back), Rose Schmulevitz (on the left) and Clara Koppold (on the right). Rose is the mother of Yetta and Clara. This photograph was taken in 1939.

7. Paula Grünbaum (13 years old) and her sister, Edith (5 years old): first day at school, *c.* 1937.

8. Abraham and Trude Grünbaum with their daughters, Paula (14 years old) and Edith (7 years old), Leipzig, *c.* 1938.

9. Clara and Adolph Koppold with their children (left to right): Harold (5 years old), Zilla (infant), Siegmar (2 years old).

10. Clara Koppold,
c. 1939.

11. Zilla, Clara's daughter,
was adopted at the age of 8 by
the Schall family in New York.
This photo was taken in
Westchester, NY, *c.* 1958.

12. Samuel Schmulevitz, grandfather; cantor of Broder Shul,
c. 1930.

13. At the Binke home shortly after the arrival of the Koppold children; taken *c.* 1939 or 1940. From left to right: Dana Binke (guarantor), Siegmar Koppold (3 years old), Zilla Koppold (9 months old), Edith Grünbaum (8 years old) and Paula Grünbaum (15 years old).

14. Leo and Eva Schmulevitz, Leipzig, *c.* June 1936. Leo was the uncle who registered the children for the *Kindertransport*.

15. Siegmar brought his family to England in 1973 to visit Elsie Mansfield who had been his foster-mother and who had 'provided him with the best home' he ever had. Back row: Siegmar and Norma Silber; middle row: Elsie, Rachel and David; front row: Miriam.

16. Greta Burkill, 1984.

17. Harry Burkill, foster child of Greta and Charles Burkill. He arrived in England at the age of eight and took the Burkill name because they became his parents. He is now Reader in Mathematics at Sheffield University.

18. Harry with his wife, Jean, Oxford, 1994.

19. Ann Sofier, foster mother to Harold Koppold (now Zvi Shaimah). 'Fostering Harold was one of the most wonderful experiences of my life,' she said. He changed his name when he moved to Israel and called his foster mother every Friday night.

20. Zvi Shaimah on his kibbutz, Nir Oz, Israel. A self-taught artist and sculptor, his work beautifies the kibbutz – much of it reflects his *kindertransport*/Holocaust experiences.

21. Siegmar Koppold Silber in his New Jersey law office. 'The simple home I had with Elsie Mansfield was the best home I ever had.' He was adopted at the age of 12 by the Silbers of Patterson, New Jersey, USA.

Six from Leipzig Today:
The Past as Prologue

Where are they now, those six from Leipzig? They are all married and have generated families of their own. Zilla, the youngest of the Leipzig six, is 63; the oldest, Paula, is 78. Among them, there are 15 children and 32 grand-children. Five of the original family are scattered across the United States: two in New Jersey, one in South Carolina, one in Michigan and one in California. One lives on a kibbutz in Israel. Milestone events in their respective families bring them together from time to time: a *Bar Mitzvah*, a wedding, a death in the family.

The youngest of the six has suffered the premature death of her husband, in his sixties. When he heard the news, her brother, from whom she had been estranged, flew immediately from New Jersey to South Carolina to be there for her during the difficult time of a final farewell. Of the three Koppold children, two live in America: a lawyer in New Jersey and a housewife in South Carolina. The third, a talented artist, lives on a kibbutz in Israel. As with his early life in England, he is once more on the edge, now in Gaza.

Paula, the oldest of the six, lost her husband a few years ago. She is writing a personal memoir about her experiences in England and Cambridge during the time between her arrival on a *Kindertransport* and her leaving for a new life in America at the age of 20. Her sister, Edith, lives in Michigan with her husband, a retired engineer. Both Paula and Edith have three children each, all of whom have college degrees in law, social work, business and medicine, respectively. Vera, having raised two daughters and supported them through college, lives with her husband in suburban New Jersey and attends to the needs of two grandsons living nearby while their single mother, trained in art, is trying to finish another degree that would enable her to teach. Both Edith and Vera talk to school-children about their experiences on the *Kindertransport*. Edith also serves as a guide at the Holocaust Museum in Detroit.

For a time, there were tensions between siblings, serious disagreements, lack of trust, hurt feelings. But shared experiences and time are great levellers. All six cousins are now in close communication and all have been interviewed by the author. About telling her story, Paula says it is both painful and healing. Arriving in England when she was 15, she could not go to school and instead worked in a variety of low-level jobs to support herself. In England she also supported her sister and her youngest cousin, Zilla. Paula says she survived emotionally because Jewish values, passed on to her by the family, were a source of strength. She hopes people can learn from the past and from the experiences of others. Her guiding principle is that people must be informed and must be good to each other.

In the process of interviewing and sharing social experiences with the six from Leipzig, I have been continually impressed by their honesty, their courage and their pain, even while I felt humbled by their efforts both to cooperate and to preserve their own privacy. Much family history resides within individual members themselves, and interviewers intrude upon closely guarded information. It is one of the difficulties and dangers of asking people to share their pasts, significant though it may be, and instructive to others as it surely is.

I find each interview I conduct a profound experience that carries with it certain obligations of honesty in reporting. There is poetic truth in everything people say about their pasts and about themselves; it is the truth of personal feeling that shapes personal memory. Often, however, the interviewee reshapes the story to coincide with a different vision of a past that might have been. My effort has been to be respectful of the feelings, while trying to discern the actual factual history.

In dealing with the Holocaust, we cannot discount the personal experiences, the eyewitnesses who survived to bear testimony to events that are so horrendous that we do not want to believe them. But, at the same time, we must try to be as objective as possible and try to corroborate if possible what people remember, so that the record is as accurate as it could be. It is only as useful as it is honest.